THE MAVERICK GUIDE TO
BALI AND JAVA

mav·er·ick (mav'er-ik), 1. an unbranded steer. Hence [col-
loq.] 2. a person not labeled as belonging to any one fac-
tion, group, etc., who acts independently. 3. one who moves
in a different direction than the rest of the herd—often a
nonconformist. 4. a person using individual judgment,
even when it runs against majority opinion.

The Maverick Guide Series
The Maverick Guide to Australia
The Maverick Guide to Bali and Java
The Maverick Guide to Hawaii
The Maverick Guide to Malaysia and Singapore
The Maverick Guide to New Zealand
The Maverick Guide to Thailand

*Information in this guidebook is based on authoritative data available at
the time of this printing. Prices and hours of operation of businesses
listed are subject to change without notice. Readers are asked to take this
into account when using this guide.*

MAVERICK GUIDE TO BALI AND JAVA

Don Turner

1992-1993 EDITION

PELICAN PUBLISHING COMPANY
GRETNA 1992

ISBN 0-88289-818-3

Maps by Michael Forsythe

Manufactured in the United States of America

Published by Pelican Publishing Company, Inc.
1101 Monroe Street, Gretna, Louisiana 70053

Contents

LIST OF MAPS

ACKNOWLEDGMENTS

Thanks to all the Indonesian people who gave their time and assistance and answered my many questions; the Indonesian Government Tourism Offices throughout Bali and Java that were vital sources of information; to Sarah and Agus Moeda in Jakarta, who have kept me up to date with city life; to Gus Perger in Perth, who coordinated the word processing of the original manuscript; and to my wife, Sien.

THE MAVERICK GUIDE TO
BALI AND JAVA

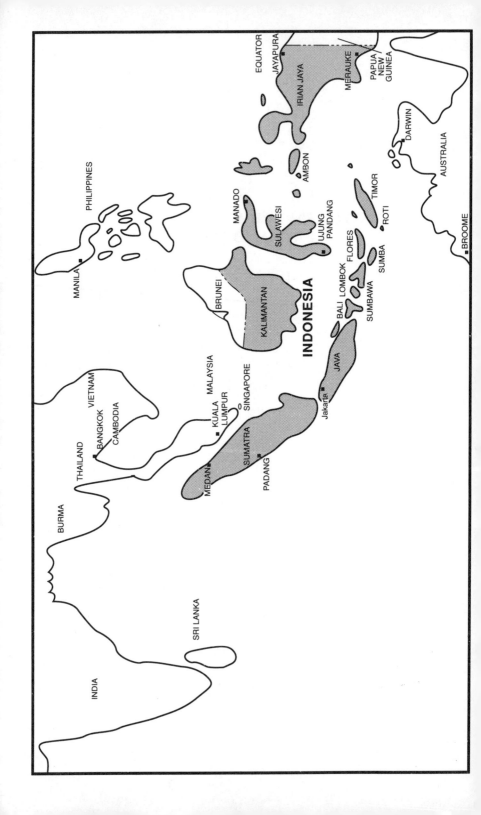

1

Why Bali and Java?

Bali, the ever-dynamic isle of festivals, greets you with a vista of blue water and swaying palms. Whether your first look is when the plane dips its wings over Kuta Reef, or sunrise as your bus rolls off the ferry from Java, you can feel the excitement growing within. You are here at last. Bali, though only a small island, offers something for everyone—water sports, hiking, cycling, arts and crafts, magnificent food, breathtaking scenery, discos, and, most important of all, the Balinese people. Java, with its ancient temples, Kraton culture, *batik* and *gamelan*, numerous volcanoes, and big cities, is a melting pot of cultural influences that date from the beginning of man's existence. All of this, together with good hotel service, excellent seafood, tropical fruit, and an abundance of things to buy, makes these two islands difficult not to enjoy.

Java's place in the evolution of man goes back some 35,000 years, since Java Man (or Solo Man) lived on the banks of the Solo River in Central Java. Wajak Man, whose remains were found on the southern coast of Java, is the earliest known form of *Homo sapiens*, the human race.

Even before this time, when a land bridge still connected Bali and Java to the Asian mainland, animals such as elephants, rhinoceri, and tigers came to the islands and have only recently been pushed to near extinction.

Java has been supporting great civilizations since the 9th century A.D., when Hindu-Buddhist kingdoms flourished and built such monuments as Borobudur and the Prambanan temple complex. By the 1400s, the last of the Hindu-Buddhist kingdoms, Majapahit, controlled most of the area that now makes up Indonesia, and possibly even parts of Malaysia and the Philippines.

Then came the Middle-Eastern religion of Islam, which mixed with, rather than erased, the Hindu-Buddhist beliefs and the animism (spirit worship) that predated them all. By the sixteenth century, Europeans had reached China and sailed around Africa, and Java and other islands of Indonesia became sources of spices such as pepper, cloves, and nutmeg. The Portuguese came first, followed by the Dutch, who dominated the spice trade and the economy of Java itself until their rule was brought to an abrupt halt by the invading Japanese forces and World War II.

To a large extent, Bali was left alone to fight its wars, grow rice, and develop a society that revolves around worshipping their Hindu gods. Only since the early 1970s have Westerners been coming to Bali in large enough numbers to influence Balinese society. Changes in Balinese attitudes are occurring, and along the coastline tourism facilities are mushrooming, but the Balinese heartland by and large remains as it was. Frankly, of the outside influences, those from Java are just as strong as those from other countries.

Bali's water sports are one of its major attractions, with hotels and resorts that offer diving, parasailing, and windsurfing. Or you may prefer to just laze around on the beach or by the pool. Artistically, Bali and Java are about equal, with painting, carving, and jewelry making, as well as traditional dance and the *wayang* epics to see on stage or at a local religious ceremony in Bali.

A Land of Leisure and the Arts

Indonesia's early history may have been violent, but with President Suharto at the helm, the country has settled into a pattern of steady growth without forgetting its cultural and artistic background. Traditional dance schools are thriving as local students seek to learn the old arts, more for their own personal enrichment than for the tourist dollar. Neither have the Javanese and Balinese given up wearing intricately patterned *batik* cloth. In fact, it has now spread from the *Kraton* palaces to the population at large.

Still, you must realize that Indonesia is not a Western country nor, for that matter, a particularly advanced country in the way that countries are now measured. Rather it is in a continual state of "controlled disorder," in which things get done, but not always in the way or at the time you had expected. Most tropical islands are like that, and Bali and Java are just a few degrees south of the equator. While it is not quite a *mañana* syndrome, the locals have their own term for it—*jam karet* or "rubber time." Follow suit, be flexible, and you'll be sure to enjoy your stay.

Prices in Bali and Java are very reasonable, and creeping devaluation of the local currency means that they have remained so. Rooms at moderately priced hotels cost around $US70 for a single (one person) and a little more for a double (two people). When it comes to luxury, name your own limit, as some of the suites are favorites of kings, queens, and movie stars. At the lower end, motel-style comfortable rooms with smiling service go for around $US40 a night. You can go all the way down to real backpacker basics, but they aren't covered in this book.

A good dinner in a good restaurant will run $US10-$15 per person, plus any drinks. I have tried to keep the restaurants listed in this book around that price level as a maximum. If that's too much, I have listed plenty of smaller cafes and Indonesian restaurants that serve a variety of local and Western food for less than $US5 a head. A bottle of beer will cost you $1, and a coke 50c. Beer is produced locally, but not wine or spirits. Much of the wine sold in restaurants is from Australia, which produces a good drop at reasonable prices.

Cooking for yourself is not possible in Bali and Java, as hotel rooms don't have cooking facilities, though you can buy fruit, bread, cheese, biscuits, and milk if you prefer not to go out to eat for a change. However, when eating out is such a pleasure and prices are so reasonable, why not make the most of the fresh seafood, spicy curries, Chinese noodles, and iced-juice drinks, as well as competently cooked Western dishes?

The roadways of Bali and Java at times leave a lot to be desired, the main problem being that they are too narrow for the volume of traffic. Other drawbacks are the unwritten "rules" of the road, the pedestrians that step out without warning, and the drop off at the edge of the asphalt. As you might have guessed, when most visitors want to rent a car they get one that comes with a driver. You are there to sit back and enjoy the scenery, so leave the driving to a local.

Terraced rice fields, pristine beaches, quaint villages, and colorful ceremonial dress make Indonesia a visual delight. In between the rice terraces are rows of coconut palms and patches of tall bamboo, with a backdrop of mountains that are often active volcanoes.

Flowers, such as hibiscus, frangipani, and bougainvillea, line the streets and flourish in the warm, wet climate. At the center of most towns and villages you will see a huge banyan tree that houses certain spirits. Most of the other trees are fruit-bearing. Much of the teak has been lost, used in the past for building traditional houses and now for woodcarving.

Of the wildlife, that which survives stays well hidden, though you do see plenty of water buffalo and, in Bali, white Brahman cattle. The same goes for birdlife, except for near the water, where you will see pelicans, cormorants, and maybe even a sea eagle. The most common winged animals are the pampered fighting cocks in Bali and ducks marching off to weed and eat the bugs in the rice fields.

In a land where cars cost many times more than in the U.S. and spare parts are hard to find, you will see all types of vehicles that long ago should have stopped running. Local ingenuity, a bit of wire, and simple tools seem to keep them going, though with frequent breakdowns. Where tourists are involved, however, the cars and buses are newer, locally assembled Australian and Japanese models.

The Balinese and Javanese are in many ways quite distinct. The main difference is their religions (Bali being strongly Hindu and Java basically Islamic), and how this affects their attitude towards life. Balinese always seem to be happy. Javanese are much more serious. In the cities and larger towns there is a significant ethnic Chinese population which dominates commerce and industry. Other outsiders have come in to do business also, notably the Americans, Australians, Italians, French, and the Japanese, but these are also concentrated in the big cities and coastal resorts.

The Confessional

Now, here are some answers about the Maverick *modus operandi* in Indonesia. How do I make my recommendations on where to stay or eat? Do I succumb to kick-backs?

Readers of other titles in the Maverick series have understood for over a decade now that the word "Maverick" guarantees that we are totally honest in our opinions on the travel scene. A dirty hotel room, poor service, and overpriced rooms are noted as such and are not stated as being otherwise. Some of the rooms recommended might not be spotlessly clean, but they will be in the budget group or not in at all.

I have never been influenced by money, friendship, or favors to say something nice. Some places I like more than others and heap them with praise. You may not agree with my interpretation, but you can be sure that I am being honest.

All opinions expressed, unless otherwise credited, are my own and I take full responsibility for them.

Sometimes, however, I may not have stayed in a particular hotel or eaten at a restaurant that is included here, but it will have been recommended to me by someone who has. On occasions I have been given a free room for a night or two, but this doesn't mean that I'll say the place is good if I don't think it is. If I hadn't thought it was good I wouldn't have stayed there in the first place.

I don't accept free meals in restaurants I am testing, and usually only tell them that I'm writing a guidebook after eating, when I ask for a business card. The same goes for hotel rooms.

Since I first visited Bali and Java in 1974, I have returned many times, including a two-year working stint in 1979-81. No airline has given me free tickets, though on one occasion Garuda did get me a seat on short notice.

The Indonesian Government Tourism Offices gave me lots of information and brochures, but no more than any other tourist who took the time to ask for them.

So that's how it is. If there's something I have written that you don't agree with, tear out the letter/envelope at the end of the book and let me know. The same goes for anything you think I have missed, especially in the accommodation and eating-out sphere, which changes so fast. I'll be sure to read every word and look into it further on my next trip.

Getting the Most Out of This Book

As in the previous Maverick guides, this one has been arranged in a smooth pattern designed for quick and easy use. Following the first four chapters on the basics of travel, nature, and people, the "area chapters" cover the islands of Bali and Java, divided into three areas each.

These are *Bali's Southern Beaches*, the resort areas of Sanur, Nusa Dua, Kuta-Legian, and the nearby town of Denpasar; *Ubud and Central Bali*, the Balinese cultural and artistic heartland; *Bali's East and North Coasts*, concentrating on Candi Dasa to the east and Lovina/Singaraja to the north; *East Java*, the city of Surabaya, the large town of Malang, and sunrise at Mt. Bromo; *Central Java*, Jogya and Solo—an area of ancient stone monuments, *batik* cloth, and the *wayang* dance-drama; and *West Java*, Jakarta—Indonesia's capital—and Bandung in the highlands.

Each of these area chapters is divided into 12 numbered sections; after you have become familiar with them in one chapter you will know where to look for information on the same subject in each of the others.

The area chapters are divided as follows:

1. The General Picture
2. Long-Distance Transportation
3. Local Transportation
4. Hotels and Lodging
5. Restaurants and Dining

6. Sightseeing

7. Guided Tours or Going It Alone
8. Water Sports
9. Other Sports
10. Shopping
11. Night Life and Entertainment
12. The Address List

We strongly suggest that you use this book in two ways. First, go over it at home to help you plan your trip to Bali and Java. In the next chapter, for example, we cover many of the choices to be made concerning airlines, tours, travel agents, and the like. The other two general chapters—one on nature and the other on people—should contribute to your knowledge of the country. The individual hotels, for which you may want to make advance reservations, are listed in the area chapters.

Second, the book is designed to be used on the scene to help you answer those tricky questions—what *bemo* to take to Solo, where to find a cool drink, and generally how to budget your time and money as you travel throughout Bali and Java.

Bagus!

To explore Bali and Java still requires a certain spirit of adventure. It's not like going to Europe, where everything but the Italian trains runs on time and happens when you want it to. Indonesia is more like Latin America. "Rubber," or flexible, time is ingrained in the national psyche, so be prepared for a few hiccups in your schedule.

The Indonesian people, though, you will find hard not to like. As long as they speak enough English to understand you, they will do their best to help you and make you feel at home. If you think they are doing a good job, enjoyed a meal or performance, or generally want to express your satisfaction, remember at least one word—*bagus*—and give the thumbs-up sign. I'm sure you'll be doing it a lot while you're away.

2

Before You Go Jalan-Jalan

Planning your trip in advance can make all the difference in regards to how much you enjoy your days or weeks in Indonesia. This chapter looks systematically at the practical aspects of traveling across Bali and Java, and tries to explain the problems and cultural differences that you may encounter when you go *jalan-jalan* (literally: "go for a walk") in Indonesia.

None of these cultural differences, however, are serious enough to keep anyone away from Bali or Java. Both islands have their traditional and tourism-oriented sectors that are quite separate, so you can travel in comfort (and even luxury) among English speakers or go off into the traditional sectors to rough it a little and see how the locals live. Forewarned is forearmed, as they say. With this in mind, I have tried to be clear about the negative as well as positive points, so you will know how to deal with most situations when they arise.

This chapter groups these details into some fourteen categories, namely getting to Indonesia, transportation within Indonesia, availability of conducted tours, choice of a travel agent, types of accommodation, sport and leisure, baggage allowances and packing, health matters, best times to go, weights and measures, security, official formalities, and where to get further information.

The Maverick Guide to Bali and Java is the second book in the series to deal with an Asian destination. Like other Maverick guides it is aimed at the traveler/tourist as well as those who have been transferred there for work. On some occasions you may feel like spoiling yourself and going for the best. On others you might need to watch your finances (for whatever reason) and so will be looking for budget-priced options, such as on a Sunday afternoon when you have spent most of your *rupiah* (the local currency) and you want to go out for a meal. Both ends of the spectrum are covered in this Maverick guide, although not down to the backpacker level. It is geared for people who have sufficient money but don't necessarily want to pay top dollar every time.

Certain words in the Indonesian language (*Bahasa Indonesia*) are used continually throughout this book, such as *jalan* (singular), meaning "street" or "road" in street addresses. (e.g., Jalan Thamrin 15). Transportation vehicles also have individual local names that are covered later in this section. In chapter four I have condensed the language section from my Australian publication, *Bali and Java: The Pocket Guide*, so that in emergencies when no one seems to speak English you will be able to make yourself understood.

Sea Routes to Bali and Java

Cruising around the islands of Bali and Java is a distinct possibility, though you will usually need to fly from your home to the starting point of the cruise. Departure points for these cruises include Singapore, Fremantle in Western Australia, and Sydney on the east coast of Australia. The *Q.E.II's* sister ship, the *Sagafjord*, calls into Bali during its yearly round-the-world cruise that takes some 111 days from New York to New York and leaves each January. Apart from the huge cost of this option, the other drawback is that you will only have two or three days in Bali. For details contact Cunard Lines at 1-800-221-4770.

Fairstar the Funship is a refurbished favorite of the P&O Fairstar company that cruises from Singapore to Penang in Malaysia, to Phuket in southern Thailand, and then south to Java and Bali. *Fairstar the Funship* anchors off Krakatoa Volcano in the straits between Java and Sumatra, then sails to Bali, where it stays for three days. From Bali, *Fairstar the Funship* heads for Sydney, stopping at Darwin, Cairns, and the Whitsundays in the Great Barrier Reef. The 25-night cruise costs around US$2000 per person. You will need to add on airfares to Singapore and back from Sydney, Australia. Ask your travel agent or contact P&O Fairstar at 1-800-421-0522 for details.

Leaving from Sydney and going in the opposite direction is the Russian cruise liner the *Belorussiya*. The 31-day cruise passes through the

Java Sea, South China Sea, Malacca Straits, to Bali, and back to Sydney via the Great Barrier Reef. Three thousand dollars is the fare per adult in a four-berth cabin. Book through your agent or C.T.C. Cruises.

The *Cora Princess* (formerly *M.V. Coral Princess*) sails between Fremantle and Southeast Asian cities, stopping at Jakarta and Bali on the way. The *Cora Princess* offers cruises that leave from and return to Fremantle (location of the America's Cup yacht races in 1987), or shorter cruises that start in Singapore and stop in Bali on the way to Fremantle. The 16-day cruise will cost you under US$2000 to make a full circle of the ship's route.

For information on the Australian ports of call you should have a look at the *Maverick Guide to Australia*, so that you can get the most out of your time there.

The Airways to the Indies

Paying big money for first-class airfares to Indonesia certainly ensures that you will be pampered for that long flight across the Pacific Ocean, but you have to ask yourself if it's worth the extra thousands of dollars that first class costs. Currently a full-fare first-class ticket with no restrictions can cost up to $5000.

Business Class. Some of you may not want to spend so much on first class, yet may not want to travel real economy. In between these two, most airlines now sell a "J-class" ticket called "business class" for around $2500-$3000 round trip. The fare costs a few hundred dollars more than economy class, but you do have quicker check-in, more spacious seating, and better meals and reading material during your flight.

Economy Class. Real savings can be had by flying economy class (or coach class), though you may get a little cramped and stiff-necked on the long Pacific leg. Some consolation to make the plane trip a little easier to bear is that the money stays in *your* pocket rather than the airline's. As well as in normal economy class, additional savings can be had by booking and paying in advance for an APEX ticket ($1500 round trip). APEX stands for Advanced Purchase Extension and is geared for those who have a firm plan to travel there and back and not change the departure date. The return trip, however, is sometimes able to be changed. If you break any of the conditions of your ticket and cancel, you could lose up to half of the fare. Full-fare tickets, while more expensive, do allow you the option of changing your travel dates or even canceling altogether and still getting a refund. Insurance against sickness causing a cancellation is a possible safety net for APEX ticket holders.

The full-fare economy-class round-trip ticket to Bali or Java now costs around $2500 from California. The price varies with the airline you travel with, how many stopovers you have, and what time of the year you fly. Some airlines are trying to cut costs by putting in smaller seats with less leg room, and even adding an extra seat to each row. If you have long legs, check in early and ask for an aisle seat. At least then you'll be able to hang your legs out for a stretch. The most cramped seats are those in the middle of the center column of the cabin (generally E, F, and maybe G).

Which Airline to Fly? You have a choice of several American and foreign airlines to fly to Bali and Java. Garuda Indonesia Airlines flies direct to Bali from Hawaii, while other airlines fly via Guam, Japan, Singapore, Hong Kong, or Australia. Most U.S. flights across the Pacific Ocean leave from Los Angeles or San Francisco.

Continental. Of the American airlines, Continental has the most direct route, leaving three times a week from Los Angeles at 8:30 A.M. The first leg is Flight 3 to Guam, then you connect to flight 900 to Denpasar, Bali. Your arrival time in Bali is 8:40 P.M. but your flying time is much more than the clock indicates, as you have crossed over the International Date Line between Hawaii and Guam. With its extensive North American network, Continental offers you good connections for your flight across the Pacific. If you don't live on the West Coast, you probably should plan to spend the night in Los Angeles. Otherwise you'll be totally exhausted by the time you reach Bali. Also, don't forget that you'll need to allow a couple of hours for check-in, since it's an international flight.

Like other carriers in the Pacific, Continental sports three classes. They are: First (16 sleeper seats in a two-two-two configuration); Business Class (28 seats set up two-three-two in the lower deck and two-two on the upper deck); and Economy (390 narrower seats arranged three-four-three, a total of 10 across).

The airline does not charge extra for headsets or drinks on any of its Pacific runs. In first and business classes the headsets are now electronic.

United Airlines. United, the largest airline in the Western world, took over the Pacific routes of Pan America in early 1986. If you leave from Los Angeles, you have a choice of some ten morning flights on weekdays and around half that on weekends to Hong Kong, Tokyo, or Singapore. From these cities you can easily connect to Bali or Jakarta on Garuda, Singapore Airlines, Cathay Pacific, or Japan Airlines. From San Francisco there are three daily flights to Hong Kong, six to Tokyo, and four to Singapore. From Chicago, United flies twice daily to Hong Kong, some five times daily to Tokyo, and three times daily to Singapore. The majority of these are morning flights that get you back on the ground in Tokyo in the mid-afternoon, Hong Kong at around 8:00 P.M., or Singapore at midnight. Connections to Bali or Jakarta can also be made with Garuda, Singapore Airlines, Cathay, or J.A.L.

Garuda Indonesia Airlines. Indonesia's national carrier is currently the only airline that flies direct from the U.S. to Bali and then on to Jakarta, the capital city. The DC-10 flight leaves four times a week from Los Angeles (via Honolulu) at 8:00 P.M. and stops for fuel at the island of Biak in Indonesia (near New Guinea). Garuda is a good value, with a combination of cheap airfares, a subsidy against your accommodation costs, knowledge of hotels and internal flights, and the charm of Asian in-flight service.

Qantas Airways. The Australian airline also flies to Bali. There are some twenty flights a week from various Australian cities to Bali and Jakarta. Getting from the U.S. to Australia is easy, with many airlines crossing the Pacific. The closest major Australian airport to Bali is Perth in Western Australia. Bali is three hours flying due north of Perth by jumbo jet. Sydney, on the eastern coastline of Australia (facing South America), is seven hours south-east of Bali by jumbo jet.

Singapore Airlines. Rated one of the world's best airlines, S.I.A. flies daily to Jakarta via Singapore, leaving from Los Angeles. From Jakarta there are connecting flights to Bali. To leave Bali you will need to go back to Jakarta and Singapore. Flights to Jakarta from San Francisco are also available. Singapore Airlines offers excellent service and newer planes, but the fares are generally a bit more expensive.

U.T.A. French Airlines. This airline offers a weekly jumbo flight from Los Angeles to Jakarta via Papeete in Tahiti and Sydney, Australia. This flight is reasonably priced, and a stop-over in Tahiti will give you an idea of what is ahead of you in Bali, as well as a rest on this long haul.

Other Airlines. Several other airlines offer services from the West Coasts of America and Canada to Asian cities and on to Jakarta and then Bali. This second leg may be with the same airline or, more likely, with Garuda Indonesia if they don't fly into Indonesia themselves. **Northwest Airlines** flies via Japan to Southeast Asia, and **T.W.A.** goes as far as Japan.

Of the Asian airlines, **Japan Airlines** leaves from L.A., San Francisco, Chicago, Vancouver, and other cities to Tokyo, Japan, and then on to Jakarta. **Thai Airways International** flies the Pacific to Bangkok, with connections to Singapore. **Cathay Pacific** flies to Hong Kong and on to Singapore.

Which airline you choose depends to a large extent on whether you want to combine other countries with your Indonesian adventure, or whether you would prefer as direct and short a flight as possible.

Transportation in Indonesia

Getting around Bali and across to Java can be as easy as catching a taxi or jet aircraft. Or you could travel with the locals and you'd be sure to have lots of experiences to tell about back home.

Garuda has a Fokker F28 jet service between Bali's only airport and a few major cities in Java, such as Jakarta, Surabaya, and Jogya. Overnight express buses leave Denpasar each afternoon for Java. The trip to Jogya is 14 hours, including a roll-on, roll-off ferry crossing. The atmosphere at the Balinese port of Gilimanuk is electrifying, as dozens of buses line up to drive onto the ferries for the 30-minute ride. A drawback is that there can be holdups up to 2-3 hours in both directions at the ferry crossing or near traffic accidents in Java.

Bali's size of 125 miles x 65 miles (200 kilometers x 100 kilometers) means that you can get anywhere in one day or around the tourist areas in a morning. There are plenty of taxis in Kuta, Sanur, and Nusa Dua, as well as 6-seater minibuses at the beaches and Denpasar. Elsewhere in Bali there are few taxis but you can negotiate a ride back to your hotel in a minibus. If you use a minibus as a taxi, it's called to "charter." This is a handy word to remember so they don't stop to pick up anyone else on the way, or wait for someone to come along and make up the numbers.

In Java the means of public and private transport are much the same. It can take 2-3 days to travel the 850 miles (1200 kilometers) between Denpasar and Jakarta, or an hour or two by jet. Taxis in Jakarta and Surabaya have meters. In other towns in Java taxis are more likely to be replaced by minibuses operating on a fixed rate system. Be sure to bargain hard before sitting down inside a "charter" minibus. If you don't fix a price before traveling in Indonesia, you can't argue about the fare being too expensive when you arrive. And some drivers like to take advantage of both local *and* Western travelers.

Domestic Air Travel Up until recently, Garuda was the only domestic airline permitted to use jet aircraft. **Merpati** and **Bouraq** airlines fly many of the same routes, but as these fleets are mostly prop aircraft the fares are lower and traveling time is longer.

Fares on Garuda around Bali and Java are quite reasonable: US$107 from Denpasar to Jakarta, US$58 from Denpasar to Jogya, and US$63 from Jakarta to Jogya. There are 6 flights daily each way between Denpasar and Jakarta and 4 flights each way between Jogya and Jakarta. This will be covered in more detail in each location under Long Distance Travel.

Airport taxes in Indonesia vary with where you're leaving from and your destination. For travelers leaving the country the tax is Rp7000 in Jakarta and Rp5000 in Bali. The domestic tax is Rp5000 and Rp3000.

Getting from the airport to your hotel is well taken care of by a taxi cooperative in Bali that has set prices to all areas of Bali. You pay in advance at the booking desk, and your allocated taxi will then come forward.

Many of the larger hotels in Bali will have an employee waiting outside as you leave the arrivals area. Inquire about this with your agent when booking your accommodation.

In Jakarta there is a similar system with a one-hour drive into the city along a toll road. Here you need to check the fare to your hotel before leaving.

Taking the Train. While train travel in Java is by no means luxurious, the route between Jogyakarta and Bandung along the southern coast and the highlands of West Java rates the best for scenery.

Daytime travel in Indonesia can be pretty unbearable due to the heat and dust, so air-conditioning is recommended. In the economy section there are few restrictions on the number of passengers allowed on board and Indonesians like to keep the windows closed. Theft of valuables when you sleep does occur.

The daytime *Parahyangan Express*, with assigned seating between Jakarta and Bandung, is definitely recommended. Another classic train is the *Bima*, which leaves Jakarta at 4 P.M. for Jogya and Surabaya. Sleepers, meals, and AC are available. Fares are $16 to Jogya or $20 to Surabaya. The day train between Jakarta and Jogya is the *Fajar Utama*. It leaves at 6 A.M. and costs $20 for first class with AC. The *Mutiara* goes from Jakarta to Surabaya via Semarang, going straight along the north coast.

From Surabaya there are day trains to Banyuwangi, the ferry terminal to Bali. Day trains stop a lot and are hot.

The meals that are available on all these trains are mostly typical Indonesian fare such as fried rice or noodles, rice, meat and vegetables, or chicken soup. It is advisable to stock up on fruit, bread, biscuits, and canned juice before you get to the station. Then you can eat when you wish.

Escorted train tours are run from Australia, catering to Australian and Dutch train buffs who are fans of the nineteenth-century train network built by the Dutch colonial government. Contact the WA Newspapers Travel in Perth, Australia (Tel. (09) 321-4757) for tour details. You can join the tour in Bali.

Buses and Minibuses. Jakarta and Surabaya have city and suburbs bus systems similar to any in the world, but no other city or town in Bali or Java does. Instead, 6 to 20-seat minibuses called *"colt"* (Mitsubishi

DISTANCES BETWEEN TOWNS IN JAVA (KM)

Km	Wonosobo	Cilacap	Tegal	Tasikmalaya	Solo	Surabaya	Sukabumi	Serang	Semarang	Rembang	Probolinggo	Purworejo	Pekalongan	Malang	Magelang	Madiun	Kediri	Jogyakarta	Jember	Cirebon	Bogor	Bondowoso	Jakarta	Banyuwangi	Bandung
Bandung	339	259	202	106	467	675	96	258	367	476	774	362	266	764	403	581	662	428	873	130	126	869	180	964	0
Banyuwangi	678	768	762	893	506	280	1060	1171	597	490	190	637	698	281	633	412	367	571	104	834	1090	128	1082	0	964
Jakarta	481	428	320	275	585	793	115	89	485	594	882	504	384	882	522	699	780	565	991	248	54	986	0	1082	180
Bondowoso	560	671	665	796	409	192	965	1074	500	393	93	540	601	184	517	315	270	474	33	739	993	0	985	128	869
Bogor	465	385	328	232	593	801	61	143	493	602	900	488	392	890	530	707	788	554	999	256	0	993	54	1090	126
Cirebon	233	203	72	121	337	545	226	337	237	346	644	256	136	634	274	451	532	317	743	0	256	739	248	834	130
Jember	565	695	671	801	414	198	977	1080	506	399	99	545	607	185	522	320	275	479	0	743	999	33	991	104	873
Jogyakarta	107	197	245	322	65	427	524	654	118	212	381	66	181	363	43	179	240	0	479	319	554	474	565	571	428
Kediri	326	437	460	562	175	124	758	869	295	206	177	306	376	103	283	81	0	240	275	532	788	270	780	367	662
Madiun	265	375	379	501	114	169	677	788	214	145	222	245	315	184	221	0	81	179	320	451	707	315	699	412	581
Magelang	64	174	202	297	108	370	500	611	75	184	443	44	138	406	0	221	283	43	522	274	530	517	522	633	403
Malang	449	560	562	682	298	89	860	971	397	275	91	429	499	0	406	184	103	363	185	634	890	184	882	281	764
Pekalongan	134	195	64	257	201	409	362	473	101	210	508	170	0	499	138	315	376	181	607	136	392	601	384	698	266
Purworejo	54	131	223	256	131	393	458	593	119	228	446	0	170	429	44	245	306	68	545	256	488	540	504	637	362
Probolinggo	487	598	572	702	316	99	870	981	407	300	0	446	508	91	443	222	177	381	99	644	900	93	892	190	774
Rembang	228	355	274	467	147	201	572	683	109	0	300	228	210	275	184	145	206	212	399	346	602	393	594	490	476
Semarang	119	246	165	358	100	308	463	574	0	109	407	119	101	397	75	214	295	118	506	237	493	500	485	597	367
Serang	570	517	409	364	674	882	203	0	574	683	981	593	473	971	611	788	869	654	1080	337	143	1074	89	1171	258
Sukabumi	435	355	298	202	563	771	0	203	463	572	870	458	362	860	500	677	758	524	969	226	61	966	115	1060	96
Surabaya	434	523	473	649	262	0	771	882	308	201	99	393	409	89	370	169	124	327	198	545	801	192	793	280	675
Solo	151	262	265	387	0	262	563	647	100	147	316	131	201	298	108	114	175	65	414	337	593	409	585	506	467
Tasikmalaya	233	153	193	0	387	649	202	364	358	467	702	256	257	682	297	501	562	322	801	121	232	796	275	893	106
Tegal	197	131	0	193	265	473	298	409	165	274	572	223	64	562	202	379	460	245	671	72	328	665	320	762	202
Cilacap	127	0	131	153	262	523	365	517	246	355	598	131	195	560	174	375	437	197	695	203	385	671	428	768	259
Wonosobo	0	127	197	233	151	434	435	570	119	228	487	54	134	449	64	266	326	107	565	233	465	560	481	678	339

Colt) follow set routes but not to set timetables. Rather, the conductor calls out to potential customers while the minibus is moving or waiting for some passengers to make up the number so it will be worth his while to continue on the route. The smaller the town, the smaller the vehicle used. In Denpasar, 3-wheeled *bemo* (pronounced "beemo") that run on 2-stroke engines putter around the town center. Reasonably comfortable 14-seaters make the 1/2-hour run to Kuta Beach or Nusa Dua. Six-seaters ply the 1/4-hour run to Sanur Beach. To towns outside Denpasar, there are village buses at set times or 10-seater minibuses on free scheduling. On Java, the situation is much the same as Bali, with the addition of man-drawn vehicles (*becak*) and horse-drawn carriages (*dokar*). These will be covered in more detail later.

As indicated, buses and minibuses run during the day between all towns and cities on Bali and Java. For longer trips from Denpasar to Surabaya, Jogya, or Jakarta, there are also overnight express buses that leave in the afternoon and arrive at around 6 A.M. An overnight express bus (*bis malam cepat*) is probably the best way to go direct to Surabaya from Bali if you don't want to fly. The journey takes around 10 hours, including a roll on-roll off ferry crossing. The direct bus between Denpasar and Jakarta is not recommended. The 20-hour trip is too long, and the towns and countryside passed through offer pretty poor scenery.

From Bali, I would suggest taking an overnight express bus to Jogya, staying there for a couple of days, and then taking the train to Jakarta. The intercity bus terminals in Jakarta are way out of town and ticket scalpers and pickpockets can be a real menace. Gambir railway station, on the other hand, is well placed in the central business district a short taxi ride from most of the major hotels. When you arrive in Jogya at the crack of dawn, you will probably need to fix a price with a *becak* driver if there is no taxi or *bemo* available for "charter." If you catch a bus to Bali from somewhere in Java, you will be let off at the Ubung bus terminal. There you should be able to "charter" a *bemo* to your hotel. Price should be around Rp5000 for the vehicle, not per head.

Day buses travel between all towns in Bali and Java at regular intervals. Locals catch them back from or to market, so there is lots of animals and produce. Sometimes they stop every few hundred yards and can take hours to get anywhere. They are okay if you have got plenty of time and don't mind getting hot or squashed.

Other Vehicles. The *becak*, the Indonesian tri-shaw (pronounced betchuck), has a two-wheeled cubicle about 3 feet wide in the front with half a bicycle attached to the back of the cubicle. It has a plastic canopy for protection against the sun or rain. The *becak* driver does not own his vehicle but rents it from a local businessman at a daily rate. For some destitute *becak* drivers in Java, their *becak* is their home. It is true that working conditions may be hard, but the pay is more than that of a process worker. Fix the price before sitting down. It is rarely more than Rp500.

Becak are not very common in Bali, and Jakarta city has been declared a *becak*-free city. This is causing great problems in some suburbs, as the *becak* is the feeder for the main bus routes to one's home. In the commercial district though, the ruling is helpful because *becak* drivers are notorious for blocking the traffic near bus stops so that they can find a passenger. Late at night they can be fun, cruising along tree-lined streets with the wind in your hair. I think it will be a long time, if ever, until *becaks* will disappear from Jakarta's streets, at least during the wee hours. This banning of *becaks* from Jakarta has meant that other Jakarta cities now have more. If *becaks* aren't moved off the bigger roads, or out of Jakarta, they end up as artificial reefs at the bottom of Jakarta Bay.

The *bajaj* (pronounced badge-I), a motorized *becak*, now reigns where the *becak* once went. The Indonesian authorities thought it bad for their country's image that human labor was used to transport people around the capital, so a motorized version has superseded the pedal-powered one. In some ways this is a positive step, but they are bad polluters and lack the exotic feeling of the *becak*. Fix the price before sitting down; it's usually about Rp500-1000.

The *dokar* (dot-car) is a horse-drawn carriage found in the smaller Javanese and Balinese towns where *becak* have not penetrated. In large towns they are usually used by a local merchant taking produce to and from a market. Once again, fix the price—usually Rp500-1000—first.

The *ojak* is simply a motorbike carrying a passenger. In Denpasar and Javanese cities a ride on the back of a 100cc or 125cc motorcycle may be the quickest way of getting around. The fare is usually Rp500-1000 for a 1-2-mile ride.

Ferries and Ships. As Indonesia is an archipelago of some 3000 islands, ferries and ships are a major form of transportation. The Bali Strait at the ferry terminal is only a mile wide and takes around an hour. Interisland buses roll on and off this ferry and all interisland ferries. There is a small ferry from Padangbai in East Bali to the island of Lombok, which takes around 6-10 hours. From Merak in West Java there are ferries to South Sumatra.

Where the distance is too great for ferries, large freight ships move produce and people, such as from Jakarta or Surabaya to all the major ports in Indonesia.

Conditions on all sea vessels in Indonesia are pretty poor, the unpleasantness increasing with the duration due to lack of sanitation and catering facilities. Think twice before traveling more than 10 hours by sea.

Motorcars and Bikes. In Bali, Volkswagon convertibles and Suzuki jeepneys are available for self-drive rental on a daily or weekly basis. The daily rate is around $20 plus insurance. You should be aware, however, that the rules of the road in Indonesia are, in practice, quite different from the rules in the U.S., or almost anywhere else, for that matter. The major difference is that *everyone* gives way to buses and trucks, and cars should also give way to bicycles or animal-drawn carriages. Keep your hand ready for the horn. Beep if anyone or anything looks remotely like getting into your way, especially pedestrians. The onus is on *you*, the driver of the oncoming vehicle, to warn them to get out of your way. Pedestrians tend not to look before crossing the road and often lack road sense, especially on village roads. Keep your speed down to 60 kilometers per hour (40 mph) except on country roads where you have visibility of over 100 yards. Then you can go up to 80 kilometers (50 mph) with safety.

Highway traffic police are rare in Indonesia but road conditions are often poor, so be careful. If you're thinking of driving while in Indonesia, get an international driver's license before leaving home, so you won't have any delays when in Indonesia. Otherwise you will have to waste half a day getting a driver's permit.

I would advise against riding a motorbike during your first week in Bali, until you get a feel for the traffic situation. By law, you must wear a helmet if on a motorbike, and shoes and jeans are advisable for added protection. Motorbikes rent for around $5.00 (Rp10,000) per day.

The ideal way to get around the slower towns of Ubud and Jogya is by bicycle. Riding a bicycle will slow you down and give you a chance to experience the local pace of life. It gives you a breeze in your face and saves you walking in the dust, too. Daily rental is around Rp1,500.

Choosing Your Rental Vehicle. Before you take possession of your rental vehicle, make sure that the lights, brakes, and horn/bell are all in good working order. If the horn or lights don't work without the engine running, the battery is flat. Insist on a new one and it will be found very quickly. Ignore these precautions and you run a good chance of having problems. Petrol stations are few and far between in Indonesia, so fill up whenever you see one.

In Jakarta you are much better off renting a car with a driver than driving yourself. Apart from knowing his way around, he will take care of the hassle of parking and avoid tampering with the vehicle by street kids.

Choosing a Travel Agent

The key to your having happy memories of your Indonesian adventure is having a travel agent who has been to Indonesia at least once. The agent will then be in a better position to suggest you may prefer Kuta to Sanur, or wouldn't appreciate the slow pace of Jogya. If you go on a Garuda package, you are able to benefit from a government subsidy of the air fare or accommodation. For this reason, package tours with Garuda should usually be cheaper than those with other airlines. Booking your hotels before you leave is definitely cheaper than booking when you arrive in Indonesia, especially during the peak seasons of July-August and December-February.

On the other hand, local tours are best arranged in Indonesia. There are plenty of reliable tour operators and most day tours are quite cheap.

Accommodations

Room rates in Indonesia vary from US$200 a night in an international-class, 5-star hotel to US$3.00 a night in a 10- to 20-room hotel called a *losmen* or *penginapan*.

The better hotels in Jakarta or the beaches of Kuta, Sanur, or Nusa Dua rate on a par with any in the world for comfort and facilities, and provide Asian service with Indonesian grace and style. If you pay more than US$50 a night in Bali or $100 in Jakarta you are reasonably sure of being happy with the room and service. As the price drops, service and cleanliness tend to suffer. It really depends on how much you care about the little things. At the Kuta or Sanur beaches you can get a well-appointed bungalow with a flush toilet and hot shower for US$50 a night.

In section 4 of each chapter of this book, I will outline the different types of accommodation available and make recommendations. Away from the major resorts and cities there are few places with basics such as flush toilets, hot water, or air conditioning. However, this in no way means that such places are not clean or pleasant to stay in. In some ways, they offer more than any 5-star hotel in terms of friendliness. If you stay in these hotels with a local or sometimes Dutch feel, you get the chance to meet middle-class locals, instead of just other Western tourists. Room rates average $US10-$20 a night.

Local Tour Operators

For all your sightseeing tours to temples, volcanoes, or shopping safaris, you can book them through an agent back home or book them when you get to Bali. If you have 1 or 2 weeks in Bali, I wouldn't worry about booking them until I got there. Most of the tours can be booked one day in advance. It would be quite a bit cheaper to pay for the tour in Indonesia, so if you are watching your dollars you will be able to save a few this way.

Sightseeing and guided tours are covered in section 6 and 7 of each location. If you know a few basic Indonesian words and phrases such as "where to go," "how much," and "what time," and you have a map, you can get around Bali and Java reasonably easily by public transportation. The only problem is the noon-day heat and the delays, so be prepared to warm up a little. When you do, grab a cool drink.

Eating Out

Indonesian cuisine is a gourmet's delight, and seafood and American and European food are so plentiful that you don't have to eat the local dishes if you don't want to. But if you do, there is plenty of it, from Rendang beef curry to fried rice, Hokkien noodles, or *sate*, as well as plenty of fruit for sale at roadside stalls. Most fruit is only Rp100 per piece, although the evil-smelling *durian* will cost you Rp5000. Kuta and Sanur each have dozens of excellent restaurants, cafes, and bars in addition to those in the bigger hotels. Poolside bars are a specialty of Bali, such as the Bali Intan Bungalows at Legian, where the bar is in the pool. It's a favorite with Australians in their 20s. Restaurants and dining are covered in section 5 of each location.

Sports and Leisure

Bali Handara Country Club, chosen repeatedly as one of the world's greatest 50 golf courses, is perhaps the only one set in the crater of an extinct volcano. The waters of Bali are well known for their colorful coral gardens and surfing breaks. You can also go parasailing or sailboarding, or just laze on any of the white sandy beaches.

If you prefer ball sports, many of the larger hotels in Bali and Jakarta have tennis courts, a gym, sauna, and sometimes a golf driving range. Squash courts are not so common.

On Java the sports cater to businessmen and expatriates rather than tourists. Jakarta has the most to offer, especially tennis, squash, golf, swimming pools, bowling, and water sports at beaches or islands 2 hours away by car or boat. In section 8 of each location the water sports will be given in more detail. Other sports are in section 9.

Nightowls will find the discos, nightclubs, piano bars, and supper clubs of Sanur, Nusa Dua, Kuta, and Jakarta very cool and relaxed. At the bigger hotels, bars, and pubs throughout Indonesia, the usual live music is jazz-rock, except for Kuta, where rock takes over. Nightlife and entertainment is in section 11 of each location.

How about taking on nature and climbing a volcano? In Bali you can do it at Penolokan. First you drive or ride a horse from the main road to the edge of a lake, cross the lake by motorized dugout canoe, and then ascend the black sand peak. Java has several. Mt. Bromo in East Java is probably the most spectacular and accessible to anyone who can climb stairs or walk along a beach. If you're a walker, you'll just love Indonesia.

Photography

Being in the tropics, glare can be a problem between 11 A.M. and 2 P.M. or with water nearby. The film best suited to daytime use is 100 ASA. Use 400 ASA for sunsets and indoors. Fuji film on Kodak paper gives good results. Color prints are very cheap in Indonesia, around Rp100 per print (6 cents).

Most Indonesians don't mind having their photos taken. If you don't have a telephoto lens for close-ups, you should ask permission first—just a simple "May I?" will do. Try not to crowd the locals, especially when they are praying. You shouldn't take photos of the military or people bathing. Photography is allowed in most places of worship, but avoid using a flash. Serious photographers should be sure to take along polarizing and sunscreen filters for single lens reflex cameras.

Airport scanners in Bali or Java won't hurt your film, but the heat and humidity can. Store your undeveloped film in a cool place in a sealed plastic canister. Cars parked in the sun or the glove box when moving can become very hot. The floor away from the exhaust pipe is the best place to keep your camera and film. Sand and salt can also damage your camera, so try to keep it in a bag at the beach.

Indonesia is like paradise for photographers, with so much beauty, color, and smiling faces.

Travel Facts and Figures

BAGS AND BAGGAGE

At home—As most of you will be leaving North America by plane, you're automatically limited on the total amount of luggage you can carry with you. Whether leaving or entering the U.S. or Canada, you will be limited to 2 pieces of baggage per person traveling (including children), plus a small amount of hand luggage.

Neither of the two checked bags may exceed 62 inches in overall dimension—adding together length, width, and height, and unless you're traveling first class, the two together may not exceed 106 inches, all told. Virtually no commercial suitcase made in the U.S. exceeds 62 inches, so you should be okay. In Indonesia most suitcases sold are within the size limitations. If in doubt, put a tape measure over it.

You're allowed one or more pieces of carry-on luggage small enough to fit under one seat (camera bag, airline bag, etc.). The maximum outside dimensions of all those pieces combined may not exceed 45 inches per person.

If you have an extra suitcase, be aware that it will cost you from about $70 (West Coast) to about $100 (East Coast) to take it to Indonesia as excess baggage. I would suggest you take 2 suitcases only half full so that you have plenty of space for Balinese clothes, *batik*, carvings, and other souvenirs. Also, airline regulations say you must put your name on the outside of your bags. If you're only staying at one address while you're away, put that on, too.

In Indonesia—Indonesia and other countries where you may plan a stopover on the way, such as Singapore or Australia, still follow the 44-pound (20 kilogram) rule (66 pounds for First Class), with no limitation on the number of bags or packages. Hand luggage is limited to one small bag plus a camera or umbrella. Depending on how full or overweight the plane is, and/or the whims of the check-in clerk, you may be charged for excess baggage. Each kilogram (2.2 pounds) is usually charged at 1% of the fare. Travel light and play it safe.

Packing I'll say it again—travel light, both in the weight of your baggage and the thickness of your clothes. On the other hand, take all the toiletries you'll need for your trip, because you probably won't be able to get them there at a reasonable price. If you're planning a sporty holiday, take your favorite racket, clubs, or goggles with you, or rent them there.

The Male Traveler Most Westerners dress very casually in Bali, to fit in with the climate and pace of life. A few supper clubs may require a jacket, but otherwise a shirt with a collar and slacks and shoes are enough. The Australians have made shorts, a t-shirt, and thongs (flip flops) the standard dress at Kuta. Javanese cities are more formal. Follow the locals and buy a long-sleeve *batik* shirt for formal occasions, with slacks and shoes.

The Female Traveler I would recommend that you wear a long-sleeved blouse or t-shirt with slacks or a knee-length skirt when away from your hotel or the beach. Indonesians, especially Javanese, have some funny ideas about the morals of women based on what they wear, even when the temperature is over 80 degrees F. and the humidity is near 80 percent. In Javanese cities you should avoid wearing tank tops or shorts. In fact, shorts are not recommended outside the hotel or off of the beach. Islamic values and these clothes do not go together, except for prostitutes, so beware.

Take a couple of light evening dresses for formal occasions. When you're out and about, slacks and t-shirts are suggested, depending on the area, and can be bought at the hundreds of boutiques and stalls in Bali or Java. Jeans tend to be a bit hot and are heavy. For shoes, a pair of comfortable tennis shoes or running shoes are the best for most times of the year. During the rainy months of December, January, and February, leather shoes are best for puddle jumping, and you should have a very light spray jacket. You may also need a light wool pullover if you plan to go into the mountains.

For Both A hat is good protection from the sun. Either take a soft one with you or buy a brimmed straw one for a dollar in Bali.

Add light underwear, pajamas or robe, and socks. As there are no laundromats in Indonesia, it may be more convenient to hand wash your underwear and socks in the evening and they will be dry by the morning. Most hotels have drying stands in each room. For dirtier clothes, room service will pick them up in the morning and return them to you ironed in the evening, for a fee.

With all the beaches and swimming pools you may need more than one swimsuit. Some people end up living in their suit during the day and only get dressed after sunset. Bali is that sort of place. (Ladies—most of Java is not.)

Apart from clothes and toiletries, take a camera. Film is quite cheap in Indonesia and color developing is especially so. A good combination is Fuji film on Kodak paper.

The radio networks are mostly Indonesian language and music, so a Walkman will let you play the cassette tapes that cost just $2.50.

A couple of last-minute warnings. If you like decaffeinated coffee, you'd better travel with it. It's available in the supermarkets but generally not served in restaurants. Don't forget to get enough of any prescription you may need before you leave, but also write down just what that medicine is. If you lose the bottle, an Indonesian doctor or pharmacist may be able to match it.

Don't pack that medication in your suitcase, either, just in case the bag goes astray. It's much better in your hand luggage. That also applies to liquid toiletries, so they are less likely to spill. Pack the liquids in small plastic bags and knot them. Oh, and your passport. Keep it in your pocket or hand luggage. When moving between countries or hotels I always keep my passport, traveler's checks, and other documents in a passport-size zippered cloth neck pouch. No matter what happens, I won't be separated from them. Make sure you're not, either.

DEALING WITH OFFICIALDOM

Officials in Indonesia aren't always good at English, so speak slowly when confronted by one. They often try to play it tough. If you are a tourist you've got nothing to worry about. For working people it's a different story. Immigration formalities for workers in Indonesia can be very time consuming, so get an agent to handle the details.

TELEPHONE BOOKINGS

Be warned. Making a booking over the phone in Indonesia is not always reliable, especially if you are speaking English. Most of the hotels and restaurants listed in this guide have phones, but you have to speak slowly and ask for someone who speaks English. Ask the person taking the booking to repeat the details back to you before you hang up.

MEDICAL SERVICES

If you have an accident or health problems do not go to a suburban or small-town doctor. The main danger in going to one of these is that they often don't use sterilized instruments. In Bali there is a Western doctor at the Bali Beach Hotel and in Jakarta go to the Wisata Building behind Hotel Indonesia. In Jogya the Bethesda Hospital has a 24-hour casualty ward. If anything serious happens, go straight to one of these or come home.

DRINKING WATER

Drink only water that has been bottled, such as soda, AQUA, or other brands of mineral water. Juices in plastic bottles or those little disposable boxes and pouches are refreshing. Water or cold tea out of a clean bottle or teapot at a hotel, restaurant, or someone's home is also generally safe, as is ice in the same places. Bali Belly (Montezuma's Revenge), if it lasts for more than a couple of days, is more likely due to bad water rather than spoiled food. Quite often Bali Belly is caused by brushing your teeth in tap water. Just to be safe, carry a small bottle of AQUA for your teeth and late-night drinks. Play it safe and you won't end up spending half your holiday in the bathroom. If you are struck down, replace your body fluids with salt and water. A recent discovery is that raspberry cordial (powder or liquid drink concentrate) will stop the runs. You can take concentrated powder with you or buy it there by the bottle.

FIRST AID KIT

In a tropical climate all cuts and abrasions have to be kept dry and treated carefully, and usually with antibiotics. Kimia Farma is a pharmacist/chemist company with branches at most towns and resort areas included in this guide. It also markets pharmaceutical products under the same name.

I would recommend that you take a small first-aid kit with a few basics such as sterile gauze, antibiotic cream (mycin), anti-biotic powder (mycin) and Elasto-plast Band-Aids.

SUNBURN

Only mad dogs and Englishmen go out in the noonday sun. The locals sure don't if they can avoid it. Avoid sunbaking between 11 A.M. and 2 P.M. At all times you should use an ultraviolet sunblock of factor 15. Take some with you. And don't *EVER* fall asleep in the sun. It could make you quite sick.

ANIMALS

Dogs and monkeys, two animals that are thought to be friendly in the West, can be vicious in Asia. Because *dogs* aren't usually regarded as pets in Indonesia, they aren't petted and cuddled. The result is that when you go to pet them they will snarl and may bite you.

This can be extremely dangerous as there is rabies in Indonesia. If bitten go straight to the nearest doctor or hospital.

The *monkey* forests at Ubud and Mengwi are beautiful places to visit, but watch out for the monkeys. If you have seen the credit-card advertisement set at a temple in Thailand you will know why. The reason that the monkey took the bag was that it probably thought there was food inside. Feed the largest male first and then the others. Don't go too near the very young ones or their mother may defend them. Don't put any food in your pocket or bag. Show them your empty hands when you have no food left and they will soon go away.

WHEN TO GO

Or, more to the point, when not to go. Avoid the second half of December, and all of January and February—the Australian peak season. These are their summer vacation months, so if you want a taste of Australia without going there, just go to Kuta Beach during these months. Indonesia and Australia have a common sea boundary, so for people in Perth or Darwin, Bali is closer and cheaper than Sydney (only 3 hours' flight). The other peak period is July-August, when the French and other Europeans and Americans have their summer break.

The rainy season goes from December through February or March. This is another reason not to go there during the Southern Hemisphere's summer.

Most of the public holidays in Indonesia follow lunar calendars. The actual day can be hard to pin down, as they fall on different dates each year. You may have noticed that I used the plural "calendars." Just to confuse the issue further, Bali and Java have their own traditional Hindu Caka calendar, plus the Western and Islamic calendars that business and government use.

You won't have any problems on Bali during the Islamic fasting month of Ramadan. Java is a different story. Food outlets and local transportation may be less regular if you are sightseeing, and DO NOT eat or smoke in public in Java during daylight hours. People get pretty irritable toward the end of the month.

Local school holidays are not much of a problem. On public holidays all government offices, banks, post offices, and many local businesses close for the whole day. On Java the Islamic influence means they all close on Fridays at 11:00 A.M. for the day. Saturdays are a half or full day.

The more important holidays observed on both Bali and Java are:

January 1	New Year's Day
Variable	Idul Adha—Muslim day of sacrifice
Feb-March	Chinese New Year—many small businesses close for 1-2 days.
March-April	Good Friday/Easter Easter Sunday/Easter
April-May	Idul Fitri/Lebaran—2 days at end of Muslim fasting month of Ramadan.
May 10	Waicak commemorates the Lord Buddha (not a public holiday).
Aug 17	Independence Day
Dec 25	Christmas Day

Bali Only

Much of Bali continues with business as usual for many of the Islamic holy days, but stops on the following:

April	Hari Raya Puputan—anniversary of the suicide/ massacre of Bali's rulers in 1910.

Other religious holidays in Bali revolve around the 210-day Balinese calendar, so they come around almost twice in one of our years. The main ones are:

Galungan	Celebration of the creation of the universe.
Kuningan	10 days later. Ancestors bidden farewell.
Nyepi	Balinese New Year's Day, no work, fires, or traffic.

Also, every temple in Bali has its birthday ceremony (Odalon) every Balinese year, and seeing as there are hundreds of temples in Bali, there are processions heading towards temples every day of the year.

INTERNATIONAL POSTAL AND TELEPHONE SERVICES

If you're making your own arrangements by mail, send everything by air and check the rate at the post office before posting. Allow two weeks each way for mail to Indonesia, especially if you're not on the West Coast. Wherever possible we have included the fax number at the end of each hotel's address so that you can take advantage of this instant method of communication. One page takes around one minute to transmit to Indonesia, costing a couple of dollars.

Phone numbers are included with the local area code, so you can phone a hotel or car rental company direct if you wish. Dial 011 (the international access code), then 62 (the country code for Indonesia), then the area code and local number. Please don't get confused, but when calling long distance *within* Indonesia the area code is preceded by zero (e.g., "0361" for Southern Bali or "021" for Jakarta). Calling from overseas this extra zero is not used.

TIME ZONES

If you start your trip in Bali and plan to visit Java too, you will have to move your watch backwards an hour when you get off the plane or ferry. Traveling from Java to Bali the opposite applies. Catch the 5:30 P.M. plane from Denpasar and you can follow the sunset to Jakarta. Bali is 8 hours ahead of GMT, Greenwich Mean Time, so if it is 6 P.M. in New York and 3 P.M. in California, it will be 7 A.M. on the following day in Bali. Each of the islands, though, has only one time zone. Bali follows Central Indonesian Standard Time, while Java falls within Western Indonesian Standard Time, which is 7 hours ahead of GMT.

Being within 5 degrees of the equator, day and night are pretty much 12 hours each, with a changeover at 6 o'clock morning and evening, and the sun is directly overhead at noon. This regularity makes telling the time by the sun an easy exercise. Also, there is no daylight savings time to confuse you. Other places in this part of the world in one of these time zones are Singapore, Hong Kong, Peking (Beijing), and Perth.

Jet Lag

At least if jet lag hits you will have a good excuse for lazing around by the pool or beach for a couple of days. That will give your body clock a chance to readjust after racing the sun halfway around the world.

Take an overnight flight and you should at least minimize its effects. Also, although you lose a day crossing the International Dateline, you gain a couple of hours of extra sleep. That's the advantage of flying west instead of east. Flying over the Pacific you may wake up when it's still dark, but your stomach will tell you it's time for breakfast. That's your body clock working. The further east you start, the worse you'll be affected. East Coasters would be well advised to spend one overnight in L.A. on the way. Here are a few things you can do to reduce the impact of jet lag:

1. Change your watch to Indonesia time as soon as you take off.
2. Sleep as much as you can on the airplane.
3. Unless you are sleeping, stand up and walk around the plane once an hour or so.
4. Take no sleeping pills and little alcohol during the flight, but eat when food is offered.
5. After you arrive at your hotel, pull the shades and try to have a good nap.
6. Schedule no business appointments, car rentals, or demanding sightseeing on your first day.
7. Eat lightly, choosing familiar foods, on your first day.

METRICS AND ELECTRICS

Generally speaking, Indonesia follows the metric system. For travelers this means distances are in kilometers (5/8 mile), the average daily temperature is 30 degrees C, petrol is sold in liters, and fruit by the kilogram.

Temperature

The centigrade or Celsius system is based on a freezing point for water of 0 degrees C and a boiling point of 100 degrees C. Indonesia's usual daily maximum temperature is 30 degrees C all year round. This is a quite hot and humid 86 degrees F. Evenings cool down to around 25 degrees C (77 degrees F), or lower in the mountains. Try to avoid too much sun between 11 A.M. and 2 P.M. For an accurate Fahrenheit equivalent, multiply by 9, then divide by 5, then add 32. It's easy . . . with a pocket calculator. Not that you need one, because temperatures vary little throughout the year, wet or dry.

Distance and Length

Bali is shaped like a triangle that is 200 kilometers across the top and 100 kilometers top to bottom. That's about 140 miles across the north and 65 miles from the north coast to Nusa Dua on the southern point. However, short distances can take quite a while to cover, as the roads are only fair and the usual traffic speed is 60 kilometers per hour.

In a market or boutique you will buy *batik*, a decorative cloth somewhat similar to tie-dye, by the meter, which is a few inches longer than a yard. A good quality *batik* will usually be at least 2 meters in length.

Volume

Liquid measure is by the liter. Around one U.S. quart equals one liter. Four liters is around one U.S. gallon. The petrol tank on a four-cylinder car holds just over 30 liters, or 7 to 8 gallons. One fluid ounce is approximately 30 milliliters (ml.).

Weights

You will be confronted with kilograms as you pack your bag to leave for Bali. Your weight limit is 20 kilograms (kg), at 2.25 pounds per kg. At the lower end, 300 grams will get you just over 1/4 pound.

Area

The area of Bali and Java is measured in square kilometers. There are 10 hectares in one square kilometer. 2.5 acres makes one hectare, which is the size of many rural plots supporting one or more extended families.

Room size is measured in square meters, roughly equivalent to square yards or 11 square feet.

Electricity

While electricity is measured in volts, the same way as in North America, there are 220 of them coming out of most sockets. In some areas the voltage can vary between 170 and 250 volts. So don't take any appliances with you except possibly a low-voltage razor. Light bulbs unscrew and electrical plugs have two round prongs. Hair dryers have a bad habit of blowing the fuses even if they are the right voltage.

Stick to a battery-operated tape recorder if you want some music while you are away.

Security

VALUABLES

It is always safer to leave your valuables at the hotel rather than carry them with you. This applies all over Indonesia. Bag snatching does occur. As long as your room door is locked at all times, you have no need to worry. If you are staying at the same place for a few days, deposit your passport and valuables with the manager and write down what you have given him. In budget accommodations in Indonesia, your room is not cleaned if you are not present. When you are away, there is always someone watching for intruders.

JEWELRY

Leave it at home, as Balinese love to slip off your rings and try them on for size. They will give them back, but you will worry about how to ask for them without offending.

CHANGING MONEY

Put your money in your bag while still inside the bank. Separate the money into two groups—one being a wad of less than $50 for daily use so you don't flash a great pile of money all the time, and so draw attention to yourself and risk theft. Keep another wad in another pocket or somewhere safe.

POSTAL

When posting letters and packets in Bali, all post offices and agencies are reliable. On the other islands, however, it is safer to make sure that the stamps are postmarked before you leave your letter.

Money, Currency, and Prices

The currency of Indonesia is the *rupiah*, commonly referred to as the "roop." The average exchange rate in early 1991 was Rp 1,900 to one U.S. dollar. There is only the one unit of currency (i.e. no cents and dollars) so numbers can get very high. This makes it confusing and hard to judge if something is cheap or expensive. Coins are 5Rp, 10Rp, 25Rp, 50Rp, 100Rp. Notes are 500Rp, 5,000Rp 10,000Rp, and 100,000Rp. Remember that 1,000Rp is about 50 cents, 5,000Rp is $2.50, and 10,000Rp about $5.00.

Hotels and restaurants in hotels and up-market shops usually quote prices in U.S. dollars alongside rupiah. This is a hedge against the devaluations that have a habit of occurring every few years.

Try to get at least 10,000-50,000Rp before you arrive in Indonesia for the taxi ride to your hotel from the airport. If you don't, you should be able to change money at the airport when you arrive.

Bargaining

Bargaining is a part of the culture in Indonesia when shopping for fruit, souvenirs, and handicrafts. At roadside stalls or markets you may be able to get them down to 1/2 their opening price, sometimes only 20% off in more upscale shops. Restaurants, cafes, hotels, buses, tours, etc. operate at fixed prices.

Haggling in the market can be fun or irritating, depending on your mood at the time. Just remember if you offer a price you can't change your mind, because it's a verbal contract.

Credit Cards

American Express is the most widely accepted credit card in Indonesia. Next come Visa, Diners, and Mastercard. You can use credit cards at the larger hotels, restaurants, boutiques, and for car rental. The exchange rates charged by the cards are quite fair, but Diners adds on a foreign exchange fee.

Traveler's Checks

These are probably the best way to go if you want to get the best value for your dollars. In Bali the best rates are from banks and money changers at Kuta, Denpasar, or Sanur. In Jakarta and other Javanese cities there are banks and money changers. Elsewhere, each town usually has only one or two banks or money changers that offer the official rates. Most of the large hotels have money changers, but the rate is 5%-10% less than the official rate. Put your money into traveler's checks of $100, so you're not always going to the bank to change more. Also carry about $100 in US$10 notes for transit stops on your flights. Banks are open for business every day except Sunday from 8:00 A.M. or 9:00 A.M. until 1:30 P.M. and until noon on Friday.

Postage

Postcard rates are about 30 cents U.S. to most countries. Generally speaking, sending mail out of Indonesia is safe, though it is advisable to get it postmarked while you watch in Jakarta. Incoming mail is a different story.

Official Formalities

Thank goodness, there's not a lot of red tape to unwind for a trip to Bali or Java. Any travel agent should guide you through the governmental guff, but here it is in brief form.

Passport

Unless you're an Indonesian citizen you'll need a passport to enter Bali or Java. Americans can apply at a passport office in major American cities or at any U.S. post office. It can take a few weeks once you deliver or send in the filled-out form with the required photographs and fee.

A potential trip-up, however, is that the Indonesians require that your passport remain valid for six months beyond the date you expect to leave the country. If it won't, you'll just have to apply for a new one a little earlier than you may have planned.

Visas

Indonesia has lifted the visa requirement for Americans, Canadians, and a few other nationalities, providing they are staying as a tourist for no more than 30 days. You can find out about conditions for other visas by applying to the Indonesian diplomatic mission in Washington, New York, San Francisco, or Los Angeles.

Vaccinations

Vaccinations against cholera and typhoid are recommended. The cholera vaccine lasts six months and typhoid three years. Both diseases are contracted through food or water contaminated with human feces. Localized cholera outbreaks still occur in Bali and Java, especially in smaller towns and villages.

Malaria had been eradicated from Bali and Java but it is now coming back. For many years quinine was the major preventative treatment for malaria; in fact, gin and tonic was the famous colonial drink because tonic contains quinine. Much of the world's quinine is produced in Bandung in West Java. Spraying the ground with DDT was also successful for a while until the mosquitoes that carry the disease developed a resistance to the poison.

Any tablets given nowadays are only effective against some ten percent of mosquito varieties. They can also increase the risk, because they reduce the signs of fever that would warn you to go to a doctor, without stopping the virus itself. This could even end up causing the person's death. Tablets can also make you feel sick and spoil your holiday.

Instead, drink tonic before, during, and after your trip to beat the virus. Cover up with long pants, shoes, socks, and long sleeves so they can't bite you. When sleeping in a non-air-conditioned room, mosquito coils are recommended. One burns for around 8 hours, so light it before you go to sleep and place it on the stand underneath your bed. Also, put insect repellent on your ankles, neck, and some on your pillow before bed.

Don't let any of this put you off, however, as the chance of getting malaria is almost zero if you are not travelling to any other island or country.

Immigration Officials

Those passport stampers in snappy uniforms will want to see a few things before they allow you any farther than the airport—the passport, of course, and the visa, if needed, and perhaps your round-trip or ongoing ticket. That's just to make sure you're not coming into Indonesia to work or to become a burden on the economy. If these chaps think there's anything out of the ordinary, of course, they're allowed to ask for some kind of proof of your financial responsibility. They're polite and efficient. No genuine visitor needs to worry about them.

Customs

You're allowed to enter Indonesia carrying items for your own personal use. You won't have any trouble unless you're loaded down with stuff like drugs, alcohol, precious stones, a dozen tape recorders, and anything anyone in his right mind knows would be prohibited. You can bring in a quart of wine and a quart of hard liquor (spirits) and a carton of cigarettes. If you're concerned at all, pick up information at a travel agent or Garuda Indonesia Airlines office.

Coming home to the U.S., of course, you have to deal with U.S. customs—an easier job now that some computer-based procedures have finally been established. We can't go into all their rules and regs here, but remember that your duty-free allowance (which can be pooled with other members of your family) is currently $400 per person. If you keep it below that, you can make a declaration to that effect instead of writing it all out.

If you're thinking of bringing back some Balinese wine or beer, the limit is now one liter (just over a quart) of alcoholic beverage per person over 21. You'll pay duty plus internal revenue tax after that amount. If you buy valuable items like jewelry, you get the best customs deal if you carry them back with you rather than mailing them home. (You must pay duty on mailed items whether or not you have used up your exemption.) You'll clear U.S. customs at your first U.S. port. On the way to L.A., that will mean Honolulu, if your plane pauses there. If you're worried about any of this, the best thing to do is to pick up a free booklet entitled *Know Before You Go* from any customs office or write the U.S. Customs Service, P.O. Box 7118, Washington, D.C. 20044 for Customs Publication No. 512.

For Canadians, the limit on tobacco is 1 carton of cigarettes or 50 cigars or 2 pounds of tobacco. You may bring 40 ounces of liquor or wine back in or 24 12-ounce pints of beer per person. Check with the Canadian Customs Service for more details at Revenue Canada Customs and Excise, Ottawa, Ontario K1A OL5.

Further Information

In her popular syndicated newspaper column "Trip Tips," Marie Mattson once wrote that the best vacation trip begins at the public library. Don't step on a plane for Indonesia or any other country until you've had a chance to read up on your destination. We'd like to think that most everything you need can be found right here, but it wouldn't hurt to crack open an encyclopedia or a *National Geographic*. The public library should have a few books on history and geography, though it may be hard to get much background information in the U.S.A. In Indonesia the government tourist offices are wonderful sources of brochures, maps, and programs free of charge.

The tourist office is by no means our only source of information, and we certainly don't expect that its personnel will agree with all of our interpretations of the Indonesian scene today. Nevertheless, these friendly, capable folks have always been very helpful.

Garuda Indonesia Airlines are good people to contact for information on flights to and accommodations in Bali and Java. Their main offices in the U.S. and Canada are:

CHICAGO
20 North Michigan Ave. 104
Chicago, IL 60602
Tel:(312) 443-0063

HONOLULU
1600 Ksiolani Bldg., Suite 632,
Honolulu, HI 96814
Tel:(808) 945-3971
   (808) 947-9500

LOS ANGELES
Indonesian Consulate
General Building.,
3457 Wilshire Boulevard
Los Angeles, CA 90010
Tel:(213) 387-3323
   (213) 387-0651

MIAMI
2011 NW 117 Terrace
Pembroke Pines, FL
Tel:(800) 248-2829

NEW YORK
51 East 42nd Street,
Suite 413-415
New York, NY 10017
Tel:(212) 370-0707
   (212) 826-2829

SAN FRANCISCO
360 Post Street, Suite 804,
San Francisco, CA 94108
Tel:(415) 788-2626

VANCOUVER
1040 West Georgia Street.,
Vancouver BC, Canada V6E4HI

3

The Living Land

Java was one of "The Spice Islands" from which Portuguese traders brought back pepper and other herbs and spices hundreds of years ago. Bali is a small, diamond-shaped island adjacent to Java in the chain of islands that run between Malaysia and Australia. These are but two of the 13,677 islands that make up the country of Indonesia, the world's largest archipelago. Other major islands in Indonesia are Sumatra, Borneo (Kalimantan), Celebes (Sulawesi), and West New Guinea (Irian Jaya). Some of the smaller ones are Sumba, Sumbawa, Flores, Ambon, Timor, and Biak. The whole of Indonesia stretches 3,200 miles (5,150 kilometers) from east to west and 1,100 miles (1,770 kilometers) from north to south, straddling the equator (10 degrees N to 10 degrees S; 100 degrees E to 145 degrees E).

Java is an oblong-shaped island, some 850 miles (1,100 kilometers) from east to west and 150-230 miles (200-300 kilometers) from north to south. Across the narrow Bali Strait to the east is Bali, 125 miles (200 kilometers) from east to west and 65 miles (100 kilometers) from north to south. For the purposes of government, Java is divided into three similarly sized provinces from east to west, namely East Java, Central Java, and West Java. The whole of Bali and some small offshore islands make up one province.

Weather and Climate

The islands' location along the equator means that the climate is tropical with a high humidity, especially in the month or so before the rains begin. Temperatures tend to be similar for most of the year, from 85 degrees F (30 degrees C) during the day down to 70 degrees F (20 degrees C) at night. What varies is the humidity. When the air is dry the weather is beautiful, but when the humidity rises air-conditioning is a must in large towns and on the coast. In the upland areas daytime temperatures are average, but evenings can drop to 60 degrees F, which is quite chilly if it's raining.

The rainy season (sometimes called simply "the wet") starts just before Christmas and has usually finished by late February or March. There is some variation between coastal and upland areas. For example, it may be fine at Sanur but when you get to Kintamani it may be raining, especially in the afternoons. The same applies to Jakarta and Bogor, where it rains nearly every day for an hour or so. The driest months are from June through September, but the greenhouse effect is making the seasons less distinct. On certain religious occasions when in the past it never rained, it now sometimes does.

A Spiritual Land

The land and its bounty are a central part of life for the rural portion of Bali and Java's population, not only in the sense of growing crops or catching fish but also as a religious/mystical power that they worship and give offerings to in Bali or see as a source of strength and energy on Java. These beliefs apply not only to the Indonesians who live in rural villages and live through farming or raising livestock, but also the some 30 percent of the population that lives in towns and cities.

Mountains and Volcanoes

In the Balinese and Javanese worldview, which has many Hindu-Buddhist elements, certain volcanoes represent the home of their gods. On Bali, this mountain is Mt. Agung, and on Java it is Mt. Merapi. The fact that both volcanoes are highly active means that affairs of state can be and have been influenced by them. Eruptions could convey the impression to both the king and subjects that something was wrong and that the gods were not happy. Remedial action was needed, such as special offerings.

Volcanoes are a big attraction in Java, such as Mt. Bromo with its famed sunrise in East Java, and Mt. Tangkuban-prahu near Bandung in

West Java. Mt. Batur and its crater lake in Bali are stunningly beautiful and easily reached by car or bus. Mt. Agung blew the top off its once-perfect cone in 1963. No roads approach very close to the steep peak, but the fit and hardy can get there on foot (see Other Sports in Chapter 7).

Natural Resources

The main resources of these two islands are their rich soil and people, which, when combined, produce an abundance of rice and other agricultural products. Industries set up on Java process the raw materials that come from the other islands. This is often a sticking point between Java and the regions that provide Indonesia's oil, natural gas, tin, coal, gold, bauxite, seafood, and timber. Java has small deposits of gold, oil, natural gas, and thermal energy, and so does Bali, but not enough for the needs of their own populations.

In terms of food production, Java and Bali hold their own, and even export rice, fruit, and vegetables to less developed islands and resource projects.

Rice Growing

The lifestyle of the rural portion of the population largely revolves around the cultivation of wet rice, which is grown in irrigated fields, as opposed to dry rice, which depends for its water on rainfall. Over the centuries, a very elaborately balanced system of wet-rice cultivation has developed in Java and Bali in the areas where the soil is fertile. It seemed that the fertility of this soil was inexhaustible, so there was no need to develop a shifting pattern of rice growing (on other islands this was not the case). Volcanic eruptions replenished the soil at regular intervals, either through volcanic ash deposits falling from the sky or by alluvium weathered from lava on the mountain slopes. This sediment is carried into the rice fields by the irrigation channels and by the occasional flooding of rivers and streams.

Rice plants begin as seedlings sprouted from special rice from the previous year's crop. The seedlings are grown to around 6 inches high in a nursery and are then transplanted into a flooded field. The water level is kept at 3 inches or so deep for a few months until the crop nears maturity. In the last month the field is drained and the bunches of rice ripen and are harvested (mainly by hand). The rice stalks are used as feed for cows and buffalo, and later burned so that the ash will fertilize the soil. Chemical fertilizer is also used nowadays. Depending on the availability of water, the fields are left fallow for a few months or straight

Rice terraces

away plowed and reflooded and the cycle starts again. Some areas are able to plant two or even three quick-maturing crops each year.

In Bali, the *Subak* is the community water committee which determines which farmers' fields receive water on which days from the irrigation ditches that run for miles through the fields. Each farmer has 5-10 acres (1-2 hectares), but farmers group together and move from field to field to plant and later harvest the crop. Agriculture in Indonesia is very much a communal exercise.

Some Other Flora, and Some Exotic Fauna

During the worst years of Dutch colonization, rice production was neglected and the land was given over to plantations growing sugar, tobacco, and hemp. This caused famine and death but enriched the coffers of the government in Holland. These three crops are still important on Java.

Sugar plantations and mills are still evident in Central Java around Solo, and *tobacco* is an important mainstay of the highlands of East and West Java. In Bali *rice* is also dominant, but as the altitude rises so does the cultivation of *corn*, such as on the way to Kintamani. This is true also of Java in the non-irrigated highlands, such as near Bandung.

Everywhere across the two islands are *coconut* palms. The meat from the young fruit has the consistency of marshmallow and is best scooped out with a spoon. Someone has to climb the tree and cut the coconuts free to eat them at this young age. Otherwise they get old and hard and are grated for desiccated coconut, or dried for copra (dried coconut), or grated, soaked, and strained to become an ingredient of many dishes. After rice, coconuts are the most important food source of the poorer rural population. Don't sit or camp under the trees though, as the branches, which weigh 20-30 pounds, have a tendency to fall off without warning. At night you can hear the thump of branches hitting the ground. Falling fruit is also a problem. Dried husks are used for cooking fuel.

Indonesia is one of the world's main sources of *tropical hardwood timber*, though there is little left on Bali and Java. Except on inaccessibly steep slopes or at sacred places, natural forest is rarely to be found, though there is a reasonable amount of secondary forest in the highlands and the occasional teak tree. What natural forest there is, is on the rugged southern coast of Java and the western most part of Bali. Sacred *banyan* trees are at the center of most towns and large villages. These are huge trees with multiple trunks.

For the locals, *bamboo* is an important building material. The largest sections are used for house uprights and irrigation pipes. These poles are also stripped into pieces and interwoven to produce wall sections. Most villages have bamboo groves that are harvested on a regular basis.

Thatched roofs are common in Bali. Long *pandanus grass* is woven with bamboo to produce 6-feet by 3-feet sections that are laid one on top of another. More are added if a leak occurs.

Flowering plants are plentiful, such as *frangipani*, which is often worn behind the ear of Balinese men in ceremonial dress. *Hibiscus* and *bougainvillea* also add a splash of color to people's gardens. *Lotus* lilies do the same to landscaped ponds.

In Bali, flowers are especially important as offerings to the gods. In the markets, women sell woven flower offerings that are placed on home altars, on dangerous sections of road, and on the sidewalk outside each house's front door.

ANIMALS

Wild animals were once plentiful in Bali and Java, but the spread of agriculture and reduction of the forest cover has meant that the Javanese *tigers*, which once terrorized villagers, are now gone or restricted to the most rugged mountain slopes where man does not go. Similarly, the one-horned Java *rhinoceros* is bordering on extinction and is only found in the wild in the Ujung Kulon National Park on the westernmost tip of Java. In more plentiful supply are monkeys, which are considered sacred animals in Bali and inhabit the forests around the temples at Ubud and Mengwi. One of the largest primates, the *orang-hutan* (orangoutang, of course) (literally meaning "man of the woods") is native to Sumatra and Borneo and is only found in Javanese zoos.

Reptiles

The most famous Indonesian reptile is the *Komodo Dragon* which is similar in size to a crocodile or alligator, though with a smoother skin and smaller mouth. Fortunately in Bali and Java they are only found in the zoo. *Crocodiles* exist in the uninhabited tidal flats of western Bali but are not seen as a threat to humans. *Snakes* are in much the same boat as other wild animals. They are plentiful in other islands but are rarely seen in Bali or Java. Harmless tree snakes, their larger cousin the python, and cobras are in the forested areas. *Sea turtles* are quite common, and though protected in the West, in Bali they are hunted for food and to make souvenirs. So don't buy any!

A smaller reptile that likes to stay near man is the *gecko lizard*. The largely nocturnal gecko comes in two varieties—a three inch one called "chik-chack," and an eight- to ten-inch "tokeh." Both have sticky pads on their feet and spend most of the time on the ceiling and walls catching mosquitoes and other insects. In Bali, the story is that if they make their loud sound seven times it means good luck.

Domesticated Animals

Water buffalo are essential for the cultivation of wet rice and are pampered as a result. After their session in the fields, a young boy is given the task of washing and walking the buffalo to a place where it can find some fresh grass. These boys even cut grass off steep slopes and feed the buffalo by hand. Motorized plows are becoming popular, but water buffalo are still the best for the job. *Horses* are also important work animals, pulling carriages with people and produce in the rural towns and villages. These horses tend to be small and stocky, and unfortunately are not always treated as humanely as one would desire.

Of the domesticated animals, *dogs* in Bali need a mention. For some reason they are often treated quite badly, to the point where sick and starving dogs can be seen wandering the streets. Don't think this is a poor reflection of the Balinese; some people do treat their dogs as pets and feed them and treat them well. Just be careful, as I mentioned earlier, about trying to pet them. *Cats* keep pretty much to themselves, feeding on small birds and mice.

What the Balinese do treat as pets are the brightly colored *fighting cocks*. These are coddled, fed well and trained until their day comes in a win-or-die cockfight. Gambling had always been an integral part of cockfights, but this was banned in the late 1970s and so were the village cockfights. Nowadays the occasional cockfight accompanies religious ceremonies where fresh blood is needed for mystical purposes. Originally these fighting cocks came from the jungle. In fact, they are considered to be the forerunner of the domestic chicken which was later taken to other parts of the world.

Birds on the Wing

Seabirds are most common in the areas that visitors stay. Seagulls, sea hawks, pelicans, and cormorants can be seen eating and nesting around Sanur, Benoa, Pangandaran, and Pelabuhan Ratu. Of the land variety, Bali and Java have some beautifully colored birds, but these are rarely seen in inhabited areas. You will need to trek into the western part of Bali or the southern coast of Java to see birds out of cages. Other islands have the Bird of Paradise, peacocks, eagles, and jungle fowl which can be seen at the Surabaya Zoo or are for sale at various bird markets (*pasar burung*). What you do see a lot of in the towns are *homing pigeons*.

Insects

Of the insects, *mosquitoes* are the most plentiful and annoying, especially during the rainy season when they have plenty of still water to breed in. Mosquitoes also carry a danger of malaria, which is coming back again in Bali and Java after being eradicated by D.D.T. spraying in the 1970s and 1980s.

Butterflies are also plentiful and beautifully colored. A traditional Balinese dance is even based on a flirtation between two butterflies.

More Than the Spice Islands

The food is one of the major attractions of Bali and, to a lesser extent, Java. Topping the list are tropical fruits, seafood, and spicy rice dishes. Fruit and seafood are served naturally, in a Western manner, or according to local recipes. Iced fruit juice drinks, which consist of crushed ice, fresh fruit, and a little sugar thrown into a blender, are fantastic (and cheap). The variety, freshness, and price of local seafood means that you can stick to it for a week or two for every meal and not get bored.

Herbs and Spices

For those who want to try the local specialties, here are some of the most commonly used herbs and spices. Black pepper and hot chili peppers (the smaller the hotter) are used to put the whammo into the food and leave you with a perspiring forehead and teary eyes. If you find your mouth on fire from hot chilies, don't try to wash it away with cold water or beer. Hot tea, plain rice, or cucumber are best.

Cloves, cinnamon, ginger, laos, coriander, tamarind, and tumeric are added for more subtle tastes or coloring. Other important ingredients are brown sugar and the strong-smelling dried shrimp paste called *trasi*. Some of these herbs and spices are also basic ingredients for the herbal medicine called *jamu*.

Meats and Poultry

Chicken (ayam) is reasonably plentiful on restaurant menus and in the markets of Bali and Java. Seeing as how the present domestic chicken probably originated from Southeast Asian jungle fowl, this is understandable. Traditional chicken dishes include *ayam goreng* (fried chicken), *soto ayam* (chicken soup), and *sate ayam* (grilled skewers of chicken pieces). Cooked the Balinese or Javanese way, these three dishes are delicious. You may want to make a note of *sate*, which is a delicious method of cooking meat on a skewer. It's everywhere in Bali and Java. The noodle dish *bakmi*, which consists of flat noodles cooked in a chicken sauce, is a local Chinese favorite. Indonesian chickens tend to be a bit smaller and more chewy than the factory-bred Western variety, but they make up for it by being tastier. Bear this in mind if ordering Western dishes.

In Bali, *duck* (*bebek*) is baked in banana leaves (*bebek betutu*). Sometimes in the countryside you will see a man or boy with a long stick shepherding a gaggle of 20 or 30 ducks along the road. They are used as environmentally safe bug-eaters in the rice fields—and it saves on feeding costs for the ducks, too. Away from the big cities of Jakarta and Surabaya, poultry is usually grown on a free-range basis. The cities' Chinese populations have their own way of baking duck and hanging them in the shop window, much like in Hong Kong.

Soy-bean curd, called *tahu* in Indonesia, is an important protein source, both in the familiar cake form and also as *tempe*, fermented soy-bean cake made with whole soy beans.

Eggs are the safest way to eat if you're in an out-of-the-way place and have to eat local food, but you're not sure about the freshness. Eggs don't go bad as fast as meat, so you won't have to worry as much about the runs. Chicken eggs are boiled, fried, curried, added to soup, and sprinkled on top of *gado-gado* (vegetable salad).

When it comes to *meat*, there are some marked differences between Bali and Java. This revolves around the fact that Java is mostly Muslim, so *pork* (*babi*) is not on the menu. At the same time though, the Chinese, who make up a large proportion of the city populations, do eat pork, so in reality it is served in many restaurants. In Bali, pork is one of their favorites, especially *roast suckling pig* (*babi guling*) and as *sate* skewers. *Beef* is grown in Indonesia on a small scale, so beef *sate* skewers (*sate daging*) and *bakso* (beef meatballs in a light soup) are on the local menu. In the better restaurants, beef for steak is imported from the U.S. or Australia. Spicy Rendang beef curry is a Sumatran specialty that is regarded as a national dish. *Goat* (*kambing*) is a tasty local alternative to lamb, turning out beautifully as *sate* skewers or soup with vegetables. *Fried rice* (*nasi goreng*) is a mix of rice, meat, and vegetables that is often eaten for breakfast by the locals. *Nasi champur* or *nasi rames* is a spicy selection of steamed rice with meat, fish, and vegetables.

Rijsttafel is a Dutch-introduced banquet in which some twenty beef, chicken, rice, and vegetable dishes are laid out in buffet style. The dishes are traditional Indonesian fare, though the method of presentation isn't.

Fish and Seafood

The seas around Bali and Java come forth with a bountiful harvest of seafood that ranges from lobsters, shrimp, and oysters to cholesterol-free fish. Cooking is frequently done on the grill, an easy and healthy way of eating Indonesian seafood. *Grilled lobster* is a delight, as is grilled fish such as *coral trout*. *Squid* is usually fried, but is also grilled on occasion, and the same applies to *shrimp*, which are big and tasty. Fresh whole fish are baked or grilled or fish pieces are used in noodle dishes, curries, and certain traditional rice dishes. *Turtle* steaks or *sate* skewers are on some menus in Bali. You should realize that if you eat turtle you are encouraging local fishermen to kill more of this endangered species.

Fruit and Vegetables

If you're a fruit lover you should think seriously about putting up with a bit of rain and going to Indonesia in December or January, when the greatest variety of fruit is waiting to be eaten. Bali and Java both offer a long list of well-known tropical fruit such as banana (*pisang*), mango (*mangga*), papaya (*pepaya*), pineapple (*nenas*), avocado (*advokat*), and guava (*jambu*), as well as others that are just as delicious. For example, there are *mangosteens* (*manggis*), which has a soft, white flesh in compartments a bit like a mandarin. Watch out for the outer skin, which stains badly. *Rambutan* (literally: hairy one) is a furry fruit with an inside that looks and tastes like lychee. *Jackfruit* (*nangka*) is the biggest of the fruits (weighing up to 50 pounds), and needs to be cut into manageable pieces with a machete. The flesh is sweet and yellow and it is cooked in the traditional Javanese dish called *gudeg*. *Salak* (*sawo*) is a small, hard fruit with an outside that looks like snake skin and a dry inside with a tart flavor. It mightn't sound too good, but it sure is different. *Starfruit* (*blimbing*), *custard apples* (*sirsak*), *watermelon* (*semangka*), and *pomelo* (*jeruk Bali*) are found here, too. Last but not least is *durian*, which has a hard, thick skin with sharp spikes protecting a moist flesh that smells like rotten-egg gas but tastes like heaven. It's also considered a bit of an aphrodisiac, as it heats you up inside.

Gado-gado is perhaps the best-known Indonesian vegetable dish. Steamed green beans, cabbage, and bean shoots are topped with chopped boiled egg and thick peanut sauce. In Jogya, *gudeg* is the local specialty, consisting of a rice base with jackfruit and various vegetables boiled in coconut milk, to which some chicken and egg are added. *Gudeg* is available in a couple of large restaurants, as well as in *warung* food stalls or from vendors on the sidewalk along Jalan Marlioboro in the evenings.

A Chinese vegetable favorite is *capcai* (meaning "five vegetables"), with fried or steamed mixed vegetables with meat or seafood. It is a good, healthy, balanced meal that is not overcooked or overspiced. Cool-climate vegetables have also been introduced to Bali and Java, such as cauliflower and carrot. One that has been around for a long time is corn (*jagung*), which can be safely bought from street vendors who cook it on a charcoal-fired grill while you wait.

Dairy Products

Dairy products have only recently caught on in Indonesia and are largely limited to *milk* (*susu*) and *yogurt*, though imported cheese is available in supermarkets. Most of the dairy herds are in the high country near Bandung in West Java and Boyolali in Central Java. The locals like their milk at night, warm and with honey and chocolate or egg. This milk is safe and fresh daily. Milk can also be bought in refrigerated tetra packs or as "ultra-milk," a local version of ultra-high-temperature processed milk. Yogurt is also sold in roadside stalls and, like milk, was introduced by the Dutch over a hundred years ago. With the emergence of an Indonesian middle class, dairy products (an important source of protein) are being fed to more children.

Cakes and Desserts

Indonesians do not normally have dessert after a meal of rice and vegetables. Rather, they would have a second helping of the main course. In the cities, shops such as Holland Bakery serve a variety of simple cakes and *Dutch pastries* (*kue*). Balinese *rice cakes* are called *kajen*. These are used for temple offerings, and after they have been blessed by the gods they are taken home and eaten. In Jogya, *roti bakar* (hot, buttered toast) is a late-night snack something like a grilled cheese sandwich in which the cheese has been replaced with a chocolate jam-like spread. Also popular are colorful, sweet, sticky-rice cakes. Western-style *bread rolls* can be bought at most resorts and larger towns, and *croissants* are served with coffee in Kuta, Sanur, and most hotels. Even in the smallest towns you can buy cans of locally made, shortbread-style Dutch cookies.

4

Who Are the People of Bali and Java?

Bali and Java are just two of the over 3000 islands that make up Indonesia. On these two islands there are three major ethnic groups that make up the bulk of the population: the Balinese of Bali, the Javanese of Central and East Java, and the Sundanese of West Java. Each of the three groups has its own distinctive language, customs, laws, arts, and traditions that have been influenced to a varying degree by Indonesia's Hindu-Buddhist past, as well as the more recent Islamic and colonial periods. On both islands there are remnants of even older civilizations.

Bali is arguably one of the most idyllic places on earth, and the Balinese are a race of people to suit. They live for their religion, their art, and their music. The climate is so kind here that most locals are able to live comfortably on a partly self-sufficient basis.

Java and the Javanese are a different story, with severe overcrowding in some areas on the central plains. There and on the north coast the influence of Islam is the strongest, which has led to simpler places of worship and more subdued religious ceremonies.

In the old Javanese Hindu-Buddhist centers of Jogya and Solo, the veneer of Islam is often pushed aside by the *Kraton* court rituals dating back 1,000 years. There *batik* and *wayang* are the dominant arts. One of the laws of Islam says that man cannot reproduce man in any form in art or architecture. The stylized *batik* is one of the results.

Batik is something like tie dyeing, using wax to stop parts of the 9 foot by 4 foot cloth from being colored by the dye, instead of tying knots. Local interest in *batik* has been intense for the past few hundred years, so techniques are quite advanced and some pieces are very highly prized and priced. This *batik* cloth is often worn instead of pants or a skirt, and then it is called a *sarong*. They are very comfortable around the house. Try it and you'll be converted.

Wayang is an art form including dance, drama, and puppetry to the accompaniment of a *gamelan* xylophone and gong orchestra. The stories are based on Indian epics about love and war so there is plenty of action, especially in the dance-drama. *Wayang Kulit* uses intricately carved buffalo-hide puppets and a light to show the story as shadows on a screen. In Bali these performances can go on from the early evening until dawn in cool, open-walled venues. At any one time some of the audience is sleeping, eating, having a cup of coffee, or watching the unfolding story. Do the same yourself. Make a night of it—a long but very interesting night.

Visit the town of Ubud, the center of the artistic energy of Bali. Or even stay there for a couple of days if you want to see how the Balinese really live—away from the beaches at the southern resorts.

Way of Life

Just how do the Balinese and Javanese live? How do they interact with one another? Well, basically, both in the cities and the rural areas, their feudal past hasn't gone too far away in these modern times. In fact, one could say that some parts of Indonesia, including Bali and Java, still very much follow a traditional feudal lifestyle based on a patron-client relationship led by the old ruling class, who still still tend to hold relatively lucrative positions in the local governments, and the new merchant class, who lord over the rest.

Religion plays a big part in the life of most Balinese. Somewhere on the island every day of the year there will be a procession and ceremony commemorating a temple's birthday or a Hindu religious occasion.

Balinese Society

Balinese society is strongly influenced and guided by its religion, Hindu Bali. This is a blend of Hinduism from old Java and the animist beliefs that existed before the Majapahit Dynasty of East Java fled to Bali in the 15th century.

Nowadays, the most noticeable parts of Balinese religion are the thousands of temples, called *pura*, that are found all over the island. On hills, on the coast, at fishing spots, rivers, lakes, and the rice fields, a temple is

Balinese cremation pyre

there to appease the protecting spirits and ward off evil ones, as well as to keep the souls of deceased villagers happy.

The visual arts of dance and the accompanying *gamelan* orchestra (a type of xylophone) are also a product of and played for the Hindu Bali religion.

Temples

Each village in Bali has at least three temples (sometimes more), which relate to a particular god or deceased persons. Hindu and Buddhist believers use the same temples. The basic temple types are:

Pura Dalem

Devoted to the god Siwa, the destroyer (*pencabut*). This is the Temple of the Dead, and is the first built in a new village. People who have died but are not yet purified or deified are dangerous and evil. Rites at the *Pura Dalem* are to restrict these influences.

Pura Puseh

Devoted to Visnu, the protector (*pemilihara*). This is the Temple of Origin, where villagers worship the purified and deified forefather or clan and village founder. The gods are venerated as owners of the ground, over which the village has only the right of use.

Pura Desah/Pura Bale Agung

Devoted to Brahmana, the creator (*pencipta*). This is the temple of the large meeting hall where the villagers assemble to worship and hold meetings. It is situated in the center of the village.

Pura Merajan

This is a family temple where one worships one's ancestors.

Cremation

Cremation plays a pivotal role in the religious cycle. By means of cremation the soul is purified and joins the group of deified beings. That is, it goes from the Pura Dalem to the Pura Puseh. The Pura Puseh is always situated on higher (*kaga*) land, and the Pura Dalem on lower (*kelod*) land.

Temple Layout

Each temple is divided into three parts or courts—the fore court, central, and inner. In one corner of the forecourt is the *kul-kul* or split wooden block which is rung at festivals or for emergencies. It is also the site of the shed that stores the temple's rice. In the inner court are the altars for the gods and *bales* where communal offerings are prepared.

Religious Ceremonies

Religious ceremonies that recur in every village include the anniversaries of the temples, the harvest feasts, and the ceremonies known as Nyepi, Gulungan, and Kuningan. Villagers make financial and manual contributions in preparation for the events. On the day before these events, men chop meat while women prepare offerings and young people perform dances.

Odalan

Once a year (Balinese or Javanese year) each temple celebrates its anniversary as the villagers seek to contact the gods of that temple. Each temple festival consists of the essential elements of bringing offering and paying homage (*membanten/mebakti*).

Nyepi

This is the Annual Purification on the Hindu-Balinese New Year, which falls at the beginning of the tenth Balinese month. It is a day of silence (no loud noises), smoking and lighting fires are not permitted, you may not go outside of your compound, and one should fast for twenty-four hours if healthy.

Galungan

This holiday lasts for a few days. On different days different offerings are made. The streets of Bali are overhung with long bamboo poles with tassels hanging off them to represent the sacred Mt. Meru. The last day is called Galungan. At this time the spirits of the ancestors return to earth and reside in the chapels, and then return to heaven. Galungan is the celebration of the creation of the universe. The supreme God is worshipped and thanked. It is held every 210 days, from Tuesday to Thursday. Galungan literally means to fight evil for three days, win and then celebrate victory.

Kuningan

Kuningan is associated with Galungan and falls eight days later. Taman Sari Temple at Mas is a popular place to watch the festivities.

Castes and Marriage

There are four castes in Balinese society, namely:

1. *Brahmana* or priest/scholar. This is the highest caste but members are often poor because of lack of experience in business.

2. *Ksatrya* or warrior/king/nobility. Formerly had more power than Brahmans because nobles had power over life and death. Obtained wealth through taxes.

3. *Weisya* or merchant. Often materially better off than both Brahman and Ksatrya because of the shift from a subsistence to a cash economy.

4. *Sudra* or farmer/laborer. Many are descendants of the original Balinese society. They are often wealthy, as they own ricelands.

While intermarriage between the castes is more common nowadays, daughters are usually prohibited from marrying boys of a lower caste. However, such romances often blossom at school or the university and the couple elopes, the girl leaving a note for her mother. When they return from their time away together, a quick marriage is arranged because such a dalliance would make her unmarriageable to anyone of her caste in any case. In this way education is having a very direct effect on the old ways.

Village Law/Adat and Land Ownership

Land within the perimeter of the village between the main temples (*mrajin*) has belonged to the village since time immemorial and cannot be sold. This land is usually divided into walled family compounds for protection, and belongs to the village and temple. It can, however, be surrendered to someone else as long as that person continues to pray and make offerings at the various temples that are his responsibility. Ricefields outside this area can be bought and sold, and houses on such land can be sold. Each household is limited to 3.7 hectares (10 acres). Before land reform in the early 1960s, some families owned up to 20 hectares, and many were landless. The very large tracts of land belonged to the temples. The rice from this land was sold and financed large ceremonies twice a year. Some temples owned up to 100 hectares, but after land reform this was reduced to 1 hectare, so large ceremonies are rare nowadays.

Water and the Land

All farmers belong to the local *subak* (irrigation committee), and water is allocated and diverted to all terraces. Interfering with irrigation ditches can lead to severe punishment.

Javanese Society

On Java, religion is less colorful, but at the same time it is in some ways more complex. There have been numerous civilizations that followed different gods over the centuries, plus spiritualism and mysticism that follow no particular god, following rather the "self." One such meditation group is called *Sumarah*, which means "to surrender."

Buddhism and Hinduism were practiced in Java from the eighth century A.D. until the early fifteenth century. Since then Islam has been the dominant religion. Confucianism and Christianity came with later traders and colonizers, namely the Chinese and the Dutch. Like the people who brought these religions, they are generally restricted to the larger cities.

The Central Javanese cities of Jogyakarta (Jogya) and Surakarta (Solo) are home to great walled palaces called *Kraton*. Within these walls in the eighteenth and nineteenth centuries Islam, Hinduism, mysticism, and feudalism were mixed together to produce a unique Javanese lifestyle, or *Kraton* culture.

Javanese Religion

In his book *The Religion of Java*, Clifford Geertz talks about Javanese society being composed of three main parts. The *abangan* are the feudal masses tilling fields and working in factories. Their religion is a mix of Hinduism, animism, Buddhism, and Islam. The *priyayi* are the old ruling class and hold with the same beliefs as the *abangans*. Many are in positions of power in the current government. The *santri* are quite a separate group in that they are often descended from Middle-Eastern traders, and so are quite strict Moslems. *Santri* are still mostly in business and live in the towns and cities. Not included in Geertz's breakdown are the Chinese who were born or descended from Southern Chinese traders and laborers. They are the dominant business class, with a religion based on a mix of Confucianism, Taoism, and Buddhism. Many have converted to Christianity.

While Islam is officially the dominant religion in Indonesia, including Java (but not Bali), in reality the Hindu-Buddhist-animist elements of their belief are dominant. One ritual central to the carrying out of this religion in Java is the *slametan*, or feast. A ritual feast accompanies all rites of passage such as birth, circumcision, puberty, marriage, or death, as well as birthdays of villages and special religious occasions.

Sorcery, witchcraft, and magical healing are also strongly held beliefs. The master of these is the *dukun*, who is somewhat like a medicine man of the American Indians.

Javanese Temples and Monuments

One of the major tasks of the *abangan* masses was the construction of stone temples devoted to the various gods. The biggest is the Buddhist-inspired *Borobudur*. Borobudur is a pyramid-shaped monument with sides around 100 yards long, its height almost twenty stories. Construction was finished in the year A.D. 807 but it was abandoned before the end of the century, when Hinduism became the preferred religion. Walk around the terraces starting at the base, and follow the life of Buddha as you ascend.

There are three main areas of Hindu monuments in Java. The Prambanan Plain between Jogya and Solo is named after the temple of the same name. Near Malang in East Java are several smaller monuments such as *Candi Singosari* and *Candi Kidal*. The Dieng Plateau in Central Java is the third, with monuments devoted to a Hindu god-king cult.

Islamic beliefs forbid the use of human or animal form in architecture, so the mosque, the Islamic place of worship, is usually a plain building with ornate arches and a tall calling tower. The central mosque in Jakarta is the largest in Southeast Asia.

Polite Behavior

Social interaction in Indonesia follows a pattern in which respect is due to age and position. This is especially so in Java and Bali. Men are usually addressed by the term *Pak* (pronounced "puck," in ice hockey), and women by the term *Bu* (pronounced "boo"). Children and teenagers are *dik* or *abang*. In Jogya or Solo, *mas* (gold) is a polite term for all young men. It is not usual to address a Javanese by his given name. In Bali the same four names rotate for all families and all Balinese, both men and women, royalty and peasant. They are Wayan, Made, Nyoman and Ketut. The first born is Wayan, the second born is Made, and so on. The fifth born is Wayan again, and so it goes. Besides one of these four names, all Balinese have other names showing family or caste. As you can see, picking the right name to call someone can be quite tricky in Indonesia, so when in doubt use *Bu* (for women) or *Pak* (for men).

Eating, Drinking, and Visiting

If you get out of the tourist bus or taxi and catch public transportation you'll soon meet a local and be invited back to their house for coffee. When you get to the house, ask whether you should remove your shoes at the door. Laces can be a real hindrance in Indonesia, so slip-ons are always a must. Inside, don't dare put your feet on the coffee table, even if the mood is quite relaxed, as showing the bottom of your feet or shoes is very rude. Don't even cross your legs, because that brings one of your feet quite high relative to the other person's head.

Tea or coffee are usually offered to guests, with no milk and plenty of sugar. The coffee is like thick Turkish or Greek coffee with three spoonfuls of coffee on the bottom. Wait for the floating bits to settle, because otherwise you'll get bits stuck in your teeth. Blow on the bits and they will go to the other side of the cup. Wait for your host to say *mari minum* before you begin drinking, and just sip it slowly. When you've drained your cup or glass you'll be offered a refill. Leave a little in the bottom when you've finished.

The same goes for food. Indonesians usually don't have dessert straight after a meal. Rather they have a second helping of rice, meat, vegetables, or whatever they were eating. So leave enough room for a second helping or you could risk offending your host.

Clean Hand

In Asia, the right hand is the clean hand, and the left the dirty. This is especially so when eating. The main reason for this is that the left hand is used with water to cleanse oneself after defecating. This may be squatting over a 3-inch hole in the bathroom in poorer homes, or in a fast-flowing stream beside the ricefields. Don't worry—you won't come across such a toilet in a hotel or restaurant that is recommended in this book, unless it is mentioned as a haunt of backpackers. Along the same lines, the head is clean and shouldn't be touched, even on young children. Your feet or shoes are a source of impurity, so don't push someone else's bag around with your foot like I did once on a *bemo* in Bali. I was shouted out royally when I helpfully nudged a cane basket farther into the *bemo*.

Entering Temples in Bali

Anytime you leave your hotel for sightseeing, wear a sash around your waist or keep it in your pocket at the ready. This is because you can't enter temple compounds without a sash. Sometimes a *sarong* cloth covering your legs is necessary. The *sarong* is traditional Indonesian formal wear. Shorts are a no-no in temples, and frankly even the male natives don't wear them much except when sleeping or for laborers in the fields.

According to ancient law, women should not enter temples during menstruation. This is not based on sexist principles but on a general sanction against blood on holy soil. You will find large signs outside some temples proclaiming this exclusion.

If you are inside a temple compound while a ceremony is taking place, do not climb on anything to take photos or to get a better view.

Be sure not to get between people who are praying or making offerings and the temple altars. There are often six or more altars in one outdoor Balinese temple. One should always stoop a little when walking past people who are praying, and extend your right hand about a foot out in front of your waist. Never stand higher than a priest conducting a ceremony, and try to speak in a hushed tone. How would you feel if a bunch of tourists waltzed their way into your local church on a Sunday morning, popping flashbulbs and milling around the altar? Not too impressed, I'm sure.

Body Language

As you have seen so far, body language is a critical aspect of personal interaction in Indonesia, especially when a Westerner's interpretation of a posture is opposite to an Indonesian's view. An example of this is standing with your hands on your hips. Indonesians take this as a sign of aggression. Likewise, pointing with your finger or shouting are considered very aggressive. Javanese point with their thumb and generally do not yell.

Walking in the street, people will ask "*Mau kemana?*" which means "Where are you going?" They don't really want a definite answer. It is more like "How are you?" A good answer is "over there" or "*jalan jalan*" (going for a walk). It is considered quite rude to ignore people who ask you, even if you've already been asked twenty times that day.

In the West, we beckon with our index finger pointed upwards and towards us. To Indonesians this is very offensive. They beckon with their whole hand pointing downwards, as in waving goodbye limply.

Bargaining

Away from hotels, restaurants, and supermarkets, prices have a tendency to vary according to who is doing the buying. Foreigners and domestic tourists alike will always pay more than the locals. The better the bargaining skills, the lower the final price. Depending on how you're feeling at the time, bargaining or haggling to fix a price can either be fun or a major hassle if you are in a hurry and don't want to pay an outrageous price. Testing the water for a price can easily lead to a tricky situation when the seller accepts your price and you don't really want to buy it. This is especially so if you have both given two prices and the seller accepts. It is too late to decide it's still too expensive or you don't want it after all. Some sellers put prices up two to four times, so you can laugh at their first price, but if you aren't really serious about buying something, don't continue to haggle.

Saying NO to Hawkers

To the dismay of Balinese and visitors alike, street hawkers have become quite persistent, and sometimes downright rude. Remember that you are under no social obligation to answer when you are asked whether you want to buy something that is thrust in front of you. In fact, you are better off not saying anything at all. The most effective response is a quick shake of your head and averting your eyes from theirs. The same applies when offered transportation, or when someone approaches you in a restaurant or at your hotel. The hawkers in Java are generally not as aggressive and stick more to the markets.

The Arts

The arts in Bali and Java have flourished for hundreds of years. While they are often based on traditional stories from India, modern styles and themes are woven in with the old. In this way, dance, drama, *batik*, painting, and carving continue to develop. The arts vary slightly between the two islands. *Batik* is a Java-based industry, *wayang* and *gamelan* are on both islands, and painting and carving are better in Bali.

THE ARTS IN BALI

The arts in Bali are generally "busier" than in Java. The *gamelan* playing is faster and louder, the costumes are brighter, and the paintings are more dynamic. There are a number of reasons for this, one of which being that Islam tends to be more conservative in regards to the visual arts than Hinduism. The result is that Javanese dance is rhythmic and relaxing and the colors are earthy, while Balinese dance is more active and the colors are brighter. The following is a run-down on the various art forms you are likely to see.

(1). *Wayang*—Generally speaking, *wayang* in Bali follows the same themes as in Java, though it is performed less often.

(2). Traditional Dance—Dance, on the other hand, is more common in Bali. Before any performance begins the stage is blessed, and later the assembled *gamelan* is purified by splashing with holy water blessed by a *Brahman* priest.

Because both sexes in the performance are often played by women, it is easiest to differentiate male from female characters by the headdress. "Men" wear a wrap-around scarf tied at the front, while a woman's is very ornate—metallic or flowery. The colors that are worn are also different. Males wear purple. Females wear red, maroon, or pink. Both sexes wear green.

A typical evening's performance is a mixture of traditional and sometimes modern dances. Some of the best-known and more regularly performed around Bali are:

1. *Legong Keraton* (female). This is a classical dance based on an event that occurred in the twelfth century. The two Legongs dance with fans.

2. *Oleg Tambulilingan* (female). This dance depicts a flirtation between two bumblebees looking for nectar in a garden.

3. *Baris* (male). This is a strenuous dance showing a warrior preparing

for battle. He imagines the fight ahead of him. As his mood varies from calm to angry, the dance speeds up as he tries to overcome his inner fear.

4. *Kecak* (male). This is a trance dance based on an ancient ritual in which a person in a trance state communicates with his or her gods or ancestors.

Balinese Painting

Two famous names in the development of Balinese painting are Ruldolph Bonnet and I. Gusti Nyoman Lempad. Bonnet moved to Bali in the 1930s and taught a few local painters how to paint using European methods. Lempad was possibly the greatest Balinese artist, and was noted for his sketches and watercolors. The town of Ubud is the center of painting in Bali. Lempad's house, on the main street, is open to the public and a few of his works are on display. Lempad's grandchildren follow his example from this house.

Before buying any paintings in Ubud, I suggest you visit the Museum of Painting (*Puri Lukisan*), in the center of town. This way you can compare the different styles. In one hall there is a permanent exhibition of great works. Another hall is devoted to local painters who exhibit on a rotating basis. These works are for sale. Scattered around Ubud and the other resort towns there are dozens of galleries. Be sure to bargain hard, because prices are very negotiable. Make your first price 40 percent of his first price and you may end up with 30 percent off. I advise this method when buying all arts and crafts.

Wood Carvings

Wood is one of the best materials available to the Balinese artists, and they use it to turn out some excellent pieces. Characters from the *Ramayana* and *Mahabarata* epics are popular, as well as abstracts of village people. Tall, elongated versions make the best of the local wood. The towns of Batuan and Mas have many workshops and galleries. Kuta and Sanur are recommended as places to buy. This is because most of the carvers live in small villages and take their work to the beach resorts to sell. Bargain hard for carvings, too. Stick to your price and wait for them to drop their price some more.

THE ARTS IN JAVA

Following the division of the Mataram kingdom in Central Java by the Dutch in 1755, the suddenly powerless rulers' interests turned from warfare to the arts and introspection. Jogya and Solo were at peace and the *wayang*, traditional dance, and *batik* flourished. The *wayang* stories are based on Indian semi-mythical stories of great kingdoms, love and war, and basically stories found in the *Ramayana* and *Mahabarata* epics.

Wayang has several different forms. *Wayang kulit* uses buffalo-skin puppets to cast shadows onto a white sheet. The puppets on the right are the good guys and those on the left are the bad guys. The same goes for the other *wayang* forms. *Wayang orang* is a dance drama in which people act out many of the same stories as in *wayang kulit*. *Wayang golek* has actors using masks. Musical accompaniment to all *wayang* forms is the *gamelan*, a sort of xylophone orchestra. The best-known dance is the *serimpi*, traditionally restricted to royal maidens.

Batik

Batik is a method of painting cloth, similar to tie dying, in which molten wax, rather than knots, is used to control the spread of each color.

It would be hard to deny that the best *batik* in the world is made in Java, and this includes both traditional and modern styles, colors, textures, and variety. But then it should be; it has been a central part of Javanese society for hundreds of years. A quotation from a 1980 publication of the Jakarta Textile Museum reads: "*Mbatik/batik* or *seratan* is understood in Java as the application of wax by hand. It is intended not just as ornamentation of cloth to be used for clothing, but as a manifestation of values and beliefs which are a small part of the culture that flourished in the Kratons of Java. It is an exercise in meditation and concentration."

Originally *batik* was only used in the royal courts, where it had an integral role in ceremonies. Some of these patterns are still used today. Just as Javanese society has been influenced by immigrants, so has *batik*, especially in the *batik*-producing towns along the north coast of Java. These are known as the *Pasisir* towns. They were the first to use chemical dyes, which gave brighter colors, and 10-inch square plates called *batik caps* to stamp the cloth.

Pekalongan is the best known of these *Pasisir* towns. *Batik* from Jogya or Solo tends to be brown, navy blue, or maroon. In the early days rice paste was used as a resist and a bamboo instrument similar to a pen was used to apply the rice paste. These days a special *batik* wax is used and it is applied by a smoking-pipe-type instrument with a copper bowl and a tiny spout. This is called the *canting tulis*. Initially *batik* was done by women at home in their spare time. As *batik*'s popularity spread, some makers sold their work. Some of these grew into cottage industries. At the same time, *batik* spread to most of the other countries in Southeast Asia. In 1815 a kind of stamp in the shape of *batik* designs was made from copper. This style of *batik* is called *cap* (pronounced "chap").

In 1966, a new technique evolved which combined *batik tulis* and a painting with brushes process as a Western artist would do. This is a freestyle *batik* painting which has its base at the Water Castle in Jogya. *Batik* is now even used in home decor, such as cushion covers, curtains, tablecloths, and napkins. Be sure to take a couple of pieces back home as a unique reminder of Indonesia.

Traditional Dance

When the Mataram kingdom was divided in two in 1755, Jogya and Solo evolved different dancing styles. These are both known as Javanese dancing. West Java has its own style, called Sundanese dancing.

Bedaya and *srimpi* are two court dances restricted to young girls. They date from the sixteenth century. The *bedaya* is a women's dance consisting of nine female dancers with no dialogue; the movements are so symbolic and refined that it is hard to follow the story, which covers historical events. The *srimpi* is danced by four girls and describes a dance between two woman warriors.

The *wayang wong* dance drama is more easily understood than these court dances, and it is more visually exciting. Another popular dance is *ketoprok*, a dance-drama of the common people.

Today many young Indonesians study traditional and modern dance. Closely related to the popular dance-drama is the *wayang*, or shadow play.

Wayang

Wayang, or shadow play, probably evolved in India, given that the stories that form the basis of *wayang* are usually adapted from the Indian epics called the *Ramayana* and *Mahabarata*. By the twelfth century it was established in the East Javanese Mamenang kingdom. The original form of *wayang* was puppetry with backlighting onto a white cloth screen; hence the name "shadow." Personally, I find the dance-drama *wayang wong* (person *wayang*) more interesting. The stage backdrops and the actors' movements and costumes and the *gamelan* orchestra hold my attention for hours, which the *wayang kulit* does not do.

The *Ramayana* and *Mahabarata* stories are a bit like an American cowboy movie, involving love and war between the goodies and the baddies. The good guys are the *Pandawa* and they are on the right of the screen or stage. The opposing bad guys are the *Kurawa* and they are on the left.

While the storyline is a traditional one, contemporary social and political comment is made in the dance drama by the clowns, such as Semar and Petruk, who act as advisors to the good guys.

Censorship and legal hassles are thus avoided and allusions are made that could not be made in the media. Unfortunately the actors speak Javanese, which makes the story line hard to follow. Sometimes the clowns make comments in English if there is a Westerner in the front of the audience taking photos, and this causes great laughter. On a deeper note, both forms can be seen as a reflection of the Indonesian (especially Javanese) philosophy of life.

The Gamelan

The *gamelan* is the Javanese and Balinese orchestra which accompanies *wayang* or dance performances, as well as religious ceremonies. The orchestra has three main sections, made up of xylophones, brass gongs, and hand-held drums. The Javanese *gamelan* is quite subdued, while the Balinese is much more energetic and higher pitched. Some of the gongs are thought to have spiritual powers and the musicians are respected members of society.

A Concise History

Prehistoric Man

Evidence of human settlement in Java dates back 35,000 years. On the banks of the Solo River near the town of Trinul were unearthed part of the skeletal remains of Java Man, scientifically known as *Pithecanthropus Erectus* (upright ape-man). Wajak Man, who was discovered on the south coast of Java near Blitar, is the earliest known example of homo sapiens, the human race.

The present inhabitants of Bali and Java are rather Chinese-looking Malay stock. These mongolian Tibeto-Burman people pushed aside earlier racial groups as they spread south. Other races continued to migrate in, such as Chinese, Arabs, and Europeans, but the Malay speakers remain the dominant ethnic group.

Early History A.D. 500 to 1700

For thousands of years ships traveling between India and China have passed through the Straits of Malacca which separate Sumatra in Indonesia and the Malay Peninsula. Near the present town of Palembang, on the east coast of Sumatra, was a great center of learning and commerce called Srivijaya. Religious scholars from the subcontinent went there to study Buddhism. We know this because Srivijaya was mentioned in Chinese histories from as early as A.D. 670.

Between A.D. 700 and 1400, Hindu-Buddhist dynasties rose and fell in different parts of central and east Java. The Mataram dynasty left the monuments near Jogyakarta and Surakarta (Solo). Near Malang in East Java was Majapahit, the last and probably greatest of Indonesia's Hindu-Buddhist societies. Escaping before the tide of Islam in the early fifteenth century, the Majapahit kings crossed the strait to Bali. The royal families of other towns in Java were converted to the new religion spread by the sultanates of the north coast, such as Demak.

On Bali, the Hindu religion came to permeate the whole of society, starting at Gelgel and Klungklung. To this day there are only a few pockets of Moslems on Bali, mostly around Denpasar and along the north coast.

The first Europeans were the Portuguese, who came in the sixteenth century. The spice trade was their main concern. The Dutch dominated the economy from the 18th century and later controlled the government. Dutch trading interests, namely the East India Company, or V.O.C., were also after spices from other islands. Plantations were later established on Java with the help of the now powerless rulers, who in effect had become the local bureaucracy with the Dutch pulling the strings. If the local rulers had spent less time fighting each other, they probably could have kept the Dutch out of Java.

The Kraton Palaces of Java

These impressive structures were originally built in the mid-1700s and expanded later. The present patriarch of the palace at Solo is the twelfth ruler in a continuous hereditary line from that date. In 1989 Hamengkubuwouo IX of Jogya died of old age, the last sultan of Mataram. He was allowed to retain his title after Indonesia became a republic because of the positive role he took in the struggle for independence in the late 1940s.

Jogya and Solo each have one major *Kraton* (palace), surrounded by 20-foot-high brick walls over 2 miles (3 kilometers) long. The Javanese kingdoms were often at war, with power shifting from one area to another. With the Dutch came peace; stability was needed for their plantations to thrive.

Balinese Kingdoms

After Islam pushed the Hindu-Buddhists out of Java and into Bali in the early fifteenth century, the first Hindu Balinese court was established at Gelgel on the southeast coast around 40 kilometers from Denpasar. It later moved inland 5 kilometers to Klungklung. Over the next few centuries, members of the Klungklung royal family set up courts in other areas of Bali such as Ubud, Denpasar, Mengwi, and Tabanan. The present-day local government boundaries follow the areas of the influence of these traditional courts.

The British Period: 1795—1816

In 1795, William V of Holland left Indonesia and commissioned Britain to take over Holland's colonies in the wake of the Napoleonic period in Europe. By 1811 Britain had total control of Indonesia, and this remained so for 5 years. Sir Stamford Raffles, the ex-governor of Singapore, was governor for most of that time and is remembered for initiating many administrative reforms.

Although most of Raffles' reforms didn't last very long, this period was a significant break in the Dutch method of rule by the East India Company (V.O.C.). After rule by the Netherlands was restored in 1816, the Company style of running Indonesia was over forever.

Restored Dutch Regime 1816—W.W. II

The collection of land tax and forced deliveries of produce were central to the economic viability of Indonesia during the 1820s and 30s. Many of Raffles' abstract ideas were pushed aside in favor of more practical efficiency. The land tax proved unsatisfactory and the "Culture System" was introduced in 1830 as a way of financing the colony and the wars that broke out in different parts of Java.

The Culture System was based on forced delivery by the regents (provincial governors) of large amounts of designated agricultural produce and was colonial rule at its worst. Usually plantation crops such as coffee, sugar, indigo, spices, or hemp were required. They took up land usually devoted to food crops such as rice and corn. Hardship and famine for the Javanese masses were the result.

In Holland, this surplus from Java paid off the national debt and financed the construction of the Dutch railway system. In Java, finally, the locals rebelled. The largest Java-based rebellion was aptly called The Java War, and lasted from 1825 to 1830. It was touched off because Prince Diponegoro of Jogyakarta had been promised the throne by Raffles when the ruling sultan died. When this didn't come to pass, Diponegoro led a guerrilla war that ravaged much of Central Java.

By the 1860s there was a serious liberal backlash in Holland to the exploitation going on in Java. As a result the percentage of land devoted to cash crops was reduced to 20%. Also, commissions paid to Europeans to deliver such cash crops were abolished. Holland started providing more infrastructure on Java, such as railways from Jakarta to Bogor, Semarang to Surabaya, and Surabaya to Malang in the 1870s. Telegraph and postal services were also introduced.

Another distinct direction in colonial policy was called the "Ethical Policy," and lasted from 1901 to 1942. This was instigated by a new Calvinist-Catholic government in Holland. The notable feature of the new policy was the official abandonment of exploitation and the beginnings of direct state intervention in the economy in order to improve the economic lot of the local population. This was to try to compensate for the money that had been drained from Indonesia during the Culture System. The major areas of government spending were irrigation, education, and emigration to less populated islands from overcrowded parts of Java. By 1918 there was even a form of local parliament.

The Great Depression hit Java hard, just as the local population was getting accustomed to a better standard of living. Soon after came an even greater blow. World War II brought the rout of the Dutch and the other European colonial governments from Southeast and East Asia and occupation by the Japanese military. The years from 1942 to 1945 were bad ones to be in Indonesia, but at least one positive thing came out of WW II. Nationalist groups that had been stifled by the Dutch were given limited encouragement by the Japanese. In fact, on the eve of the Japanese surrender in 1945, the Japanese allowed Sukarno and Hatta, Indonesia's first president and vice-president, to proclaim Indonesia's independence.

Bali was relatively free of the Dutch until after the Java War. By the middle of the nineteenth century the Dutch had established themselves at Buleleng (Singaraja) and started to use local conflicts as a reason to interfere in Balinese affairs. The massacre of the royal courts of Denpasar and Klungklung occurred in 1906 and 1908 respectively. In Denpasar, on the open field opposite the present-day museum, the king and his court chose certain death to surrender in what is known as "Puputan." Armed with only their sacred *kris* daggers, the warriors lined up in front of the Dutch cannons.

Sukarno and Nationalism

President Sukarno learned about politics at an early age growing up in the house of Umar Sayed Cokroaminoto, a nationalist, in Surabaya. He arrived in Surabaya in 1916 when he was fifteen and stayed for ten years. By the late 1920s competition was increasing between the Islamic nationalists and Indonesian communists (PKI) for control of the local political groups. In the 1930s attempts were made to bring the divergent nationalist groups together so that they could be more effective.

Sukarno and Hatta were very active politically, but the Dutch government cracked down and exiled Sukarno to Flores and Dutch New Guinea in 1934, where he stayed until 1938, and then to Sumatra. Although he was physically separated from the growing tide of nationalism, Sukarno kept informed and contributed by writing articles for newspapers and journals.

In 1942 the Japanese army overran Indonesia and showed that Asians need no longer be subservient to Europeans. The Japanese were in favor of an independent Indonesia within the Japanese sphere of influence. It was during this period that Sukarno became the leading Indonesian politician, working so closely with the occupying forces that he was sometimes called a collaborator rather than a patriot.

When it became obvious that Japan was about to lose WW II, plans were made to proclaim independence before the Japanese surrendered. The Republic of Indonesia was proclaimed on August 17, 1945, but it was independence in word only. The British aided the return of the Dutch, thinking that Asia would return to the old colonial status quo. Battles raged throughout Java for 2 years, until finally the Indonesian guerrillas, led by Sukarno and General Nasution, were triumphant and Sukarno became the official president of the Republic of Indonesia.

The early 1950s were the golden years of parliamentary democracy in Indonesia. Unfortunately, there were too many competing factors, and the parliament became a shambles. By the 1960s, Sukarno had come to exercise almost total control, balancing the army and the communists just as the puppeteer balances the *wayang* puppets. His policies became more extreme (such as invading Malaya), and the economy was a mess of hyperinflation and famine.

In declining health, Sukarno could no longer maintain stability. The era was almost at an end.

The Coup

The crunch came on the evening of September 30, 1965. Seven army generals were killed and their bodies dumped in a well outside Jakarta. The attempted coup (*gestapu*) was led by an army colonel with the name Untung (lucky), but his had run out. No one is quite sure whether his group was in collusion with the PKI (communist party) or it was just an uprising by disgruntled junior officers. Colonel Suharto, who was in charge of the Jakarta army garrison at the time, for some reason was not targeted by the plotters. He quickly took charge of the situation.

Like the rest of the military establishment, Suharto laid the blame on the communists. The result was a wave of systematic killing and jailing across the whole of Indonesia, especially Java and Bali where the PKI was strongest. Just whisper the word "communist" and a personal enemy could be shot or hacked to death. In Bali many Chinese were victims. Within a year around half a million people were killed, and this is a conservative estimate. Several million more were jailed or confined to prison islands. Millions lost their jobs and were ostracized by their friends for fear of being painted by the PKI brush. Compared to Indonesia in 1965, McCarthyism was like a picnic.

For the first few days after the coup, Sukarno seemed to side with the plotters. So did some of the air force. Sukarno hoped he could still maintain the balance of power. This was not to be, as control was quickly grabbed by Suharto and all resistance crushed.

Suharto's New Order:
1965 to the present

The New Order period (*Orde Baru*) has been successful in terms of economic growth as well as political stability. Suharto has always maintained and continues to maintain overriding control of the military and economic policy. Major decisions concerning all aspects of society go to him for final approval or veto. He and his family have taken on a role similar to the former rulers of Mataram or Majapahit, which is not necessarily a bad thing. At least now the ruler is a local again, not a European.

Anyone who was involved in the war for independence or the military since then has benefited greatly from the New Order. In 1957, when all remaining Dutch interests were nationalized, the local Chinese were able to expand their role in the economy. Indonesians who were in positions of power and were able to obtain business concessions or monopolies teamed up with the Chinese, who had much more experience in accounting and marketing. To this date, such business alliances dominate the local economy. The Chinese have also been favored partners in joint ventures by overseas investors, in association with a silent Indonesian partner who facilitates government permits.

The rural population has also benefited from the stability. Irrigation, roads, recreation, and health improvements keep the peasant masses content, and generally they appreciate their rising standard of living under Suharto.

The Modern Economy

Indonesia's economy has always been based on agriculture and resources. This trend continues today, though in recent years there has been a diversification away from oil and gas to manufacturing and downstream processing of other raw materials such as timber, glass, plastics, and textiles.

When the last of the Dutch-controlled assets were nationalized in 1957, the Indonesian government had gained control of the largest banks, plantations, utilities, oil installations, and manufacturing infrastructure. Most of these sectors have grown steadily for the past 30 years as the private sector moved into these areas too, often with overseas partners. With the rise of the Japanese and Taiwanese currencies in the late 1980s, the latest growth area is light manufacturing for export. Tourism is also an important industry, bringing in foreign exchange, creating many jobs, and stimulating local cottage industries.

Effects of Tourism on Balinese Society

Tourism is having some positive effects on the Balinese Arts. The increasing tourist flow is helping to rejuvenate local arts and crafts, such as dance and wood carving. Also, money is being spent on up-market bungalows that are constructed according to the traditional architectural specifications, though with modern bathroom facilities. Such bungalows are the Oka Kartini and Puri Saren Bungalows at Ubud, which are a wonder to behold with their intricately carved reliefs, doors, and roof supports and beautiful gardens with peacocks and fountains. Of the larger hotels, the Nusa Dua Beach Hotel is outstanding, the front section reminding one of a great temple. Buildings such as these ensure that the traditional skills are not lost.

Many towns in Bali are renowned as being the center of a particular art or craft, e.g., Ubud for painting, Peliatan for dance and *gamelan*, Mas for woodcarving, Gianyar for weaving, and Celuk for silver. Craftsmen from the surrounding villages work at home and bring their finished products to Kuta or Sanur to sell.

In a way, the desire of visitors to watch dance and gamelan and buy souvenirs has led to a resurgence of local interest and pride in the traditional Balinese arts and crafts, though in a modified form.

Language

No one language is spoken by all Indonesians. Most Javanese and Balinese know *bahasa Indonesia*, the official national language. However, many of the elder rural people only speak their local language. The urban older generation often speak Dutch, *bahasa Indonesia,* and a local language, as well as English.

Those under twenty years old speak reasonable English if they can get over their fear of making mistakes. In the large towns and cities there are sizable Chinese populations who speak some of the above-mentioned languages plus Mandarin or Hokkien. Strict Moslems may also speak Arabic. Such a large number of languages led to the creation of *bahasa Indonesia* (national language), which is largely based on Malay but with words from all the other languages spoken. The words and phrases we have included are *bahasa Indonesia*, so they should be understood by anyone you want to talk to.

Conversational Indonesian

The most practical words to learn are in *bahasa Indonesia*, the national language of Indonesia. Most Balinese and Javanese speak it, except possibly some elderly folk who did not go to school. The easiest thing about *bahasa Indonesia* is that there are no tenses—you just add "before" or "will" to the verb. The trickiest part is deciding which word to use for "you," so stick to *Pak* for men and *Bu* for women.

Pronunciation is 100 percent regular, though vowel sounds are quite different from the American way, namely:

    a = like *u* in up
    e = the *e* in women
    i = the *i* in hit
    o = the *o* in hot
    u = the *oo* in moon

Some tricky consonants are:

    c = like *ch* in champ
    j = *j* in jump

Here I've listed some of the most useful words and phrases for travelers. If you want to learn more, you can do a six-week intensive language course at Salatiga in Central Java each December-January. Contact :

        Language Department (Bagian Bahasa)
        University Satya Wacana
        Salatiga
        Jawa Tengah
        INDONESIA

GREETINGS

selamat pagi—good morning (before 10 A.M.)

selamat siang—good day (10 A.M. to 3 P.M.)

selamat sore—good afternoon (3 P.M. to 6 P.M.)

selamat malam—good evening (6 P.M. to 3 A.M.)

selamat tidur—good night

halo—hello

selamat jalan—goodbye (said by person staying)

elamat tinggal—goodbye (said by person going)

COUNTING

1	—*satu*
2	—*dua*
3	—*tiga*
4	—*empat*
5	—*lima*
6	—*enam*
7	—*tujuh*
8	—*delapan*
9	—*sembilan*
10	—*sepuluh*
11	—*sebelas*
15	—*lima-belas*
20	—*dua-puluh*
70	—*tujuh-puluh*
100	—*seratus*
150	—*seratus-lima-puluh*
400	—*empat-ratus*
1,000	—*seribu*
3,600	—*tiga-ribu-enam-ratus*
10,000	—*sepuluh-ribu*
48,000	—*empat-puluh-delipan-ribu*
100,000	—*seratus-ribu*
1,000,000	—*sejuta*

ASKING QUESTIONS

boleh tanya ?	—may I ask a question ?
tahu	—to know (rhymes with cow)
ada . . . ?	—Have you got . . . ?
apa	—What
kenapa	—Why
bagaimana	—How

FOOD

makan	—to eat
minum	—to drink
makanan	—food
lapar	—hungry
kenyang	—had enough, full
enak	—tasty, nice
tambah	—more, another serving
nasi	—rice
daging	—meat, flesh of . . .
sayur	—vegetable
buah	—fruit
ayam	—chicken
babi	—pork
ikan	—fish
udang	—prawn, shrimp
air putih	—drinkable water
panas	—hot
dingin	—cold
es	—ice
mau pesan	—I'd like to order
mau bayar	—I'd like to pay
saya mau makan	—I'd like to eat

SHOPPING, ETC.

mau beli . . .	—I want to buy
saya mau . . .	—I will (or) I want to . . .
saya cari . . .	—I'm looking for . . .
mohon . . .	—please
terima kasih	—thank you
boleh saya . . .	—may I . . .
tidak bisa	—can not
bagus	—fine/well
baik	—good
tidak	—no, not
tidak bagus	—not happy with something

tidak jadi	—no thanks, I've changed my mind
berapa harga ?	—What's the price/how much is it ?
mahal sekali	—very/too expensive
tidak murah	—not cheap
bisa kurang	—can you reduce the price ?

GETTING AROUND

dimana	—(at) where
kemana	—(to) where
bemo	—minibus
charter	—to hire as a taxi
bis	—bus
kereta api	—train
teksi	—taxi
mobil	—car
becak	—pedal-powered trishaw
bajaj	—motor-powered trishaw
dokar	—horse and carriage
dekat	—near
jauh	—far
belok	—to turn
kiri	—left
kanan	—right
terus, lurus	—straight ahead
pergi	—to go
ayo!	—let's go!
berangkat jam berapa ?	—departs at what time ?
sampai/tiba jam berapa ?	—arrives at what time ?
berapa kilo sampai . . . ?	—how many kilometers to . . .?
naik bis dimana ?	—where do we catch a bus ?
mau kemana ?	—where are you going ?
dari mana ?	—where have you been ?
jam tiga	—3 o'clock
setengah jam dua	—1/2 hour before 2 o'clock

| *jam dua setengah* | —2 o'clock plus 1/2 hour |
| *se-per-empat* | —1/4 (hour) |

Indonesia cannot be considered an English-speaking country, so I think it is necessary to go a little deeper into the local language than in previous Maverick guides. First you can read through the word lists, and then I will show you how to use them by way of typical conversations that you may need to have with a local. If you are not getting your message across, as a last resort you can show them this book and point to the relevant word or sentence. The language in Indonesia is written in Roman letters also, so most locals will be able to read it.

The dialogues cover the common situations of greetings, looking for a hotel, asking directions, catching a *becak*, ordering a meal, and going shopping.

GOOD MORNING—Dialogue 1.

Steve:	*Selamat pagi, Bu.* (Good morning, ma'am).
Ibu:	*Selamat pagi. Mau minum kopi sekarang?*
	(Good morning. Will you have your coffee now?)
Steve:	*Terima kasih, Bu.* (Thank you, ma'am).
Ibu:	*Dari mana, Tuan?* (Where are you from, sir?)
Steve:	*Saya asal dari Amerika.* (I come from the U.S.)
Ibu:	*Sudah berapa hari di Bali?* (How many days have you been in Bali?)
Steve:	*Sudah lima hari.* (Already five days.)

VOCABULARY

Ibu	madam, mother
dari	from, of
mana	where
Tuan	sir
asal	to come/originate from
sudah	already (past tense marker)
mau	will (or) want to
minum	to drink
kopi	coffee
sekarang	now
saya	I, me
lima	five
hari	day

FINDING A HOTEL—Dialogue 2.

Sopir
(driver) taxi: *Mau cari hotel dimana, Pak?* (Where do you want to look for a hotel?)

Steve: *Lihat dulu di Kuta.* (We'll look first in Kuta.)

Sopir taxi: *Hotel ini cukup murah.* (This one is reasonably cheap.)
Sayu mau tanya dulu. (I will ask first.)
Ada kamar, Bu? (Do you have a room, ma'am?)

Ibu: *Ada.* (Yes, we have.)

Steve: *Berapa semalam?* (How much for a night?)

Ibu: *Semalam lima-puluh-ribu.* (50,000 per night.)
Kamar mandi ada di dalam. (The bathroom is inside.)

Steve: *Boleh lihat dulu?* (May I have a look?)

Ibu: *Boleh. Kamar ini bersih.* (You may. The room is clean).

Steve: *Ya, jadi, Bu.* (Yes, I'll take it, ma'am).

VOCABULARY

mau	will
dimana	where
lihat, melihat	to look at
Ibu	madam, mother
cari	to look for
dulu	before, formerly
semalam	one night
di dalam	inside
cukup	enough, sufficient
ini	this
disini	here
di	at
ada	have
boleh	may, permitted to
murah	cheap
bersih	clean
kamar	room
mandi	to bathe, wash

jadi   okay, it will happen, it's done (as
                                    in making a deal)

DIRECTIONS—Dialogue 3.

Petani: *Mau kemana, Tuan?* (Where are you going, sir?)
Steve: *Mau lihat candi, Pak.* (I'm going to look at some
          temples.)
          Candi lewat jalan mana, Pak? (The temples are along
          which road?)
Petani: *Candi Jago lewat jalan ini, Pak.* (The Jago temple is
          along this road.)
          Lempang saja jalan-nya. (Just go straight ahead).
Steve: *Apakah candi itu sudah dekat?* (Is the temple near here?)
Petani: *Masih lebih jahu lagi.* (It's still farther.)
Steve: *Terima kasih banyak, Pak.* (Thanks a lot.)

VOCABULARY

petani	farmer
candi, pura	temple
lewat	via, by
lempang	straight ahead
dekat	near, close
jauh	far, distant
lebih jahu lagi	even farther still
kemana	(to) where
lihat	to look
jalan	track, road
saja	only, just
apakah	question maker
banyak	much, a lot

CATCHING A BECAK—Dialogue 4.

Steve: *Berapa, Pak, ke Jalan Raya?* (How much to the
              main road?)
Tukang becak: *Jauh, Pak, biasanya seribu perak.* (It's very far,
              usually 1,000Rp.)
Steve: *Masa!* (How could it be!)
              Saya sering kesini. (I come here often.)
              Biasanya saya bayar tiga-ratus saja. (I usually
              only pay 300Rp.)

Tukang becak:	*Delapan ratus, ayo.* (I can do it for 800Rp.)
Steve:	*Tidak bisa.* (Can't do it.)
	Lima-ratus paling tinggi. (500 is the highest I can go.)
Tukang becak:	*Tidak bisa.* (Can't do it.)
	Delapan ratus tidak mahal. (800Rp isn't expensive.)
Steve:	*Kalau begitu, saya harus cari becak lain.* (If that's the way it is, I'll have to find another *becak.*)
Tukang becak:	*Mari naik, Pak.* (Come and get in.)

VOCABULARY

tukang becak	trishaw driver
jalan	road, street
barat	west
harus	should, must
naik	to get in
perak	silver, Rp, money
masa!	how could it be!
kesini	(to) here
ayo	let's go
paling	most, -est
mari	come on
lain	other, different
sering	often
biasanya	usually, normally
bayar, membayar	to pay
tinggih	high
kalau, jikalau	if, when
begitu	like that, so
ratus	hundred
ribu	thousand

THE MENU—Dialogue 5.

Steve:	*Boleh saya pesan makanan?* (May I order something to eat?)
Pelayan:	*Boleh. Mau pesan apa?* (Sure. What would you like?)

Steve: *Disini nasi campur pakai apa?* (What do you put in
            your combination rice?)
Pelayan: *Pakai daging sapi, tempe manis, tahu goreng dan sayur-
            sayuran.* (It includes beef, sweet tempe, fried tahu,
            and vegetables.)
After a while, the waiter returns to his table.
Pelayan: *Sudah kenyang, atau mau tambah lagi?* (Have you had
            enough, or would you like some more?)
Steve: *Saya masih lapar sedikit, Pak.* (I'm still a bit hungry.)
            *Mau tambah nasi setengah piring sama tempe yang enak
            itu.* (I'd like half a plate of rice with some of that
            tasty tempe.)

VOCABULARY

pelayan	waiter
pesan	to order, to leave a message
makanan	food
daftar	list
enak	tasty
lapar	hungry
kenyang	full, had enough
sekali	very (after adjective)
sangat	very (before adjective)
nasi	steamed or boiled rice
campur	mixed, combination
pakai, memakai	to use, to utilize
daging	meat
sapi	beef
tempe	soybean rissolé
tahu	soybean curd (tofu)
manis	sweet
sayur-sayuran	vegetables
sepiring	a plate of
segelas	a glass of
setengah	one half
pedas, pedis	spicy hot
sama	and, with
tambah	some more, another

SHOPPING—Dialogue 6.

Penjual: *Cari apa, Tuan?* (What do you want, sir?)
Steve: *Lihat-lihat saja, Bu.* (Just browsing, ma'am.)
Penjual: *Mau beli apa?* (What do you want to buy?)
Steve: *Tidak, lihat-lihat saja. Boleh?* (No, just looking.
            May I?)
Penjual: *Silakan.* (Please, go ahead).

VOCABULARY

penjual	seller, stall holder
cari, mencari	to look for
apa	what, general question marker
lihat-lihat	browsing
saja	just, only
Bu	ma'am, you (female)
mau	will, want
beli, membeli	to buy
tidak	no, not
boleh	may, permitted to
jual, menjual	to sell
silakan	please, go ahead

MORE SHOPPING—Dialogue 7.

Steve: *Ini berapa harga-nya?* (How much for this?)
Penjual: *Itu dua-ribu.* (That's 2,000Rp.)
Steve: *Bisa kurang?* (Can you come down at all?)
Penjual: *Bisa sedikit.* (A little bit.)
Steve: *Berapa?* (How much?)
Penjual: *Anda berapa?* (What's your price?)
Steve: *Seribu bisa?* (How about 1,000?)
Penjual: *Tidak bisa.* (I can't.)
Steve: *Bisa berapa?* (How much can you do it for?)
Penjual: *Seribu tujah-ratus lima-puluh.* (1,750Rp)
Steve: *Terlalu mahal, Bu. Seriba duaratus bagaimana?* (That's
         too expensive. How about 1,200Rp?)
Penjual: *Tidak bisa. Paling murah seribu enamratus.* (Can't do it.
         The cheapest I can go is 1,600Rp.)
Steve: *Tidak bisa kurang lagi?* (You can't come down any
         more?)
Penjual: *Nggak bisa, Tuan.* (No I can't, sir.)

Steve: *Wah, masih mahal.* (Oh, that's still too expensive.)
        Tidak jadi. (I won't take it.)

VOCABULARY

penjual	seller, stall holder
harga	price
-nya	the, its
itu	that
dua-ribu	two thousand
wah!	oh!
kurang	less, reduce
sedikit	a little (bit)
se-	a, one
ribu	thousand
dua	two
enam	six
tujuh	seven
ratus	hundred
lima-puluh	fifty
terlalu	too, overly
mahal	expensive
tidak, nggak	no, not
paling	most, -est
murah	cheap
lagi	again, more
masih	still, continue

5

Bali's Southern Beaches

1. The General Picture

Bali's beaches and sea are world-famous, and rightly so, whether for active sports such as swimming, diving, or surfing, or just lazing around soaking up the sun. The three best beaches, namely Sanur, Kuta-Legian, and Nusa Dua, are within twenty miles of each other. In the middle of them is Bali's international airport and its largest town, so you can have a good look around without too much travel no matter where you're staying. A little more than an hour's drive will take you into Bali's heart with its thatched hut villages, temples, rice farmers, an active volcano, painting studios, and woodcarvers.

Sanur

Sanur is situated to the east of Denpasar, Kuta, and the airport. For a holiday by the beach in more luxurious surroundings than Kuta provides, Sanur is the place. In the past, budget travelers stayed at Kuta-Legian and package tourists, families, and honeymooners at Sanur. This distinction is now changing, as there are several quality hotels around Kuta and younger tourists stay at Sanur to avoid the hustle and bustle of Kuta.

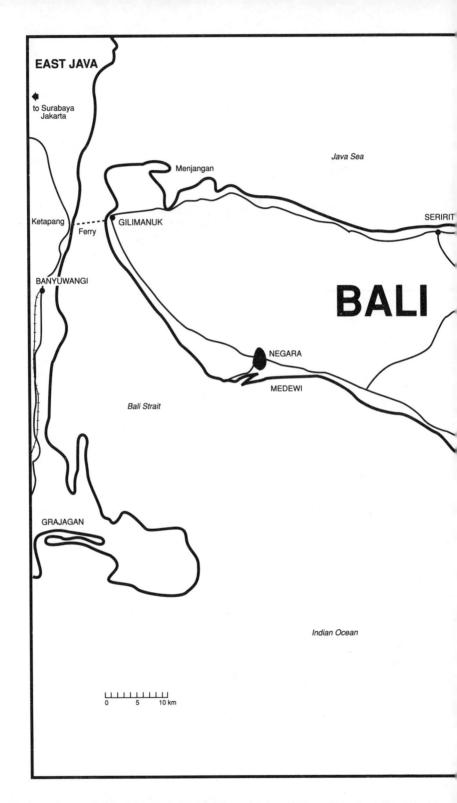

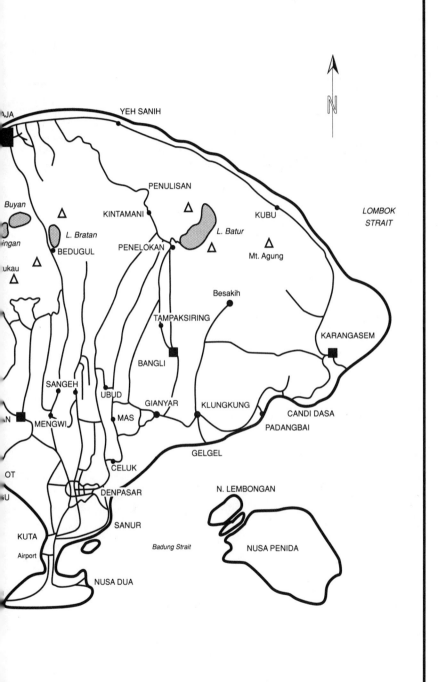

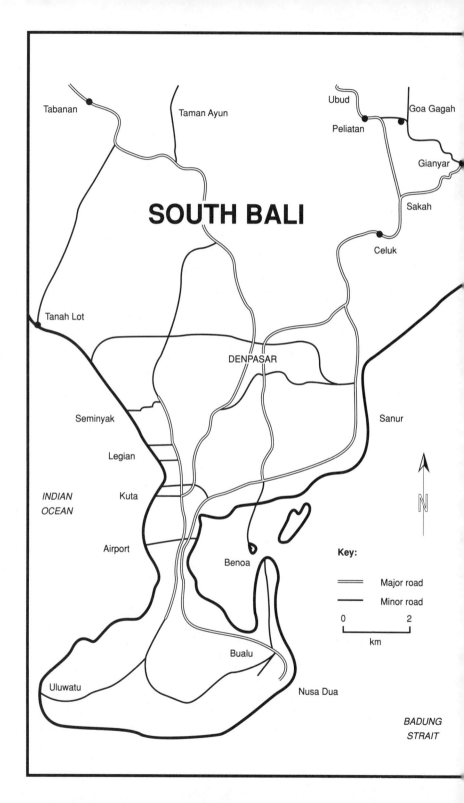

Kuta Beach, looking towards Legian

View of Sanur Beach from the Bali Beach Hotel

Sanur is ideal for water sports, as most hotels offer windsurfers, snorkeling, scuba diving, water scooters, and water skiing. Other facilities include a golf course, tennis courts, gymnasiums, badminton, spas, and saunas. Most hotels have a pool if you just want to laze around, unwind, and sip a cool drink.

Good restaurants abound at Sanur, especially along Jalan Sanur Raya, Jalan Tanjung Sari, and at most hotels. They offer a wide variety of cuisines. There are also quite a few bars, discos, and supper clubs.

Accommodations cater to all markets, ranging from the upscale Bali Hyatt at Sindhu and the Sanur Beach Hotel at Semawang and the exclusive Tanjung Sari Hotel at Batu Jimbar, to the budget-priced Hotel Taman Agung and Tourist Beach Inn at Sindhu. Most hotels face the long, sheltered beach.

Europeans have been staying at Sanur since the 1930s, studying Balinese society and the arts. Sanur is classier than other Balinese resorts, and succeeds in retaining a relaxed atmosphere, especially at the southern end.

Kuta-Legian

In the 1960s Kuta was a quiet fishing village on the road from the airport to Denpasar. At that time, most Western tourists stayed at Sanur Beach. By the early 1970s Kuta had grown into a major center for budget travelers because of its convenient location, long, sandy beach, and cheap homestay accommodations. Recently, the accent in tourist promotion has been towards package tours to fill the hotels that line the beach. Kuta and Legian have now become one continuous belt, and the buffalo that used to graze amongst the beachside coconut plantations are no more. On the other hand, if you're looking for nightlife there are now plenty of discos, pubs, and restaurants open till the early hours.

You can meet all kinds of people at Kuta and Legian. Apart from tourists and travelers, there are also many people engaged in the clothing and handicraft export business. In the next village of Seminyak, which is quieter than Kuta and Legian, there are many losmen (traditional guesthouses) among the trees and bungalows on the beach. In Seminyak there are also bungalows available for rental on a monthly basis. Regular visitors have even built houses for themselves.

Nusa Dua

Nusa Dua is the place to stay if you want a relaxing holiday in Western luxury, lazing around by the pool, on the beach, or enjoying water sports. There are many luxury tourist facilities at Nusa Dua, which currently has five hotels and more planned. Nusa Dua Beach Hotel, possibly the best hotel in Bali, and Hotel Bualu opened in 1983, and the others

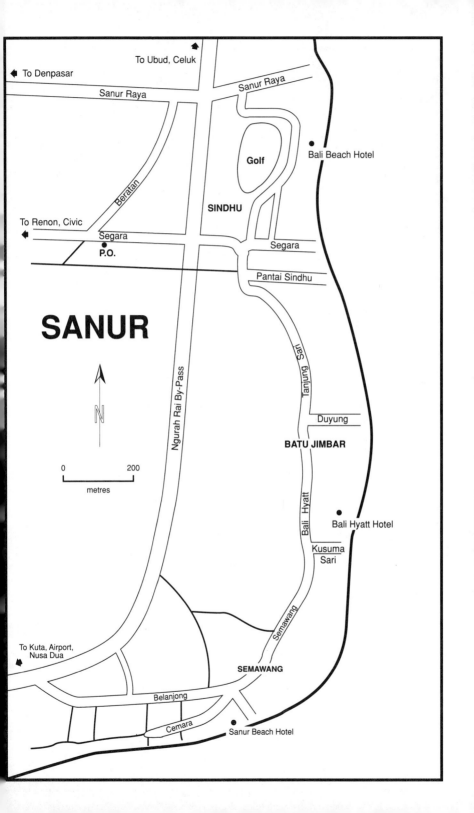

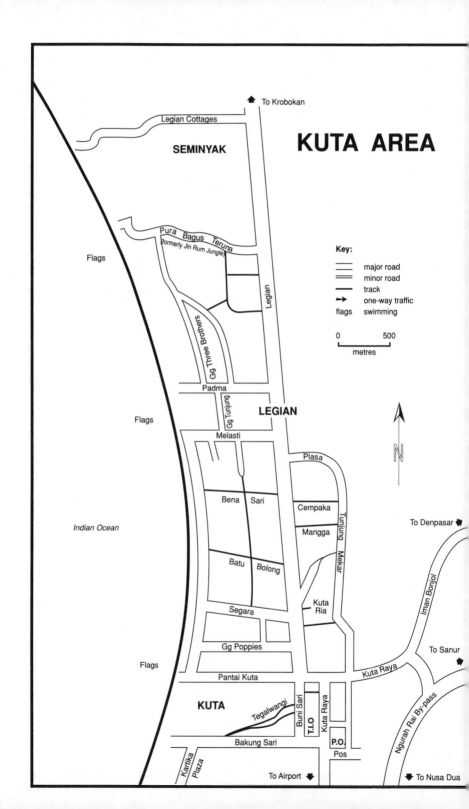

followed soon after. The most recent was Club Med, opening in December of 1986.

The area does have a few drawbacks, however, the primary one being its isolation from the rest of Bali. Nusa Dua is situated on Bukit Peninsula some twenty kilometers from Kuta and the airport. Another problem is that the food and drink in the hotels is rather expensive and there is little choice outside. Many people find themselves spending more on eating and taxis to Kuta and Sanur than the cost of their package. The exception is Club Med, where all meals are included and all sports facilities are provided free.

Nusa Dua is well laid out, with wide avenues and bicycle and jogging tracks linking the different hotels. There is an Amenities Center with a few shops situated between the Bali Sol Hotel and the Putri Bali. Other moderately priced shops and restaurants are on the road leading from the Hotel Bualu to Bualu village, near Made's Restaurant.

Denpasar

Denpasar, the largest town in Bali and its capital, is a twenty-minute drive from both Kuta and Sanur by car or minibus. Jalan Gajah Mada is the main street where the banks, tourist information office, and the main market are situated. Some of the government services, such as the G.P.O. and immigration, have moved to the new Civic Center at Renon.

The royal family of Badung (the province) is famous for its stand against the Dutch invaders in 1906. The field opposite the museum was the scene of Puputan, which was a mass suicide of Balinese men, armed with their traditional weapons, who chose death rather than subservience to the Dutch.

The main market, which is next to the river, was totally rebuilt in 1984. It is easy to spend hours wandering amongst the stalls. On the lower level is the food market and upstairs are clothing and material. Pasar Kumbasari, on the opposite side of the river facing the main market, has a wide variety of merchandise, especially *batik*.

There is more variety of clothing at Kuta or Legian, but Denpasar is the best place to buy fresh fruit. In Indonesian markets all people selling similar products are grouped together, so competition is intense. The cross streets between Jalan Gajah Mada and Jalan Hassanudin house shops selling clothing material, gold and silver, and books.

2. Long-Distance Transportation

Coming from the U.S.A., customs clearance may be done at Biak Island. In Bali the approach is over the ocean, passing between Sanur and Nusa Dua before banking over Kuta Beach and landing. Budget

NUSA DUA

Benda Harbour

Mangroves

Mangroves

to Kuta,
Airport, Denpasar

Bemo
Terminal

P.O.

Pol

Club Med

Nusa Dua Beach Hotel

Bualu

Bali Sol

Shops

Shops

Putri Bali

Bualu Hotel

0   1

km

DENPASAR

To Java
Tabanan Lovina

UBUNG

COKROA MINOTO

MARUTI

AHMED YANI

NANGKA

To Klungkung
Ubud

SUPRATMAN

PATI MURA

SETIA BUDI

SUTOMO

NAKULA

KEDONDONG

Phone

KARTINI

ARJUNA

VETERAN

RAMBUTAN

KEPUNDUNG

MELATI

KAMBOJA

P.O.

GADUNG

PELAWA

WAHIDIN

GAGAH

MADA

TIO

SURAPATI

HAYAM WURUK

KERENENG

THAMRIN

Market

SULAWESI

SUMATRA

UDAYANA

WISNU

AGUNG

SANUR

To Sanur

BATUR

HASSANUDIN

DEBES

TAMBORA

SUTOYO

TEGAL

DIPONEGORO

Key:

TEGAL   Bemo Terminal

➡   One-way Road

IMAN BONJOL

YOS SUDARSO

Civic

PATIH JELANTIK

Immigration

SANGIH

SUDIRMAN

RAYA

PUPUTAN

G.P.O.

SANGLAH

To Sanur

To Kuta
Nusa Dua
Airport

travelers coming overland from Java cross the strait and land at Gilimanuk before bussing to Ubung Terminal on the northern outskirts of the city. How to get from Ubung to the tourist areas is covered in the next section.

Airline offices for international carriers are at the Bali Beach Hotel shopping arcade in Sanur. Local carriers are at the Hotel Bali on Jalan Veteran, Denpasar or along Jalan Melati in Denpasar. Garuda, the national carrier, is at Jalan Melati 61, Denpasar (Tel.: (361) 27825, 22788, and 22028). It is always best to go and make your booking in person. When you check in for your flight, be early in case too many tickets have been sold for that flight, as often happens. This occurs because many ticket offices in smaller towns or travel agents don't have computers, and bookings are posted in or taken by hand. Try to get the agent to call in your booking while you're waiting, and confirm it 72 hours before the flight. From Ngurah Rai Airport in Bali there are flights to the U.S., Australia, Japan, and Singapore. Until not long ago, all international flights had to be boarded in Jakarta, but fortunately that can now be avoided in many cases. There are also domestic services to Jogyakarta, Semarang, and Surabaya in Java, and to other islands, including Lombok and Sulawesi. To some of the other islands prop-driven aircraft may be in service. If you want a jet aircraft, pay the extra and go with Garuda. There are no train services in Bali. If you want to get a train through Java it would be best to connect in Surabaya or possibly at Banguwangi.

Interisland boats also leave from Surabaya to Sulawesi, Kalimantan, and the islands stretching out towards Papua New Guinea. From the port of Padangbai on the east coast of Bali there are regular ferries to Lombok.

If you're heading for Java and looking for a bit of adventure at a budget price, take an overnight express bus. There are reasonably large buses with individual tilt seats, air-conditioning, and sometimes meals and toilets. They are a very popular form of intercity transport for locals and backpackers between Bali and Jogya, Malang, or Surabaya. Jakarta is a bit too far, so the trip should be broken for a day at Surabaya or Jogya. Buses leave each afternoon from the Ubung Bus Terminal in Denpasar. Some buses take on passengers a couple of hours earlier at Kuta. Here is a schedule of the better bus companies that run to Java, showing departure times from Denpasar and 1990 fares. This table sets out destinations in Java, bus company names, departure times from Ubung Bus Terminal in Denpasar, and usual arrival time at that town in Java. VIP designation means bus is a luxury type, usually with air conditioning, a toilet, videos, and snacks provided.

Overnight Bus to Java

Destination & Bus Company	Departure	Arrival
Denpasar—Jogya/Solo	All leave at 3:30P.M. and	
Cakrawala (AC); Bali Express;	arrive the next morning	
Puspasari; Bali Indah;	at 7P.M.	
Surya Indah;		
Restu Mulia (AC and non-AC)		
Denpasar—Malang		
Bali Indah (AC and non-AC)	7P.M.	5A.M.
Malang Indah (AC and non-AC)	6P.M.	4A.M.
Pemudi (AC and non-AC)	6P.M.	4A.M.
Denpasar—Surabaya		
Nilam Indah (AC)	6P.M.	4A.M.
Surya Indah (AC)	6P.M.	4A.M.
Cakrawala (AC)	6P.M.	4A.M.
Bali Indah (non-AC)	7P.M.	5A.M.
Bali Express (AC)	8P.M.	6A.M.
Lorena (VIP)	6P.M.	4A.M.
Denpasar—Jakarta		
Cakrawala (AC)	8A.M.	6A.M.
Bali Express	6A.M.	5A.M.
Lorena (VIP)	6A.M.	5A.M.
Denpasar—Bandung		
Jawa Indah (AC)	6A.M.	5A.M.

Fares to Java	VIP	AC	Non AC
Denpasar—Jogya/Solo	Rp24,000	Rp12,000	Rp15,500
Denpasar—Malang	Rp12,500	Rp9,500	
Denpasar—Surabaya	Rp13,200	Rp12,000	Rp9,500
Denpasar—Jakarta	Rp36,000	Rp36,000	Rp18,000
Denpasar—Bandung		Rp36,000	

Tickets to most destinations can be bought throughout Bali. Check departure time and place, especially if you're not buying your ticket from the town of departure.

3. Local Transportation

If you've decided to be adventurous and rent a self-drive car, then you'll be able to get around the southern beaches easily. You are also within two hours' drive of most places on the island. Linking Nusa Dua, the airport, Kuta, Sanur, and bypassing Denpasar is a freeway that makes movement between the three resorts quick and easy. Except for in central Kuta, parking is plentiful. The main problem with rental cars is the lack of filling stations, so gas up whenever you have a chance, such as on the freeway.

Most self-drive cars are Volkswagen convertibles or Suzuki "mini-jeeps." At Sanur you can rent a car through your hotel or these companies: **Bali Setia Motor**, Jalan Tanjung Sari, Sindhu; **Sanura Car Rental**, Jalan Cemara, Semawang; or **Wirasana**, Jalan Bali Hyatt, Batu Jimbar. A gas station is near the Bali Hyatt Hotel and another is on the freeway (bypass). The daily rate is around Rp30,000 ($20), plus gas, which is cheap in Indonesia. At Nusa Dua car rental is usually done through one of the major hotels.

In Kuta, Volkswagens are rented from the V.W. rental office opposite the filling station on Jalan Kuta Raya or **Yasa U-Drive** on Jalan Bakung Sari. In Legian try **Agung Raka**, Jalan Legian, or **Rena Car**, Jalan Legian. Between Kuta and Legian on Jalan Legian are **Bali Jawa Car**, **Mega Jawa**, and **Central**. For motorbikes try **Sewa Motor** in central Kuta on Jalan Legian (on the corner of Poppies Lane). In Kuta people will offer to rent you a motorbike, but chances are they got it from Sewa Motor. A few hundred yards from Kuta's petrol station are some car repair shops and mechanics.

Avis has an office at the Nusa Dua Beach Hotel (Tel. (361) 510679). There's a fuel station on the freeway near the airport.

Toyota Rent-a-Car (Tel. (361) 275656) in Denpasar operates well-maintained cars and minibuses with English-speaking drivers. Rates start at $55 a day for a 4-cylinder Corolla.

Local commuter services are geared to take people to and from Denpasar. **Minibuses** run at not always regular intervals from before 6A.M. until around 10 at night, taking the locals to market, school, or work. They're good to use to get to Denpasar and back, but getting from resort to resort is not so easy. You'd be better off to catch a **taxi** (of the 4-door sedan variety).

Hotels at Sanur or Nusa Dua have taxis waiting for fares. Taxis can be hired by the hour or for a scheduled fee to each destination. Make it clear to the driver that you know the fare before you leave. (Incidentally, in Bali these taxis don't have a light on the roof.) When hiring a taxi away from the major hotels, you must set the price before you get into the vehicle. At Kuta beach you will have to haggle with the driver if you don't want to get ripped off. At Sanur you can get a better price by walking to the hotel's carpark and negotiating directly with the taxi drivers. If the taxi has been allowed into the hotel grounds, then the driver is trustworthy. However, this doesn't necessarily mean that he won't try to charge you the highest amount possible at the time.

By midday most of the 4-door sedan taxis will have been taken, so then you'll need to "charter" a *bemo* minibus if you're away from a hotel. "Charter," as mentioned before, means to book it like a taxi with a driver and to go to a set destination or for a set period of time plus petrol. These minibuses may at times be used on the local commuter services. At Kuta or Legian if you want to "charter a *bemo*" for the next day it's best to organize it the afternoon before at around 4 to 5 P.M. The guys are hanging around and you can bargain for a good price and allow yourself to get away early the next day. Give them your hotel name and room number. They'll probably forget your name. These drivers are generally trustworthy, as are the other 4-door sedan drivers. When visiting temples and other sites the driver will usually look after your valuables in the car.

Now for a few distances so that you will be able to haggle a bit more strongly when setting your fare:

Sanur—Kuta	14 kilometers / 9 miles
Sanur—Nusa Dua	26 kilometers / 16 miles
Kuta—Nusa Dua	9 kilometers / 5.5 miles
Sanur—Denpasar	6 kilometers / 4 miles

In 1990 the taxi fare from the Nusa Dua Beach Hotel to Kuta was set at Rp8,000 ($4). To Sanur from Nusa Dua cost Rp14,000 ($7) one way. Charter a *bemo* and it will cost around half that.

Hotels in Nusa Dua have **shuttle buses** leaving every 2 to 3 hours to Sanur, Kuta, or the airport. Some are free and others charge $3 each way.

Commuter minibuses, called *bemos* (pronounced beemos) are the main form of public transportation in Bali. These are usually Japanese vans seating 6 to 15 squashed passengers with a door on the side or rear. At Sanur, *bemos* start from the terminal outside the Sanur Beach Hotel at the southern end, follow the main road past the Bali Hyatt to Sindhu, across the bypass, and along Jalan Sanur Raya to Kereneng Terminal in central Denpasar. This trip will cost around Rp600 (30 cents) in one of the cream-colored *bemos*. Kuta and Nusa Dua are on another *bemo* line. These are 15-seater dark blue vans that operate from the Tegal Terminal. For Nusa Dua catch the one marked "Tegal—Kuta—Bualu." The normal fare from Nusa Dua (Bualu) to Kuta is Rp500 and to Denpasar Rp800. The terminal at Bualu is around half a mile from the hotels, and the Tegal terminal in Denpasar is around half a mile from the main street, Jalan Gajah Mada.

DISTANCES BETWEEN TOWNS IN BALI (KM)

Town (diagonal label)	Distances, as printed left → right
Antosari	
BANGLI	80
Besakih	101, 42
Batubulan	53
Bedulu	19, 17
Bedugul	62, 109, 73
Batukaru	43, 85, 106, 53, 70, 65
DENPASAR	40, 40, 61, 8, 25, 48, 45
GIANYAR	13, 34, 7, 75, 27
Gelgel	82, 24, 35, 90, 43, 15
Gowalawah	28, 40, 96, 48, 21, 11
Gowagajah	64, 42, 1, 72, 24, 29
Giiimanuk	168, 136, 148, 128, 176, 172
KARANGASEM	118, 70, 126, 78, 51, 30, 206
Kemenuh	21, 42, 10, 67, 64, 19, 8, 24, 29, 11, 147, 59
Kuta	49, 17, 57, 9, 36, 57, 137, 28
Kintamani	108, 28, 60, 116, 68, 41, 56, 79, 70
Kesiman	43, 37, 56, 5, 51, 48, 3, 40, 45, 131, 16, 65
KLUNGKUNG	18, 21, 40, 88, 40, 13, 3, 8, 168, 38, 49, 37
Mengwi/Tamanayun	28, 56, 78, 24, 41, 32, 16, 43, 64, 116, 94, 35, 84, 56
Mas	62, 45, 70, 22, 11, 32, 62, 31, 19, 24, 38
NEGARA	135, 156, 103, 115, 95, 122, 143, 33, 173, 114, 104, 163, 135, 83, 117
Padangbai	36, 48, 104, 56, 29, 19, 37, 24, 62, 16, 72, 151
Perelokan	100, 61, 52, 108, 60, 33, 48, 188, 78, 41, 48, 40, 76, 155, 48
Pura Luhur	91, 78, 75, 30, 57, 73, 54, 128, 98, 70, 125, 90
SINGARAJA	73, 119/138, 30, 78, 92, 107, 85, 137, 52, 98, 112/128, 60, 108
Sanur	43, 64, 55, 7, 30, 46, 51, 27, 135, 81, 22, 16, 72, 7, 43, 23, 25, 102, 59, 37, 85
Sangeh	61, 82, 43/69, 21, 48, 69, 99, 89, 61, 11/37, 116, 77, 81, 51, 99, 28
Sempidi	47, 68, 41, 7, 34, 41, 85, 16, 47, 9, 88, 71, 14, 28
TABANAN	61, 82, 43, 21, 48, 69, 45, 107, 99, 30, 89, 24, 61, 9, 43, 74, 77, 81, 51, 92, 28, 42, 14
Celuk	29, 3, 59, 11, 16, 37, 139, 67, 57, 29, 27, 106, 41, 89, 14, 32, 18, 32
Tampaksiring	77, 48, 85, 82, 37, 15, 13, 36, 65, 46, 28, 27, 53, 132, 23, 67, 107/115, 40, 58, 44, 48, 26
Tanah Lot	71, 92, 51, 31, 58, 79, 109, 50, 40, 99, 71, 19, 126, 87, 81, 38, 52, 16, 42, 68
Ubud	23, 44, 5, 73, 25, 10, 27, 4, 153, 8, 48, 28, 4, 120, 45, 103, 28, 46, 46, 14, 15, 56
Tuban	53, 53, 74, 61, 13, 40, 37, 91, 81, 53, 108, 73, 91, 20, 34, 20, 34, 24, 50, 44, 28
Benoa	51, 51, 72, 19, 36, 59, 56, 11, 39, 54, 59, 35, 139, 89, 30, 7, 79, 14, 51, 27, 33, 107, 67, 71, 26, 89, 18, 32, 18, 32, 22, 48, 42, 36, 10

At Kuta it's quickest to walk to the main airport's Denpasar road (Jalan Iman Bonjol) to catch a *bemo*. Otherwise you may have to wait until the van is full before take-off. From Legian in the mornings and afternoons there is a small *bemo* shuttle to *bemo* corner in Kuta. Walk 100 yards to the main road and grab the dark blue one to Denpasar. *Bemos* to Denpasar are run on a co-op basis and are efficient during daylight hours. After 7 P.M. they are sporadic and you may be asked to "charter."

Denpasar Bemo Service

Denpasar is a small but busy town. Public transportation is by 3- or 4-wheel *bemos* which follow set routes that run in a clockwise direction around town. Different routes link up with the other *bemo* terminals at Kereneng, Tegal, Ubung, and Sanglah. Some, but not all, go along Jalan Gajah Mada, the main street, which is the shortest route from Tegal Terminal to Kereneng Terminal, or Jalan Hassanudin from Kereneng to Tegal. From Ubung buses go to Tabanan and the Gilimanuk ferry terminal. Buses and minibuses to all other destinations in Bali leave from Kereneng Terminal (central bus station). Here is how to get to a few places around town if you're in the main street of Denpasar:

1. Airline Offices on Jalan Melati—catch *bemo* to Kereneng via Jalan Patimura, alight at Jalan Melati.
2. A.S.T.I. Dance Academy, Jalan Ratna—to Tohpati via Jalan Supratman, alight at Jalan Ratna.
3. General Hospital—to Sanglah, get off at terminal, and walk a short distance.
4. International Phone Calls on Jalan Kedondong—to Kereneng via Jalan Veteran, off at Jalan Kedondong, and walk to office.
5. Post Office Kereneng, Jalan Kemuning—catch to Kereneng and walk out the way that your *bemo* came into the terminal.

3- or 4-Wheel Minibus Routes

Route	Bus color	Via
1. Tegal-Kuta-Legian Tuban-Buala	navy blue	Jalan Iman Bonjol
2. Tegal-Kuta-Pecatu	blue/white	Uluwatu airport
3. Kereneng-Sanur	green	Jalan Sanur Raya Tanjungbungkak
4. Sanur-Renon-Sanglah	cream	GPO & Immig.
5. Sanur-Renon-Panjer	cream/red	as above
6. Suci-Sanglah	gray	Jalan Diponegoro
7. Suci-Kampus-Panjer	gray	Jalan Sudirman

8. Kereneng-Tonjo-   red/yellow   swimming pool
   Nonongan-Topati

Bemo and Minibus Terminals

Kereneng	Jalan Kamboja
Tegal	Jalan Iman Bonjol
Ubung	Jalan Cokroaminoto
Suci	Jalan Hassanudin
Sanglah	Jalan Diponegoro

Bemo Fares in Bali 1990

South   (terminal name in brackets) ..... Rp

Kuta	—Denpasar (Tegal)	500
Kuta	—Legian	250
Nusa Dua/Bualu	—Denpasar (Tegal)	850
Sanur (B.B.H.)	—Denpasar (Kereneng)	360

Central

Denpasar (Kereneng)	—Ubud	600
Ubud	—Sakah	250
Ubud	—Gianyar	750
Ubud	—Teges	180
Teges	—Goa Gajah	180
Teges	—Tampaksiring	500
Gianyar	—Klungkung	600
Gianyar	—Penelokan (L. Batur)	750
Gianyar	—Bangli	300
Gianyar	—Besakih	1800
Gianyar	—Singaraja	1500

East

Denpasar (Kereneng)	—Klungkung	550
Denpasar (Kereneng)	—Candi Dasa	1500
Denpasar (Kereneng)	—Karangasem (A'pura)	1800
Candi Dasa	—Klungkung	550
Candi Dasa	—Karangasem	250
Karangasem	—Tirtagangga	300

North

Denpasar (Ubung)	—Singaraja (Bedugul)	2100
Singaraja (Banyuasri)	—Lovina (Kalibukbuk)	250
Singaraja (Banyuasri)	—Bedugul (L. Bratan)	420
Singaraja (Buleleng)	—Karangasem	1700

West

Denpasar (Ubung)	—Tabanan	500

Denpasar (Ubung) —Negara.................. 1200

Nusa Dua is ideally suited for riding a **bicycle** between the hotels and the village of Bualu and its cafes and restaurants. Each of the hotels rents bicycles at around Rp3,000 per hour. Made's Restaurant does so too, but at Rp3,000 a day. At Legian, Jalan Melasti, Jalan Padma, and the beach road are good for a ride. Give way to the motorbikes that sometimes hurtle along at breakneck speed. Kuta itself is too busy for bicycles, unless you're on the beach road heading towards Legian.

There are now two forms of Javanese transportation at Kuta. The *becak* (tricycle) and *dokar* (horse buggy) are popular with the tourists, especially at night when moving between the restaurants and bars or the mile between Kuta and Legian. Fares are extremely negotiable; Rp5,000 would be a reasonable fare late at night for a horse and buggy or Rp2,000 for one person in a tricycle. Try to ride on one if you're not going on to Java. They can get up a good speed when there's not much traffic around. The beach road between Kuta and Legian is lovely on a moonlit night by *becak* or *dokar*.

4. Hotels and Lodging in South Bali

Sanur was one of the first places that Westerners stayed in Bali, especially artists and the rich and famous. The local village is still there and many of the residents work in the hotels and bungalows. Service on the Sanur strip is arguably the best in Bali. There are many places to stay in Sanur, including a few first-class hotels and around twenty moderately priced hotels.

Backpackers and surfers in the 1960s started renting rooms with the local fishermen at the village of Kuta, on the road from the airport to Sanur. Kuta's 100 yards of white sand stretches into the distance. It's no wonder that it's been such a success with those beach lovers of the Pacific, the Australians. As more Australians and other Westerners came to stay at Kuta, villagers built rooms inside their compounds.

By the late 1970s top-quality bungalows were sprouting up along the sunset-facing beach. To all intents and purposes, Sanur had stopped growing. Kuta was the center of the action, joining together with Legian Beach as it spread northwards towards the Bali Oberoi bungalows. Nowadays there are literally hundreds of moderately priced hotels or bungalows to stay in, and hundreds more budget-class traditional *losmen* guesthouses from the early 1970s.

Bali's popularity continued to grow, so a new growth area had to be found. Sanur had run out of space and, despite a definite improvement,

Kuta was still a little down-market. A new location had to be found that wouldn't displace local villagers. Nusa Dua was ideal, with its untouched white beaches, few locals, and convenience to the airport. The results have been as impressive as everything that the Balinese do. The first group of major hotels built were the Hotel Putri, the Bali Sol, and the Nusa Dua Beach Hotel, which is built in the style of a Balinese palace. They are all truly magnificent.

A few years ago Club Med arrived, and two other hotels have just opened. Rates quoted in this book will be in U.S. dollars, because all price lists for better hotels in Indonesia use the U.S. dollar for their pricing. However, you can of course pay in local currency.

EXPENSIVE HOTELS

These hotels are the best in Bali and, for that matter, probably the best in Indonesia, given that Jakarta doesn't compete with Bali as a place to have a vacation. The better hotels in Bali could be compared to somewhere like Tahiti—tastefully appointed rooms in well-designed hotels that use local tropical themes and colors. And while precision is not a word that could be applied to Bali or Java, service is excellent due to the nature of the Balinese people themselves.

The Nusa Dua Beach Hotel (Tel. (361) 71217) is the classic Balinese-style hotel, set in twenty acres of tropical gardens. Tall by Balinese standards, the four-story hotel stands up above the coconut trees, but is forgiven for that because the main entrance and lobby are magnificent. All of the 450 rooms are centrally air-conditioned, and each has a private balcony. Standard rooms start at around $110 a night. Suites range from $500 to $2,000 a night and are fit for visiting kings and presidents. There are some eight places to eat and drink within the hotel, such as a 24-hour coffee shop, poolside bar, cocktail bars, a seafood and à lá carte restaurant, and a discotheque. Sports facilities include a gym, tennis and squash courts, a jogging track, and mini-golf. For water lovers there's a pool, beach, sailboarding, catamarans, snorkeling and parasailing nearby. Reserve through an agent or write the hotel at P.O. Box 1028, Denpasar, Bali, Indonesia. (Fax: (62) (361) 71229)

Adjacent to the Nusa Dua Beach Hotel is the **Melia Bali Sol** (Tel. (361) 71510), with 500 rooms and suites in a 25-acre setting. The Bali Sol Hotel also has tennis courts, squash courts, a beautiful beach for all manner of water sports, a vast swimming pool, indoor games, and a gym. A single room for a night (one person in the room) starts at just over $130 and cottage suites go up to $700 a night. There is no need to leave the hotel grounds to eat; just try any of the three main restaurants that specialize in seafood, Oriental, or à lá carte cuisine. For more relaxed dining and snacks, there's the Banji Coffee Shop or the poolside cafe specializing in *sate* (barbecue meat on a skewer). After dinner, disco the night away or meet some people at the piano bar. While the architecture of the Bali Sol may not be as impressive as the Nusa Dua Beach Hotel, the service is as excellent as one would expect from a Spanish-owned resort. Booking can be made direct to Melia Bali Sol, P.O. Box 1048, Tuban, Bali, Indonesia, or through Utell International worldwide. Visible across the water from the hotel, but twenty-five miles by highway past the airport and Kuta, is Sanur, the first and still the most sophisticated tourist area in Bali.

Bali Hyatt (Tel. (361) 88271) gets my pick as the best hotel on Sanur Beach, mainly due to the hotel's location and its setting amongst the coconut palms and gardens that have had years of growth behind them. The lobby is a Balinese-style building, with xylophone (*gamelan*) music drifting through the warm tropical air. Being outside the main Sanur strip of Sindhu, the Bali Hyatt has a less crowded beach, but then also there are fewer shops nearby. Not that you need to go far, given that there is a selection of restaurants and drinking holes at the hotel, as at the hotels along Nusa Dua Beach. Telaga Naga is acknowledged as the best Chinese restaurant in Bali. Then there's the Spice Island, serving Continental and Indonesian cuisine, the Fisherman's seafood place, a pizzeria, coffee shop, beach bars, and a disco. The Matahari disco is probably another best for Bali.

The rooms are decorated with Balinese fittings. The thirty-six acres of garden overflow with orchids, hibiscus, frangipani, and bougainvillaea. Book at any Hyatt Hotel in the states or Canada, or go direct if you have some special requests to P.O. Box 392, Sanur, Bali Indonesia. (Fax: (62) (361) 87683)

At the other end of Sanur is the first Western-style hotel built in Bali, and the only real high-rise, the **Hotel Bali Beach** (Tel. (361) 8511). Another wide, sandy, stretch with a breakwater at one end, the beach outside the Bali Beach Hotel stretches over several hundred yards of reef that once had colorful coral outcroppings. Unfortunately the coral is all gone, used for building roads and houses or sold to tourists. The Swiss Restaurant has a good reputation, as has the Bali Hai Supper Club. The other main attraction is the 9-hole golf course, one of only two in Bali. The hotel also has bowling and most of the international airlines' Bali branches. Rooms in the highrise tower start at around $100 a night, and garden suites at $200 per person. This hotel is part of the Hotel Indonesia chain. For bookings write to the Hotel Bali Beach, Sanur, Bali, Indonesia, or call their Jakarta office (Tel. (21) 320107).

Far from the madding crowd, two miles along the beach from Kuta past Legian and Seminyak, is the **Bali Oberoi** (Tel. (21) 51061). Offering intimate and luxurious accommodations, here is Balinese design and decor at its best. Set in twenty-five acres of lush gardens overlooking the beach, the hotel's single rooms (one-person occupancy) start at $150 per night. Villas right on the beach are $200. The great attraction of the Bali Oberoi is the sophisticated and exclusive atmosphere, together with the famed Kuta sunset. Eat at the Kura Kura Restaurant, surrounded by a fish pond, or at the beachside Frangipani Cafe. For shopping hop on the hotel's shuttle bus into Legian or Kuta. The Oberoi is the classiest place to stay in Bali. Write for reservations to Bali Oberoi Kuta, Bali, Indonesia. (Fax: (62) (361) 52791)

Other expensive hotels and bungalows that are also recommended are **Tanjung Sari** (Tel. (361) 884414), with its exquisitely decorated bungalows on central Sanur Beach ($200 a night); **Hotel Putri Bali** (Tel. (361) 71020) at Nusa Dua ($90 a night); and **Pertamina Cottages** (Tel. (361) 51161) at the southern end of Kuta ($120 a night).

Several first-class hotels are currently being built or are planned for southern Bali, such as a **Regent, Sheraton, Dusit Thani,** and **Ramada.**

MODERATELY PRICED HOTELS

There are now around 200 places to stay in the 5-kilometer strip north of the airport. Most of these are bungalow-style or cheaper *losmen*/homestays. At either end there are first-class bungalows, namely the Pertamina Cottages 400 meters from the airport and, at the northern end, Bali Oberoi. In between there are thirty second-class complexes averaging US$40 to 60 per night and over 170 budget-priced complexes averaging US$6 to 15 per night. Discounts of around 20 percent are offered in the off season.

Because there are so many alternatives, choosing a place can be difficult, especially if you have not been to Bali before or had somewhere recommended. If you fly in direct, it is suggested to get a package that includes accommodations as it is much cheaper that way. You could also pre-book just three nights so that you will have a base while looking for somewhere more suitable or before you move away from the southern beaches. The Indonesian Hoteliers Association has erected signs near all side streets towards the beach off Jalan Kuta Raya and Jalan Legian detailing the names and locations of all accommodations in that area. This makes some of the more out-of-the-way places easier to find, as many of the smaller roads and lanes don't have names.

At the Kuta end, facing the beach, are the **Sahid Bali Seaside**

Cottages and the **Kartika Plaza Beach Hotel**. These hotels are members of competing Indonesian hotel chains that will give a local feel to your holiday. **Sahid Bali Seaside Cottages** (Tel. (361) 538 5572) has cottages, each with air-conditioning and a bar fridge, and a high-rise building. The hotel offers secure postal, fax, and telex services, baby-sitting and a 24-hour restaurant. As is normal in Bali, there's an oversized swimming pool with a handy pool-level bar. The postal address for booking is P.O. Box 1102, Tuban, Bali, Indonesia. (Fax: (62) (361) 52019)

The Kartika Plaza Beach Hotel (Tel. (361) 51067-9), on the street of the same name in central Kuta, while on a smaller scale of 82 rooms, still offers well-appointed rooms with motel-style facilities and a 24-hour coffee shop. Management has recently been taken over by the group that runs the Nusa Dua Beach Hotel, and they are raising the standard to 5-star quality. Prices will probably rise also from the current rate of US$60 a night. Write to P.O. Box 84, Denpasar, Bali, Indonesia (Fax: (62) (361) 52475), or go through Garuda Indonesia airline or your local agent.

For a quieter stay try the **Kuta Palace Hotel**, (Tel. (361) 51461-2), which is actually along the beach at Legian rather than at Kuta proper. The hotel grounds front what is in reality a private beach, Legian Beach. Not far along the beach is that famous night spot, Chez Gado Gado. Rooms in the two-story hotel overlook the pool and the Indian Ocean and cost around US$50 a night. The rooms are air-conditioned with bath, shower, fridge, and balcony. The old name for the road that leads from this hotel to Jalan Legian (the main road) was Rum Jungle. It's now named after a small stone altar called *Pura Bagus Terana*, which is to the north of the road just a few hundred yards outside the hotel grounds. Traveling along the beach to Kuta is around two miles; by road it's three. Book direct to Kuta Palace Hotel, P.O. Box 244, Denpasar, Bali, Indonesia. (Fax: (62) (361) 52074)

Poppies Cottages (Tel. (361) 51059, 51149) are well located in central Kuta, but in a secluded location with a wonderful Balinese feel. The broad Kuta Beach is 100 yards away down the lane the cottages are named after. Poppies has been around since the early days of Kuta, before it had spread northward to Legian. The cottages' decor is very Balinese and the rooms are light and airy, set amid a delightful garden with a swimming pool and spa. Bathrooms are the unique Balinese garden variety. All of this goes for only US$50. Write for a brochure to Poppies Cottages, Gang Poppies, Kuta, Bali, Indonesia. (Fax: (62) (361) 52364)

Over at Sanur most of the hotels facing the beach would fall into this moderately priced category, with room rates ranging from $50 to $90.

Segara Village (Tel. (361) 87409) is typical of these, a blend of resort living, Balinese-style bungalows, and motel-style rooms set in a romantic tropical setting. Each room is individually decorated with intricate carvings and original paintings and furnished with rare antiques. You can choose from the fine Indonesian, Chinese, or European cuisine at the Wantilan Restaurant or, for Italian seafood cuisine, try the laid-back beachfront Le Pirate restaurant. There are several bars, too, each with their own special atmosphere. Facilities also include a nearby golf course, two pools, and a fully equipped recreation center. Balinese-style villas for four or more persons are available. Single rooms start at $70 a night, suites at double that. Write for reservations to Segara Village Hotel, Jalan Segara, Sanur, Bali, Indonesia.

Bali Sanur Bungalows (Tel. (361) 88421) are in two locations on the beach in central Sanur. For around $50 a night you get air-conditioning, a phone, a bar and restaurant, a swimming pool, and a balcony or terrace on which to relax and sip a cool drink or an afternoon coffee.

At the far southern end of Sanur are the **Santrian Bali Beach Bungalows** (Tel. (361) 87101) and the **Hotel Sanur Beach** (Tel. (361) 88011), offering facilities similar to the others in this class. Santrian Bungalows starts at $50 a night; Hotel Sanur Beach starts at $90.

Nusa Dua's moderately priced hotels are the **Club Med** and the **Hotel Club Bualu**. Both include all sports facilities and meals in their set fee of around $100 a night per person.

Some people may prefer the hustle and bustle of town life or may have business to attend to, and so choose to stay in Denpasar. You should note, however, that apart from banks, offices, and basic shopping, there is little else in Denpasar. There are few restaurants and no night life. An oasis in the center of this boredom is the **Bali Hotel** (Tel. (361) 5681-5), with older-style colonial buildings on a wide thoroughfare. There is also a more modern section across the road. Rooms cost from $70 to $100 a night, suites $150. Some of the colonial-era rooms may still be cooled by ceiling fans and thick walls. Even if you don't stay there, the Bali Hotel on Jalan Veteran, Denpasar, Bali, Indonesia, is a good place to cool off while exploring the town. It's on the corner of Jalan Gajah Mada.

BUDGET ACCOMMODATIONS

In Indonesia, whether in Bali, Java, or any of the other islands, budget accommodations are the norm rather than the exception. Included in the "budget" category are the hundreds of small hotels called *losmen* or *penginapan* that the locals use in Java, and the dozens that survive from the early 70s era at Kuta and Legian. Room rates at these are in rupiah—just Rp5,000 to Rp10,000 a night ($3 to $5) for a room with two single beds and possibly an Indonesian-style bathroom. (When I say a single room, I am referring to a room that may have two beds in it but is occupied by only one person. The same room for two people will usually be a bit more.) In this book, I'll be staying above that level; rates will average $20 to $30 a night and rooms will have twin or double beds, a Western toilet, and a shower. Some may have A/C wall units or a fan. A breakfast of coffee, bananas, or a pancake will probably be free. Drinking water will be supplied, but you'll have to go outside the hotel to eat.

There are now dozens of these bungalow complexes at Kuta-Legian, catering largely to the Australian market. It's hard to find an Australian who hasn't been to Bali. Many go there every year, as it's cheaper than traveling within Australia. And it's no longer limited to the young—families find that they can afford it, too.

Bakung Sari Cottages (Tel. (361) 51868) and **Rama Cottages** (Tel. (361) 51-557) in Kuta are safe bets, as is the **Bruna Beach Inn** (Tel. (361) 51564-5) at the Legian end.

On the Sanur side, the best of the budgets is **Alit's Beach Bungalows** (Tel. (361) 88567), renowned for the family atmosphere provided by Mr. & Mrs. Alit for many years. This hotel is within 200 yards of the Bali Beach hotel and golf course, faces the beach, and yet costs only $30 a night. Other acceptable cheapies are **Swastika Bungalows** (originally a Hindu symbol) and the Gazebo Cottages at around $30 to $40 a night for singles. Bookings at these Sanur hotels can be done through Garuda Indonesia airlines, who can arrange packages that subsidize your airfare if you pre-book your accommodation through them also. The same applies to the more upscale hotels and bungalows, so if you want to save a little, book with Garuda.

5. Restaurants and Dining

Seafood and tropical fruit-juice drinks would have to be the highlights of the Balinese dining experience. Add to them tasty free-range chicken, wonderful vegetables, East Indies spices, and a cool beer to wash it all down. Additionally, eating and drinking are made easy for you, with open-air terrace restaurants and bars everywhere outside the hotels at Kuta, Legian, and Sanur. Nusa Dua is the exception, with few restaurants outside the hotels, so go to another hotel for a change. Throughout Bali, prices are very reasonable, $5 to $15 being the average price for a main course per person. You can eat even cheaper, but anything more expensive is rare outside the first-class hotels.

Chinese cuisine is best represented by the **Telaga Naga Restaurant** at the Bali Hyatt Hotel at Sanur. Reasonable restaurants/cafes outside the major hotels at Sanur are the **Blue Moon**, **Blue Diamond**, **Kali Pathara**, **Kul Kul**, and **Legong** restaurants. **Roda Mas Padang** serves hot Sumatran food on a "pay for what you eat" system. A number of bowls are brought to your table, and you are charged for whatever you try; if you sample a taste from a bowl, you are charged for the whole thing, unless it contains chicken, meat, or fish, which are charged by the piece. Untouched bowls are returned to the counter and given to someone else. Restaurants tend to have the same all-encompassing menus, with a selection of seafood, American, European, Chinese, and Indonesian meals. This is especially so at Kuta and Legian in the budget-price range of $3 a meal.

Dining at Kuta-Legian is very informal. **Poppies** (Poppies Lane) is one of the oldest and best-known restaurants in Kuta. **Made's Warung** on Jalan Pantai was Kuta's original cafe. It's still popular with backpackers.

Seafood at Kuta is cheap and fresh at the Chinese-run **Viva** and **Mini** restaurants on Jalan Legian leading to Legian from Kuta. In Legian the **Orchid Garden** on Jalan Melasti and Southern Cross on the beach road are two of the many seafood restaurants. There are plenty of cafe/coffee shops on Jalan Legian. **Yudit** is a 24-hour spot with its own bakery. For Mexican try **T.J.'s** on Poppies Lane in Kuta. Reservations haven't caught on in Bali yet. If one place is busy, just keep walking and find somewhere else.

6. Sightseeing

Two of Bali's most visited temples are in south Bali. One is **Uluwatu**, overlooking a fantastic surfing break far below. The other is at **Tanah Lot**. Both are stunning at sunset, as are the **Kuta** and **Legian** beaches. At Sanur, tours take you over to **Turtle Island**, a small island 200 yards offshore where turtles come to breed, or you can walk along the **breakwater** beside the Bali Beach Hotel. In the town of Denpasar, the **main street** itself is an interesting walk. Meaning "south market," Denpasar has a vast **central market** off Jalan Gajah Mada next to the river. On the corner of Jalan Veteran is the **Governor's building**. The square opposite is the scene of the *Puputan* mass suicide of the Balinese royalty in front of Dutch colonial guns in 1906. Those warriors preferred death over surrender to the Dutch. Before that date Dutch influence in Bali was limited to the north coast.

Facing the square on the eastern side (Jalan Wisnu) are the **Denpasar Museum** and the **Pura Jagatnata temple**. Most of your sightseeing will be done away from the beach, so look for details in the next two chapters.

7. Guided Tours and Going it Alone

One way to see Bali is to book accommodations at one of the beaches in the south (Kuta, Nusa Dua, or Sanur) and make day trips by motorbike, taxi, or local transportation. An alternative is to spend some of your time at the beach and make trips through east, north, and central Bali by local buses and pickups, staying one or two nights in the towns along the way, and experiencing the Balinese lifestyle in its natural setting. I'd recommend stops in the popular Ubud, Candi Dasa, and Lovina Beach, for starters.

The Ubud area is usually the first stop when moving away from the south. There are accommodations there to suit all budgets, and there's much to see around town, not to mention beautiful walks in the surrounding rice fields. You might want to rent a bicycle and travel farther afield.

By bus from Ubud to the rim of **Mt. Batur** takes two to three hours. The view of the volcano and lake from the main road is spectacular, but the nights are cold and the local people at Kintamani and Penelokan are quite unfriendly, even hostile if you don't buy something they want to sell you. Still, it is worth staying there to cross the lake and to visit the **Pura Sukawan temple** at Penulisan, which is often shrouded in mist.

It is also possible to travel to Singaraja in north Bali via Klungkung, Padangbai, and Tirtagangga along the eastern slopes of Mt. Agung. The countryside around **Tirtagangga** rates amongst the most beautiful in Bali. Behind Tirtagangga to the north, the semi-active **Mt. Agung** symbolizes the ultimate power of nature over man—the volcano. The old royal capital of Karangasem, also known as Amlapura, was almost destroyed in the devastating eruption of 1963, in which a great river of lava just missed the town. Following the eruption there was a mass exodus from the town, as it was thought that the gods no longer looked upon them favorably. Tremors still occur, but it is the frequent eruptions that give Bali its rich soil, which enables the Balinese to devote so much of their time to art and religion.

From Tirtagangga the road winds around the side of Mt. Agung and meets the Lombok Strait near the village of Culik. The **road from Culik to Tianyar** is absolutely awe inspiring, being cut in places where the volcanic slopes meet the sea. In the wet season it may be difficult to pass along this route to Singaraja (King of the Lions), the seat of another Balinese royal family. There are a number of hotels and *losmen* in town, but **Lovina Beach**, eleven kilometers out of town, is a better place to stay. Whereas at Kuta-Legian the famed sunset is over the ocean, at Lovina the sun sets behind the towering peaks of East Java.

For those who prefer organized tours, most of the bigger hotels have tour operators on hand. Two operators at Sanur are **Pacto Tour** (Tel. (361) 87479) and **Tunas Indonesia** (Tel. (361) 8511/8056/8581). At Kuta and Legian there are many operators on Jalan Bakung Sari and Jalan Legian, such as **Care Free Bali Holidays** (Tel. (361) 5081-5) (Kuta Beach Hotel), **Easy Rider Tours & Travel** (Jalan Legian) (Tel. (361) 51672) or **Perama Tour** (Tel. (361) 51551) (Jalan Legian). The Government Tourist Office on Jalan Bakung Sari near the airport road is a good source of maps and free information.

Water Cruises

A cruise boat that operates tours on a daily basis is the **Bali Hai** (Tel. (361) 34331) **catamaran** that leaves from Benoa Harbor. This 90 foot catamaran is air-conditioned and has two bars. When you arrive at the offshore islands, you can hop into glass-bottom boats and gaze at the luxuriant coral and abundant fish life. Also try the **Bali International Yacht Club** (Tel. (361) 88391), which operates from Benoa Harbor near Sanur.

8. Water Sports

Many people go to Bali primarily for the water sports. Initially it was **surfers** from Australia, who found the waves of Uluwatu, Padang-Padang, and Medewi. Then came **scuba divers** and **snorkelers** to swim among the colorful sea gardens of coral that are best preserved on the east and north coasts, away from the larger settlements. Coral reefs are under threat in Indonesia, mainly because the reefs are being systematically broken up at low tide and the pieces carted off to be burnt for powder. This is used in building and as whitewash. Larger coral pieces are used for road building. Most coral that is less than 3 to 4 feet deep at low tide is long gone. Despite these problems, Bali still has many beautiful reefs. **Gloria Maris Dive** (Tel. (361) 51730/51403/51853) at Kuta is PADI registered, as is **Balina Diving** (or **Bali Pro**) (Tel. (361) 8777,8451) at Sanur.

These companies supply air and other equipment for experienced divers. If you stay for a week or two, even novices can learn to dive. Diving and meals cost around $100 a day. Snorkeling is beautiful under Balinese conditions. Just hire a local dugout sailboat, called a *prahu*, for a few hours and sail across the bay from Candi Dasa to Padang Bay, jumping in on the way.

The Bali Diving Center of Semawang has compiled the following descriptions of locations in Bali. Most other diving groups go to these, too.

Looking across to Sanur from Benoa Point

1. NUSA DUA
Beach : white sand
Topography : slope and flat bottoms
Entry : from the boat
Depth of diving : 10 to 60 feet (3 to 20 meters)
Object : sea view, spearfishing, photography

Comments:

Facing the northern and southern sea opposite Bualu, Nusa Dua offers gigantic underwater panoramas and various types of sponges and fish. Fully covered with rich and colorful corals, satisfies the most seasoned diver. Dives between 10 and 60 feet will be the most rewarding.

2. SANUR
Beach : white sand
Topography : slope and flat bottoms
Entry : from the boat
Depth of diving : 10 to 75 feet (3 to 25 meters)
Object : view under the sea, photography, spearfishing

Comments:

Located in front of Sanur's tourist beach. Dives at 6- to 40-foot depths will be rewarded by beautiful underwater panoramas. Table- and trophy-shaped coral and sponges. Thousands of colorful fish swim by in kaleidoscopic profusion.

3. PADANG BAY
Beach : white sand
Topography : slope
Entry : from the beach or boat
Depth of diving : 5 to 60 feet (3 to 20 meters)
Object : underwater panorama, photography, spearfishing

Comments:

Located about 45 miles northeast of Denpasar, this picturesque bay is surrounded by majestic cliffs and hills. Ideal for divers at 10- to 60-foot depths. Here water is strewn with a full growth of coral, fish, and whatnots which will surely guarantee an impressive underwater adventure.

4. TULAMBEN
Beach : stony
Topography : slope
Entry : from the beach

Depth of diving : 10 to 90 feet (3 to 30 meters)
Object : shipwreck (cargo ship *Liberty*)

Comments:

Located about 70 miles (110 kilometers) northeast of Denpasar, this trip includes a drive through truly idyllic Balinese countryside. On location you will see the remnants of a U.S. merchantman sunk during World War II. The wreck is fully grown over with all kinds of anemone, gorgonia, sponge, and coral.

5. GILI TOAPEKONG
Beach : sharp cliff
Topography : drop off
Entry : from the boat
Depth of diving : 40 to 120 feet (13 to 40 meters)
Object : sea view and spearfishing

Comments:

A tiny island adjoining Bali. Located about 30 miles (50 kilometers) north of Denpasar. Reachable by motorboat. Three hundred yards from the mainland. Suitable for expert divers and fully overgrown with a variety of colorful corals, sponges, plants and fishes. Suitable for spearfishing.

6. AMED
Beach : stony
Topography : slope, then drop off
Entry : from the beach
Depth of diving : 10 to 100 feet (3 to 33 meters)
Object : underwater panorama, spearfishing

Comments:

Located about 62 miles (100 kilometers) northeast of Denpasar. A beautiful, solitary beach with many anemone, gorgonia, and sponges, as well as small to larger fishes, make this underwater part of Bali ideal for beginners and professional divers.

7. SINGARAJA
Beach : black sand
Topography : slope
Entry : from the boat
Depth of diving : 10 to 80 feet (3 to 27 meters)
Object : underwater panorama, photography

Comments:

Located about 50 miles (80 kilometers) due north of Denpasar, where the calm water of the Bali Sea creates poollike conditions ideal for leisurely snorkeling. The best locations are Lovina Beach (suitable for beginners) and Gondol Beach (having slight currents and from 15- to 50-foot depths.)

8. PULAU MENJANGAN

Beach : white sand
Topography : drop off from the beach
Entry : from the beach or from the boat
Depth of diving : 15 to 120 feet (5 to 40 meters)
Object : photography

Comments:

The tiny island 75 miles (120 kilometers) northwest of Denpasar is accessible by a boat ride of only 10 minutes from the mainland. This area is suitable for all-season diving. Magnificent underwater vistas will surprise even the most seasoned diver. It is rich with all kinds of sponges, sea plants, coral, and fish. The area is considered the diver's paradise in Bali and words alone cannot describe its true beauty.

Parasailing takes off from Benoa Point, not far from Nusa Dua. At Lake Bratan near Bedugul in the central highlands there's also parasailing and **water-skiing**. The setting is inside an extinct volcano. Be warned that it can get extremely cold at night, especially after you have become used to lazing around at the beach.

Sailboards or windsurfers, different names for the same thing, can be hired at most of the hotels at Sanur and Nusa Dua. Surf conditions are too rough at Kuta and Legian. That noisy sea monster, the **jet ski**, also has enthusiasts at Sanur and Nusa Dua.

Surfing Breaks

Bali has been a must for **surfers** since it gained popular fame in the movie *Morning of the Earth* in the early 1970s. The sight of Stephen Cooney riding the waves of the then unknown Uluwatu still inspires surfers to go to Indonesia to look for new breaks. The number of known breaks is slowly being added to. **Medewi** near Negara has been ridden, for many years, as has **Nias Island** off North Sumatra. More recently, **Nusa Lembongan** off Sanur in Bali and **Grajagan** on the eastern tip of Java have been added to the surfing trail.

With three exceptions, all of the following spots are in southern Bali. I thought it best to put them in with these because most surfers seem to stay in Kuta-Legian. For the location of all the breaks included in this section, see the map of Bali on pages 92–93. Take your own repair kit with you, as none are available in Indonesia. Many surfers have lost good boards because they haven't been able to fix simple dings.

Getting to the Break: It is best to "charter" or hire a *bemo* with two or three other surfers to share costs. Organize the bemo the afternoon before you want to go. This is the best time to make a deal with *bemo* drivers because it is a slack period, and you will have more time to bargain and play one *bemo* driver against the other. Apart from the fact that you want an early, hassle-free start, there are not as many idle bemos in the morning and they are hyped up for the day's work. The price you will have to pay depends on how far you want to go and how long you want the bemo to wait. Always charter for the return trip. You have to pay for the return gas anyway, and the surcharge for waiting isn't much. If you don't arrange for the *bemo* to wait, you may have great trouble finding another *bemo* when you have finished surfing, and the driver will know he has you at his mercy as far as the price goes. Besides, who wants to haggle with a *bemo* driver after battling an exhausting surf?

1. Uluwatu

This break is situated at the bottom of the cliff near the temple of the same name. The temple is at the terminus of a regular *bemo* route. There are usually Balinese hanging around who will show you how to get down to the water and carry your boards for a negotiable fee. The break is quite variable and very dangerous because of the coral reef over which the waves break. Many a surfer has been rushed onto the next available plane home with jagged coral pieces embedded in his back. Be very careful.

2. Padang-Padang and Kuta Reef

These two reef breaks are quite far offshore between Uluwatu and the airport. They are best reached by chartering an outrigger. Padang-Padang is off the distant headland that is visible to the south of Kuta.

3. Kuta & Legian Beach breaks

These vary a lot depending on the banks and the season. Restrictions similar to those in the U.S. are in force, with the Kuta and Legian Surf Clubs setting up flags each day. There are a few hot locals who get possessive about the waves, so try to get to know them and reduce the tension.

4. Cangu

Cangu is a few kilometers along the beach north of Legian. At low tide it is possible to reach it by motorbike along the beach. By *bemo*, follow Jalan Legian towards the coast. From Legian it is vaguely visible as the center of the arc of the beach that stretches north. If there is no swell the break will disappear.

5. Nusa Lembongan

This is an island off the east coast of Bali which is reached by motorized outrigger from Sanur Beach. The last boat usually leaves by 9A.M. and costs Rp6,000 per person one way. Charter a *bemo* one way from Kuta or Legian to leave at 8A.M. or earlier. A boat returns most days from Lembongan at 6A.M. On the island there is a variety of accommodations stretching from the village up to the shipwreck. There is a left-hander near the wreck and a long, right-hand break on the center of the bay. The swell usually picks up around the new moon. Try not to worry about the sharks that feed near the left-hander. There are so many fish for them to eat that they don't bother trying to take a bite out of surfers. Still, pandemonium breaks out every morning as the surfers race for shore and then spot the fins. Hire an outrigger for a day and look for waves near Nusa Penida.

6. Medewi

Medewi is situated near the town of Negara about two hours' drive from Kuta. It is approximately halfway to the Java ferry terminal at Gilimanuk.

7. Grajagan

Kuta Surf Club arranges tours to Grajagan, which is in a national park on the eastern tip of Java. Grajagan itself is approximately 50 kilometers, south of Banyuwangi, which is on the Java side of the ferry. Altogether the trip will take around six hours, depending on how long you have to wait at the ferry.

9. Other Sports

One doesn't have to be interested in temples, markets, and the beach or pool to enjoy one's stay in Bali. One could pass one's time engaged in the sporting life—as long as you're into participation sports, that is, because basically there aren't any spectator sports worth talking about.

Ball sports such as **tennis, squash, badminton, table tennis**, and **volleyball** are well represented at the better hotels in Sanur, Nusa Dua, and to a lesser extent at Kuta-Legian. Tennis court surfaces are either concrete or synthetic grass. **Golfers**, too, can make their sport the centerpiece of their holiday. Sanur and Nusa Dua have one course each, but the best course is in the central highlands. Bali Handara Country Club, chosen repeatedly as one of the world's greatest 50 courses, is perhaps the only one set in the crater of an extinct volcano. The challenging 18-hole championship course, 100 hectares (247 acres) of gently sloping, tree-lined fairways and greens, was designed by Peter Thompson. Located in the cool, lush, and green highlands of central Bali at 3,700 feet above sea level, and with an average temperature of 70 degrees F., Bali Handara offers the ultimate getaway, though it's only thirty miles from Denpasar. The clubhouse is a mixture of traditional Balinese and modern architecture set on a hill surrounded by rainforest. The restaurant, lounge, and conference center all overlook the golf course. Facilities include a sauna, massage, gym, tennis courts, driving range, practice greens, and a pro shop. The luxuriously appointed cottages for overnight or weekly stays are close by the clubhouse and the first tee. Daily greens fees are around US$60 and caddy fees around US$6 per round. Room rates range from US $60 to $100 per night.

10. Shopping

Brush up on your bargaining and haggling skills before you arrive because in Indonesia the seller's first price is usually negotiable. This is especially so for souvenirs, artifacts, paintings, jewelry, earrings, batik cloth, fruit from a market stall, or clothing. Western-looking shops such as supermarkets, boutiques, and galleries at Sanur and hotel shops work on a fixed-price system. Other fixed-price goods are household items, small goods, cassettes, toiletries, food, and drink—both cheap and expensive. When in doubt, haggle to test the situation. You've got nothing to lose, except a few dollars if you don't.

Woodcarvings, paintings, and **silver jewelry** would have to be the best buys of the local arts. Villagers at Batuan and Mas near Ubud carve at home and then get their children or friends to sell the finished products to shops or direct to tourists at Kuta and Sanur. Ebony and teak are two of the better local timbers used for beautiful abstract, religious, or Indian characters. Around Ubud there are dozens of galleries and hundreds of artists. Some of their work makes it to Kuta and Sanur, but you will have a bigger selection to choose from if you shop at Ubud.

For silver jewelry, the best places are Celuk and Kuta-Legian. Celuk is on the main road out of Denpasar on the way to Ubud. Avoid the silver shops with parking lots big enough for tourist buses. Their prices will be higher. In Kuta have a look in *Mirah Silver* on Jalan Buni Sari or *Yusuf Silver* on Jalan Pantai Kuta. In Legian on Jalan Plasa try *Mila* and *Mitra*, or on Jalan Legian *Gerinsing* and *Moon Silver*. Near the Bali Hyatt Hotel in Sanur try *Kangguru Mas* and *Queen Silver*.

Cassette music tapes are another good buy. You'll find a wide selection at around $3 each. They have a bit of tape hiss but for the price you can't complain. The quality of the ones made in Bali is much inferior to the tapes from Jakarta. Ask when buying. Kuta and Legian have the widest range. Tape shops are concentrated on Jalan Legian, Jalan Bakung Sari, and Jalan Buni Sari. At Sanur try *Bohny X*, *Bagus Store*, *Sriyani*, or *Wirasana Store*, which are all on the main road leading to the Hyatt Hotel.

Bali is also a good place to buy so-called **tribal art** from the islands of Sumba, Sumbawa, Flores, Timor, and Kalimantan. This is mostly dark, woven blankets and cane baskets, as well as sometimes sinister-looking dark wood carvings. The Kuta-Legian road offers the best selection at good prices if you haggle.

Cool clothing is another great buy at the beaches, especially Kuta and Legian for the young at heart. There are hundreds of boutiques and stalls selling t-shirts, pants, beach shorts, and trendy shirts. In Bali you can wear this type of clothing on the beach and around town in the tourist areas without attracting attention. In Java keep it in your suitcase.

Leather has caught on in a big way in the last few years. It's mostly kid leather for jackets, but there are also shoes, sandals, and belts. Legian is the place to shop for leather.

As you may have noticed, Kuta-Legian is the commercial heart of southern Bali as far as tourists are concerned. People from all over Indonesia and the world have set up shop here to supply all of the things mentioned earlier to tourists, travelers, and also commercial buyers. The two-mile-long Jalan Legian, which goes from the *bemo*-corner in Kuta to Seminyak, is a bargain shopper's dream. Notice I say "bargain shopper." This is not Rome or Paris, but the prices are around one quarter of the ones found there. And don't be timid about bargaining. Expect to reduce the price by 30 percent to 50 percent depending on the season.

Bookshops are the *Bali Beach Hotel* news agency at Sanur, *Kerta Bookshop* on Jalan Legian in Kuta, and *Bali Purnama* on Jalan Legian in Legian.

Foodstuffs that you may want to take home are coffee, chili nachos, and Bali wine (*arak*), which is more like a spirit. For imported cookies, etc., try the *Galael Supermarket* on Jalan Kuta Raya in Kuta or the *Loji II Store* in Legian. In Sanur the general stores are *ABC*, *Padmi*, and *Tina*, all on the Bali Hyatt road.

Before you bring any foodstuffs back home, though, you should check with U.S. or Canadian Customs to see what is allowed and what isn't.

11. Night Life and Entertainment

Each of the southern beaches has its own style of nightlife. Nusa Dua has more of a supper club and disco scene based at the main hotels. Kuta-Legian is bars, loud rock music, and discos. Sanur is somewhere in between, with clubs and discos at the hotels as well as very relaxed bars and taverns set back on the main road. There is the **No. 1 Disco** and **Subic Nightclub** on Jalan Tanjung Sari and the **Matahari Disco** inside the Bali Hyatt. The **Bali Hai Supperclub** is inside the Bali Beach Hotel and the **Kedaton Supper Club** at the Sanur Beach Hotel.

At Nusa Dua most of the entertainment is at the **Nusa Dua Beach Hotel**, **Putri**, and **Bali Sol**. The Putri Bali and Nusa Dua Beach Hotel each have a disco. The Putri Bali also has the **Khayangan Supper Club** and the **Paseban Bar** for live music (often light jazz). Each of the hotels has a lobby and poolside bars.

Kuta-Legian is action. There are people everywhere, and many are intent on getting drunk and having a good time—with whatever that may entail, including sex, drugs, and rock and roll. Yes, Kuta-Legian is Bali's version of a red-light district, especially late at night when the tourists have gone. Sophistication is not a word one would use in describing entertainment at Kuta or Legian, but it does have lots of relaxed bars and rough and rowdy bars such as the **Rivoli** on Jalan Plasa, Legian, or the **Bruna Hard Rock Cafe** on Legian's beachfront road.

Around midnight the in crowd drives up to **Chez Gado Gado** bar and disco at Seminyak, about 5 miles from central Kuta.

Moviegoers will find Bali a year or two behind in movie releases. In Denpasar two modern cinemas are the **Wisata Theatre** on Jalan Thamrin and **Gajah Mada Theatre** inside Pasar Kumbarsari market on Jalan Gajah Mada.

Local dance and drama is one of the highlights of many people's visit to Bali. The dances are colorful and dynamic. At night they are usually staged at the local community hall, the *bale banjar*. During the day you can sometimes see villagers involved in religious ceremonies at the local temples or people from other villages making offerings at the beach.

At Sanur, **temple dances** are staged every day at the Pura Dalem Temple on Jalan Sanur Raya in Tanjung Bungkak (towards Denpasar). The other main venue for traditional dance and drama is at **Batu Bulan**, a few miles out of Denpasar on the way to Ubud. Nusa Dua has the **Ambara Open Stage** at the Putri Bali Hotel.

12. The Address List—Bali's Southern Beaches

Wherever you are in Bali, you are probably better off using these contacts and not the local ones. These are more reliable, having better phone and computer services.

Airline Offices—Bouraq Indonesia, Jalan Sudirman 19A, Denpasar (Tel. (361) 34947). Bouraq Indonesia, Airport, (Tel. (361) 51011), ext. 255). Cathay Pacific, Bali Beach Hotel, Sanur, (Tel. (361) 88576). Garuda Indonesia, Jalan Melati 61, Denpasar, (Tel. (361) 27825). Garuda Indonesia, Jalan Pantai Kuta, Kuta, (Tel. (361) 51179). Garuda Indonesia, Nusa Dua Beach Hotel, Nusa Dua, (Tel. (361) 71444). Garuda Indonesia, Jalan Sanur, Sanur, (Tel. (361) 88243). Garuda Indonesia, Airport, (Tel. (361) 51178). KLM Royal Dutch Airlines, Bali Beach Hotel, Sanur, (Tel. (361) 87460). Malaysian Airlines, Bali Beach Hotel, Sanur, (Tel. (361) 88716). Merpati Nusantara, Jalan Melati 57, Denpasar, (Tel. (361) 22864). Pelita Air Service, Jalan Merpati 2, Denpasar, (Tel. (361) 51071). Qantas Airways, Bali Beach Hotel, Sanur, (Tel. (361) 88331). Scandinavian Airlines, Bali Beach Hotel, Sanur, (Tel. (361) 88141). Singapore Airlines, Bali Beach Hotel, Sanur, (Tel. (361) 87940, 88511). Thai Airways Int'l, Bali Beach Hotel, Sanur, (Tel. (361) 88141). UTA French Airlines, (Tel. (361) 27769, 28161).

Ambulance—Tel. (361) 118/26305.

Banks—(Note that money changers at Sanur and Kuta-Legian may give better rates than these banks) Bank Duta (Visa), Jalan Roya Hayam Wuruk 165, Tanjungbungkak. Bank Central Asia (Mastercard), Jalan H.O.S. Cokroaminoto 39, Denpasar. Bank Duta Bali (Mastercard), Jalan Gajah Mada, Denpasar. B.N.I. 1946, Jalan Gajah Mada 30, Denpasar. Bank Bumi Daya, Jalan Veteran 2, Denpasar. Bank Dagang Negara, Jalan Gajah Mada 3, Denpasar. B.N.I. 1946, Jalan Legian, Kuta.

Consulates—American, Jalan Segara, Sanur (Tel. (361) 8478) (Larger U.S. diplomatic missions are the embassy in Jakarta and the consulate in Surabaya.) Australian, Jalan Raya Sanur 146, Tanjungbungkak, (Tel. (361) 25998). Canadian—nearest is in Jakarta. Please see Chapter 10. Italian Hon., Jalan Padanggalak, Sanur, (Tel. (361) 8372). Japanese, Jalan Raya Sanur 124, Tanjungbungkak, (Tel. (361) 25611).

Fire—Tel. (361) 113.

Hospital/Doctor—There is a Western doctor at the Bali Beach Hotel, Sanur. Sanglah Public Hospital, Jalan Nias, Denpasar, (Tel. (361)

27911). Wangaya Public Hospital, Jalan Kartini, Denpasar, (Tel. (361) 22141).

Pharmacy/Apotik—Apotik, Jalan Segara, Sanur. Apotik, Jalan bypass, Sanur. Apotik Sadah Karya, Jalan Gajah Mada 41, Denpasar. Apotik Gajah Mada, Jalan Gajah Mada 28, Denpasar. Apotik Kresna Farma, Jalan Gajah Mada/Jalan Thamrin, Denpasar. Apotik Mada Sandhi, Jalan Kuta Raya, Kuta.

Phone Operator—Local Information (Bali), (Tel. 108). Indonesia (other islands), (Tel. 100). International Operator, (Tel. 102). International Phones/Telex on Jalan Kedondong, Denpasar; Jalan Tanjung Sari, Sanur; and Jalan Legian, Kuta.

Police—(Tel. (361) 110).

Post Office—G.P.O. Jalan Puputan Raya, Renon. P.O. Kereneng Jalan Kemuning, Denpasar. P.O. Sanur Jalan Segara, Sanur. P.O. Kuta Jalan Pos, Kuta.

Tourist Information—Main Office, Jalan Surapati, Denpasar, (Tel. (361) 23602). Kuta Branch, Jalan Bakungsari, Kuta.

6

Ubud & Central Bali

1. The General Picture

Ubud is the first stop for most people who move away from Kuta or Sanur, and is the only place in Bali where there is a wide variety of accommodations not on a beach. Walking amongst the ricefields you catch a glimpse of Balinese life as it really is, not the hybrid version that has been created in the south of the island.

Ubud is famous as the center of Balinese painting, and one kilometer towards Denpasar is Peliatan, home of the best dance and *gamelan* troupe in Bali. Places of interest include the museum at Bedulu and the former royal capitals of Gianyar and Bangli.

One of the best places to stay so you can fully enjoy the peace, tranquility and cool climate of Ubud is at Oka Kartini's. Oka's bungalows are built according to the traditional building specifications with intricately carved reliefs and roof supports, together with the best of Western bathrooms, hot water, and fans. Located half a kilometer from the center of Ubud, Oka's is for those wanting a quiet retreat at a reasonable price.

While Ubud may not have the nightlife and variety of shopping of Kuta or Sanur, it does offer a look at Balinese art and culture in a natural setting without the hustle and bustle. For starters, most of the original Balinese painters come from Ubud and many of them still live and work there. In the 1970s Ubud was at the center of the revival of Balinese painting. The so-called "young artists" follow both traditional and modern styles, and their paintings are much cheaper than those by the masters.

To get an idea of Balinese art and wood carving before buying, visit the art gallery Puri Lukisan Ratna Warta (entry fee Rp300). The gallery was set up with money donated by Europeans and consists of three buildings set in beautiful gardens and rice fields near the center of Ubud. Two house permanent exhibitions, and one is run by the local painters' cooperative.

The works at the cooperative hall are for sale, and prices are negotiable. Each month a different local group shows their work, and each painter can show only one painting. However, if you like a particular painter's style, make a note of his name and village and track him down later. The biggest group is from the village of Padangtegal, which is between Ubud proper and the monkey forest.

At Lempad's house on Jalan Raya, his grandsons carry on the traditions and put out some good work. Lempad, who died in 1978 at age 97, had a very distinctive sketching style. Some of his sketches are on show at his house. Jalan Monkey Forest has quite a few galleries with reasonably priced traditional and modern art. One of the modern forms is the Japanese-influenced screens. There are also quite a few galleries on the main street, some of which do not offer value for the money.

The growth of tourism in Ubud has promoted a resurgence of local interest in studying the Arts. As a result, it is now possible to watch cultural performances each night at one of the local community centers. As well as these arranged shows, which consist of a medley of dances normally restricted to special religious occasions, the traditional arts of dance and drama with *gamelan* music still play an integral part of any religious holiday or ceremony.

The atmosphere of *Peliatan* village is reminiscent of Ubud in the early 1970s—just a few places to stay, not many shops or hawkers, limited Western food outlets, and a colony of artists nearby. Peliatan is one mile on the Denpasar side of Ubud, so it is easy to travel or walk between the two towns. There is a Bank Indonesia branch in Peliatan, but the money changers in Ubud offer a better rate.

Puri Agung, within the compound of the former palace, is a delightful place to stay. Or just call in for a chat with Bapak Agung, the patriarch of a friendly and open family. Ratih Agung, his daughter, is a well-known dancer who has traveled with the Peliatan Dance Troupe to Europe, the U.S., and Japan.

There are plenty of wood carver's shops in Peliatan, but that is about all. In Peliatan proper there are only a few places to eat, though halfway

Ratih Agung at entrance to family temple, Peliatan

to Ubud at Terbesaya is the Ubud Raya Coffee Shop, which serves Japanese and Western food.

2. Long-Distance Transportation

There are no long-distance connections as such out of Ubud or anywhere else in central Bali. The **airport** near Kuta is the only one in Bali. Should you be staying at Ubud the night before you fly out of Bali, be sure to phone *Garuda* (or whichever airline it is) yourself to make sure that you do have a confirmed booking. You may need to phone from the telephone office on the main street of Ubud to make an interlocal call if your hotel cannot get through. Confirmation of bookings is one serious lacking in Indonesia, so always be doubly sure. Don't just rely on a local travel agent.

Buses to Java leave from the Ubung Terminal in Denpasar. You can buy a ticket in Ubud and would be advised to confirm your seat here, too. These overnight expresses leave Denpasar in the late afternoon each day. See the section on long-distance travel in Chapter 5 for timetables and fares.

In Ubud you can book a bus seat at *Bali Coach Tour* on Jalan Monkey Forest, Ubud.

Buses to Java also leave from Singaraja on Bali's north coast. This route is only recommended if you plan to stay on the Lovina Coast and then go overland direct to Java.

Taxis and rental cars are not available to travel outside Bali, though you should be able to catch a **bemo** to the ferry terminal at Gilimanuk for travel to Java or to the Padangbai Ferry Terminal for travel to Lombok.

If you need other long-distance travel information, try *Bali Goro* agency near Nomad's on Jalan Raya or *Mumbul Tour* on Jalan Raya opposite the Tourist Information Office.

3. Local Transportation

Ubud is a very small town, so you can **walk** from your lodgings to the restaurants, galleries, or dance places. **Bicycling** around Ubud is also good for a day, as the center of town is quite level. The main road back to Peliatan is more of a gentle slope. So is the road to the monkey forest. Bicycles can be rented from *Alit's*.

Car rental can be done through *Mumbul Tour* on Jalan Raya near the Tourist Information Office, from *Gusti's*, also on Jalan Raya near Nomad's, or from *Purpa Car* on Jalan Monkey Forest.

Motorbikes can also be rented from Purpa Car. Gas is available from *Kios Benzin* on Jalan Raya in Ubud or *Purpa* on Jalan Monkey Forest, or at a small shop next to *Baligoro* on Jalan Cok Gede Rai, opposite the Mandala Cafe.

There are no **taxi** ranks as such in Ubud. What you can do is "charter" a **bemo** (local van) by the hour plus petrol. See page (24) for details on how to do this.

4. Hotels and Lodging

EXPENSIVE ACCOMMODATIONS

Luxury bungalows overlook the valley of the Agung River in the village of Kedewatan, which is two miles out of Ubud. There, long grass waves in the wind towards the distant sea. There is plenty of space and tranquility, especially suited to groups of four people who wish to take advantage of the multi-level bungalows.

Kupu Kupu Barong Bungalows (Tel. (361) 95479) are built in the traditional Balinese style, yet offer the ultimate in luxury living. Positioned for total privacy, each bungalow features two double bedrooms, combined lounge/dining area, superbly appointed bathrooms, plus upstairs/downstairs balconies for uninterrupted views of cascading rice terraces and the meandering Ayung River some 150 yards below. Bungalow daily rates are $200. A shuttle bus takes guests to the Ubud town center. Book direct at: Kupu Kupu Barong Bungalows, Kedewatan, Ubud, Bali Indonesia (Fax: (62) 361 95079, 23172).

Nearby along the valley are **Cahaya Dewata Bungalows** (Tel. (361) 95495), the first luxury bungalows built on this side of Ubud in the mid-1980s. These bungalows are not quite as luxurious as Kupa Kupa Barong but have a similar style, such as two or three bedrooms, 2 bathrooms, and sitting areas. If you stay here you will need to rent a vehicle. Staying here alone is expensive, but sharing with another couple makes it more affordable. Book by mail at Cahaya Dewata Bungalows, Kedewatan, Ubud, Bali Indonesia (Fax: (62) (361) 52777).

MODERATELY PRICED BUNGALOWS

The accommodations in this next group are really the best places to stay in Ubud. Two are in the center of town and the other is a fifteen-minute walk away. **Puri Saren** (Tel. (361) 28871) is the name of the palace of the former royal family of Ubud. When the old king died in the mid-1980s, his wooden cremation tower was the biggest seen for many years. Guests' bungalows are within the palace walls, each having hot showers, tasteful furnishings, and the traditional royal Balinese building style. Single rooms are around US$50 a night. Book through Garuda or write direct to Puri Saren Agung, Ubud, Bali Indonesia.

Siti Bungalows (Tel. (361) 28690), run by Hans Snel, are set in well-manicured gardens. These are a bit more Westernized, with a well-known cocktail bar and restaurant. All bungalows have hot showers but no air conditioning, as none is needed in Ubud's cool climate. The same goes for everywhere else in central Bali. Singles cost around $50 a night and reservations can be made by mail to P.O. Box 227, Denpasar, Bali Indonesia.

Oka Kartini is the name of the wonderful lady who runs **Oka Kartini Bungalows** (Tel. (361) 95193, 95040), formerly known to European visitors as Koeperus. Oka is from a Brahman family and everything about her is Balinese elegance.

In the mid-1980s she oversaw the building of new bungalows in the traditional royal style coupled with imported Italian marble and fittings in the bathrooms. During different visits I watched tradesmen hand chiseling scenes from the *Ramayana* Indian epics into the cement panels on the outside walls. It is people like Oka who keep the old masonry skills alive. The largest, most impressive bungalow goes for around $60 a night; the smaller ones are a lot less. In another section of the compound are larger, plainer rooms for as low as $20 a night.

All bathrooms have hot showers and a light breakfast is provided. Across the road is the Ubud Raya Coffee Shop for meals if you don't feel like going into town. The walk into town is a short 10 to 15 minutes, depending on how fast you go.

Book directly at Oka Kartini Bungalows, Terbesaya, Ubud, Bali Indonesia.

BUDGET ACCOMMODATIONS

There are a multitude of very hospitable places to stay in this price range in and around Ubud. All have that characteristic Balinese feel about them, either coming from the people running them, the building style, or the location in the rice paddies or beside a temple. Booking in advance may not be 100 percent reliable.

Tjanderi's (or Canderi) was one of the first places to stay. Started by a lady called Tjanderi in the early 1970s, the rooms have continually been upgraded and are now up to motel standards for $10 a night. Quite spartan, Tjanderi's is really still a backpackers' place to stay. Write to the Tjanderi Losmen, Ubud, Bali Indonesia.

Farther along Monkey Forest Road is the **Ubud Inn.** Comfortable and away from the busy town center, Ubud Inn is a short walk from the monkey forest. Rooms are around $20 a night. There is an adjoining restaurant and others nearby. Book directly at Ubud Inn, Jalan Monkey Forest, Ubud, Bali Indonesia.

The **Menara Hotel** is on the main street, opposite the art museum. Central to restaurants, shops, and galleries, the Menara Hotel is now a bit dated in its building style, but its later rooms are okay. Room rates are $10 to $20 a night. Hot water is not always guaranteed to be flowing, but you don't really need it in Indonesia. Write to the Menara Hotel, Jalan Raya, Ubud, Bali Indonesia.

The **Cecak Inn**, in a quiet location overlooking the Campuan River, is about a fifteen-minute walk up a hill to the town center. The young family that owns and runs these bungalows is descended from the royal family. The building style is traditional Balinese and so are the surroundings. Single rooms are $10 to $20 per night. Book directly by writing to the Cecak Inn, Ubud, Bali Indonesia.

5. Restaurants and Dining

The road that leads from Denpasar through Peliatan to Ubud and Champuan is littered with dozens of memorable eating places, starting with **Mandala** in *Peliatan*, which was one of the first eating places in Bali that catered to foreigners. This family has been involved from the start, teaching traditional dance and renting rooms out. On the *Ubud* side of the Terbesaya roundabout is the **Ubud Raya Coffee Shop**, which serves some Japanese dishes. As you enter *Ubud* proper, on the left is **Nomad's**, an expansive, terraced restaurant which opens till late as a cocktail bar. It's a cool place to be on balmy nights.

A few hundred yards farther and you're at the center of town—the market. The Ubud main market opens every *second* day. There are stalls selling hot, spicy meat, vegetables, rice, and noodle dishes at around $1 a small main course. Each *warung* (food stall) has only a small selection. Be warned that eating at these stalls may give you the runs, both from chili peppers and lack of refrigeration.

Continuing along the main road (Jalan Raya) past the temple, you'll see set in beautiful gardens the **Cafe Lotus**, possibly the number one eating place in Ubud. The location in the gardens at night with the spotlights on is stunning.

Another few hundred yards on, restaurants are on terraces over the road, such as **Griya**. Next point of interest on the eating trail through Ubud is **Murni's Warung** at the main river crossing, alongside the Dutch colonial-era suspension bridge.

To this point prices have been very reasonable, main courses rarely costing more than $5 or Rp10,000. But now, crossing the river, we move into *Campuan* (pronounced "champuan"), the more upmarket side of town. Main courses around Campuan cost under $10. A beer is $3 to $4.

Ubud market

Carrying the shopping basket at Ubud

Shopper at Ubud market

Market day at Ubud

Beggar's Bush and the **Campuan Hotel** are the first over the bridge on the right and both are open until late for drinks and snacks. Recommended for afternoon coffee or a few drinks is **Cahaya Dewata Restaurant** and bungalow complex. There is a fantastic view over the Ayung River valley towards the sea. And the food's good, too—very well presented Western and Indonesian meals, at higher prices. Cahaya Dewata is in the village of *Kedewatan*, about 15 minutes' drive from Ubud. Back in town, on Jalan Kajeng, is **Hans Snel Garden**, with a late-night cocktail bar.

The other main road in Ubud leads from the central market to the monkey forest, and so Jalan Monkey Forest it is named. **Canderi**, one hundred yards down on the left, was the first *warung* where Westerners ate in the early 1970s. It caters to backpackers with its $2 all-day breakfast, $1 fruit juices, and some Indonesian and Chinese meals. Also on the left side at equal intervals before the monkey forest are **Harry Chew's**, serving budget-priced Chinese and Indonesian meals, and the upscale **Ubud Restaurant**, recognized as the best Indonesian food in town.

Most of you will be driving to the volcanic crater rim at *Penelokan* and looking down into Lake Batur. While you're there, grab a cup of coffee in an Indonesian-style cafe near the parking lot, or warm up with a bowl of soup. Prices are less than $1. A mile farther on at the village of *Batur* are the up-market **Kintamani Restaurant** with a buffet lunch and the **Puri Selera Restaurant** serving Balinese fried chicken. These two and the **Puri Astina Inn** at *Kintamani village* all have stunning views of the lake and the new volcano cone rising out of the crater of the original one. Your restaurant is perched on the rim. For a budget meal there is **Superman's Restaurant** in the village of *Batur*.

6. Sightseeing

AROUND UBUD

Ubud is an ideal town for walking. The main road passes through *Peliatan* village on the way from Denpasar, goes through the center of the town past the market, former palace, the art museum, and then runs on to *Campuan*. Turn left at the market and a bit over a mile away is one of the best **monkey forests** in Indonesia. Try to be there when there is a ceremony at the **Pura Dalem temple**, which is on the far southern edge of the forest. Other outstanding temples are near the former palace, (now Puri Saren Bungalows), at Terbesaya next to Oka Kartini Bungalows, and on an island in the river near the bridge at Campuan. Some

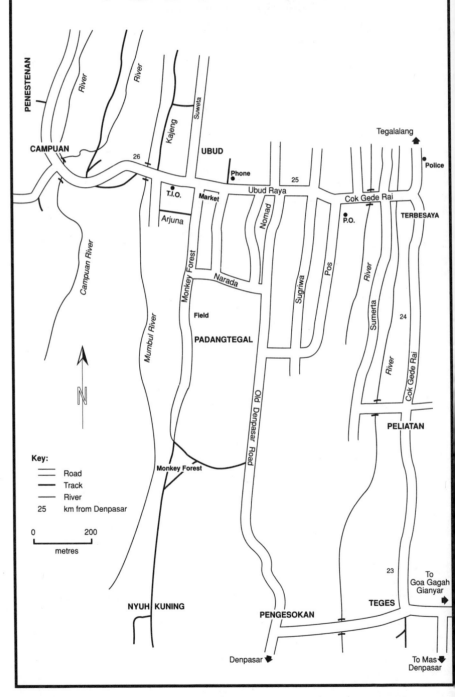

UBUD AREA

PENESTENAN

River

River

Kajeng

Suweta

CAMPUAN

UBUD

26

Phone

25

Ubud Raya

Campuan River

T.I.O.

Market

Cok Gede Rai

Police

Tegalalang

TERBESAYA

Arjuna

P.O.

Nomad

Monkey Forest

Narada

Sugriwa

Pos

River

Sumerta

Mumbul River

Field

PADANGTEGAL

24

River

Cok Gede Rai

N

Old Denpasar Road

PELIATAN

Monkey Forest

Key:

Road

Track

River

25   km from Denpasar

0   200

metres

NYUH KUNING

PENGESOKAN

TEGES

23

To
Goa Gagah
Gianyar

Denpasar

To Mas
Denpasar

people like to head off along small walking tracks that lead from the main roads into the villages and rice fields, into the real Bali.

The **tourist information office** is on the main street (Jalan Raya) 100 yards past the market on the left-hand side. They will give you a free map of the town and surrounding areas. Last time I was there, the map had lots of interesting and humorous anecdotes, all written in English by a local. With this map in hand you'll be in a better position to walk your way along the back tracks of Ubud and Peliatan.

Opposite the market and surrounded by an eight-foot stone and brick wall is **Puri Saren**, the home of the former royal family. Royalty went out with Indonesia's independence in 1945. In one of the outer courtyards there are now bungalows and in another is the venue for their own dance group's nightly performance. The side streets around the former palace have the best temples in Ubud, which is normal seeing as how the royal families in Bali had the most wealth to devote to their Hindu gods.

Follow the main road away from Denpasar a few hundred yards, and on your right is the entrance to the **Art Museum Puri Lukisan**, set in beautiful gardens. On display is a blend of traditional and modern paintings. Some are on permanent display and others are exhibits from the local villages on a rotational basis.

The road to **Campuan** is over a mile down a reasonably steep incline, across the colonial-era footbridge, and uphill again to Campuan. Give yourself a few hours and walk there. You'll enjoy it (except at noon, of course). **Peliatan** is around 1.5 miles (2 kilometers) back towards Denpasar from Ubud along the main road, a bit too far to walk but okay by bicycle. The village has a very peaceful air about it.

SCENIC WALK—UBUD TO PADANGTEGAL

Start at the Ubud market and head towards Denpasar. The second street after Nomad's turn right, past Masih Homestay, dip through a bamboo grove, and emerge into the ricefields. Bear right past a small temple and turn left onto an asphalt road. Take the first right fork and continue to the monkey forest. Take the main road back to market.

TEMPLES IN UBUD

Here is a list of the better temples in Ubud and Peliatan and their locations. *Pura* means "temple" in Balinese. Be sure to wear a sash around your waist when entering any temple compound. Otherwise you will be confronted by very irate locals.

Pura Campuan	under bridge, Campuan
Pura Dalem	Jalan Raya, Ubud
Pura Desa	Jalan Kajeng, Ubud

Puri Saren, Ubud

Pura Sakenan	Jalan Raya, Ubud
Pura Merajan	Jalan Suweta, Ubud
Pura Batur Sari	Jalan Suweta, Ubud
Pura Dalem	past Monkey Forest, Padangtegal
Pura Dadya Pasek Gelgel	Jalan Cok Gede Rai, Terbesaya
Pura Panetaran Pande	Jalan Cok Gede Rai, Peliatan
Pura Merajan	Jalan Cok Gede Rai, Peliatan
Pura Desa Gede	Jalan Cok Gede Rai, Teges

OUTSIDE UBUD

One of the advantages of staying at Ubud is that when you want to visit other towns and cultural sites in Bali you don't have to go through the hassle of traffic congestion. This will save you an hour's drive each way. In this section I will divide places to visit outside Ubud into four groups, the first three of which are: (a) those around the **Goa Gajah** archaeological sites, (b) **Lake Batur** volcanic highlands, and (c) the busy market towns of **Bangli** and **Gianyar**. Visits to all of these places can be arranged through a local tour company in Ubud or at the southern beaches if you are staying there. Try *Bali Goro* or *Mumbal Tours*. The fourth area is (d) **Bedugul-Lake Bratan**, which is in the highlands on the other road from Denpasar to Singaraja. This road crosses the mountains to the west of Kintamani and it may be easier to go back to Denpasar than to travel cross-country direct from Ubud, or go direct from the southern beaches.

(a) Goa Gajah

This ancient site is named after a cave used for meditation by Buddhist monks near the Gajah River. It dates from around A.D. 1000 and was first mentioned in a royal chronicle of Kertagame in 1365. Like other sites in the area it has a Buddhist and Shivaist background. Beside the *T*-shaped cave there are three large water spouts and pools. Follow the path down towards the river past a waterfall and fallen rock carvings. Goa Gajah is in a very tranquil setting only 2.5 miles from Ubud. If you are feeling energetic early in the morning it makes a nice walk through Peliatan, Teges and 1.5 miles of ricefields. At the Teges intersection take the road to Tampaksiring and Gianyar, not Denpasar. Stalls selling handicrafts and fruit at Goa Gajah can be a bit of a rip-off.

Yeh Pulu

Not far from Goa Gajah, on the steep bank of a small river, is a fourteenth-century stone sculpture measuring 14 yards long and 3 yards high. The sculpture shows peasants at work, and is one of the oldest to deal with non-religious themes. To get there, take the next road to the right after Goa Gajah and follow it until it turns left at the school building. There you turn right and follow it to its end. Cross the ditch, go through the rice paddies, cross another small stream, and you are there.

Bedulu

Half a mile from Goa Gajah and left at the intersection is the Purba Kala Archaeological Museum, also known at the Gedong Arca. Built in 1960, it is a small but well-laid-out museum with lines of sarcophagi (stone coffins) in a garden setting. In the fields opposite the museum is the Buddhist Pura Kebo Edan (crazy buffalo temple), with a 10-foot statue of Dancing Bima. Another half mile up the road is the Pura Panataran Sasih temple at Pejeng, where a famous gong was found.

Candi Tebing

This is an ancient Buddhist hermitage in the Pakerisan Valley near Desa Tegal-Lingah village, which is half-way between Goa Gajah and Gianyar.

Tampaksiring

The temple of Pura Tirta Empul, situated in a valley near Tampaksiring, is built around a holy spring, the waters of which are said to have curative powers. The temple complex, which was founded in the tenth century, includes two bathing places which derive their water from the holy spring in the inner sanctuary of the temple. At special times of the year, people come to this temple to bathe in the holy water and pray for good health and prosperity. The water from the holy spring itself can only be taken by a priest. Regular ceremonies are held at this temple when the Barongs from nearby villages come to be purified with the holy water. The temple and shrines are beautifully decorated and maintained. Tampaksiring is also noted for its bone and ivory carvings.

(b) Lake Batur Area

Lake Batur is a must for visitors to Bali. The morning view from Penelokan over the lake is fantastic. In the afternoon or the wet season, the lake, volcano, and Penulisan Temple at Kintamani are often shrouded with mist. You can cross the lake by boat and stop off at a Bali Aga village or walk across the lava flow to the small hot spring that emerges on the edge of the lake.

Unfortunately, you should be watchful of the locals at Penelokan as they are pushy and rude. The village of Batur is prettier than Penelokan or Kintamani. The mountains are extremely cold at night, so make sure that you have plenty of blankets if you stay in one of the basic hotels overlooking the lake.

Getting there by bemo

The intersection to Batur and Kintamani is at the 31-kilometer post, which is 2 miles past Gianyar. Wait for a *bemo* here. This *bemo* may stop at Bangli on the way and then go straight to Penelokan or Kintamani. If coming from Ubud catch a *bemo* going to Denpasar, and alight at Sakah where you first meet the highway. From Sakah catch a *bemo* direct to kilometer 31.

From Kereneng Terminal at Denpasar catch a *bemo* or bus going to Klungkung, which takes you direct to kilometer 31, or even better, one to Bangli or Kintamani.

Temples

On the mountain is Pura Sakawan at Penulisan, which is an important pilgrimage for the Balinese. Pura Batur at Batur is still not finished.

Other temples on the way past Gianyar and their locations:

Pura Dalem	Sidan	Km 35 post
Pura Puseh	Sidan	Km 35.5 post
Pura Panetaran Gaga	Sidan	Km 36.5 post
Pura Panetaran Cempage	Bangli	Km 42 post
Pura Kehen	Bangli	Km 43 post

(c) Gianyar

Gianyar is the second largest town in Bali and a center for weaving and textiles. Opposite the open field on the main street is the old palace. Three miles from Gianyar on the road to Bangli is Pura Sidan temple, which looks back over the ricefields to the coast. Another half mile up the road in the village is Pura Puseh.

Bangli

This is another former capital past Gianyar on the way to Lake Batur and Kintamani. The road from Gianyar climbs slowly as corn and oranges replace rice and the air becomes cooler. The market street is a bit run down, but Pura Kehen temple one mile out of town is a major attraction. Follow the road to Batur to the *T*-junction and turn right. The temple is 300 yards away. Artha Sastra Inn, in the grounds of the former palace, offers basic rooms with inside and outside bathrooms. One of the buildings in the private section is intricately carved and painted. There are many outstanding houses and smaller temples between the market and Pura Kehen. There is a waterfall 300 yards to the left of the *T*-junction. Bangli is 30 miles from Denpasar.

Pura Ulu Danu temple, Central Bali

(d) Bedugul/Lake Bratan

There is an orchid market and botanical gardens at Bedugul. The Pura Ulu Danu temple was flooded by the rising level of the lake in the 1970s but has since been reclaimed. The lake is good for water-skiing and the Bali Handara golf club is nearby at Panca Sari. There are accommodations around the lake, bungalows in the forest, a hotel on the edge of the escarpment 1.5 miles towards Denpasar, and luxury villas at Bali Handara. The area is very cold at night.

7. Guided Tours and Going It Alone

Visits to all of the places discussed in the previous section can be arranged through a tour company in **Ubud** or at **Sanur, Kuta,** or **Nusa Dua** if you are staying there. In Ubud there is a travel agent next to Nomad's on the main road. Across the road is *Baligoro Tours.* Closer to the center of town, opposite the tourist information office, is *Mumbul Tours.*

Getting around town to the temples and monkey forest is best done on foot or bicycle. Out-of-town visits to **Mt. Batur, Kintamani,** and **Penelokan** can be done by public transport via the towns of **Gianyar** and **Bangli.** While close to Ubud, **Goa Gogah** is a bit far to walk or bicycle unless you leave early in the morning. Public *bemos* run from **Teges** to **Goa Gogah.** More details on getting to all these locations is given in the previous section. The easiest way is to "charter" a *bemo* for a set fee for a set number of hours (plus gas) so that you don't waste time or get lost between places. Pick up a *bemo* at the intersection opposite the main market at Ubud. You may need to pay for gas as you go, but pay your fee when you get back to your hotel or wherever you want to stop.

8. Water Sports

Lake Bratan, near the town of Bedugul, is the place to go for water sports. For **water-skiing** there are power boats and ski equipment on hand for a reasonable price. **Parasailing** is also possible. Lake Bratan has a beautiful atmosphere about it—the lake, temples, and steep cliffs fronting the lake on one side are all set in an extinct volcano. Bali may be a hot place, but this water is cold. So it wouldn't hurt to take your own short-sleeved wetsuit if you plan a visit into the mountains. Lake Bratan is a couple of hours' drive out of Denpasar to the northwest. Depending on the traffic this trip could be longer.

9. Other Sports

Also within the extinct crater of the volcano, on the other side of the town of Bedugul, is the **Bali Handara Country Club**, a must for golfers. You can visit for a game if you're staying at one of the beaches or you can experience a few days of bliss and book into the country club as part of your stay in Bali. Accommodations and greens fees are very reasonably priced. Lots more information about this 18-hole paradise, including greens fees, can be found on pages 124 and 125.

Bali Handara has been included in the Southern Beaches section so that no golfer will miss out.

Bush walkers and trekkers can go to Penelokan for walking on the outside slopes of Bali's other extinct volcano. There is a specially designated "tourist forest" off the main road just before you arrive at Penelokan coming from Denpasar. This forest extends up to the rim of the volcano. Another open forest is 1.5 miles past Kintamani on the way to Penulisan Temple. Off to the left from the main road, the forest stretches into the valley across to Mount Batukau. A third walk leads from Pura Batur temple down into the old volcano towards the lava flow. This track is not passable during the wet season.

10. Shopping

Ubud and the surrounding towns of Mas and Batuan are the centers of **printing and woodcarving** in Bali, and Ubud is the best place to shop for them. Vendors are less aggressive than at Kuta or Sanur and there is plenty of competition here with the painters and carvers themselves trying to beat the galleries to the tourist dollar (or rupiah). After you've been to Puri Lukisan Art Museum you'll be ready to appreciate what's good and bad about Balinese art. The main areas for galleries are: 1) on the main road in Ubud and Terbesaya, 2) on the road to the monkey forest, and 3) at Pengesokan artists' village, which is near Peliatan.

The better **oil and watercolor canvasses** (up to 6 feet square) sell for hundreds of dollars. **Wood carvings** may also reach such prices, but only for exceptional pieces. There are some small wood carvers on the main road at Teges as you approach Peliatan and Ubud.

There are too many *galleries* to name any and risk keeping you away from others that may have better works on display. Just remember to shop around before you buy and start with an opening price that is half of their opening one. There are no fixed prices in the art market.

The main *Ubud market* meets every second day. This is the place to buy Balinese **woven fabrics**. There is a wider range of fabrics and clothing in Ubud than at the Denpasar market and it doesn't get as hot or smelly.

Batik is not made in Bali but there is a good selection here and prices aren't much more than in Java, so if you aren't going to Jogyakarta you could do worse than buying *batik* in Ubud. The reason that there is so much *batik* in Bali is that Balinese women like it almost as much as Javanese women, so the markets cater more to them than to the foreigners.

For **photographic supplies** try *Tiro* general store on the main road or the *Kodak Shop* run by Gusti outside of the main market.

The only **bookshop** in town is the *Ubud Newsstand*, which is on the main road near the tourist information office.

11. Night Life and Entertainment

Nighttime entertainment is not one of Ubud's attractions, unless you include **traditional dance-drama** that is performed somewhere in the area every night. I have written about the types of dances on pages 69 and 70 in Chapter 4. Be sure to see at least one performance.

Here is a list of the sites for each dance performance. When you get to Ubud there will be people selling tickets on the streets the afternoon before each show.

a) *Legong Dance* at Puri Saren, Jalan Raya, Ubud
b) *Gabor Dance* at Banjar, Jalan Monkey Forest, Ubud
c) *Rajapala Dance* at Menara Hotel, Jalan Raya, Ubud
d) *Wayang Kulit* next to Oka Kartini, Jalan Sumerta, Terbesaya
e) *Legong Dance* at Mandala, Jalan Cok Gede Rai, Peliatan
f) *Legong Dance* at Banjar Kawan, Jalan Raya, Teges

The night-life scene consists of a few laid-back bar-*cum*-restaurants such as *Nomad's, Hans Snel* or the *Campuan Hotel*. Otherwise one sits around in restaurants or cafes, drinking beer or coffee and talking about your latest adventures or tomorrow's plans with the other travelers.

12. The Ubud and Central Bali Address List

Bank/money changer—Tiro shop, Jalan Raya, Ubud. Bank Indonesia, Jalan Cok Gede Rai, Peliatan.

Consulates—There are no diplomatic missions in Bali away from the southern beaches. The nearest American Consulate is at Sanur (Tel. (361) 8478). The closest Canadian Consulate is in Jakarta. Please see Chapter 10.

Doctor—Go to the Bali Beach Hotel at Sanur. For simple things there is a doctor next to the Telephone Office in Ubud.

Freight to send your paintings and carvings home—Baligoro, Jalan Raya, Ubud. Diana Express, Jalan Cok Gede Rai, Peliatan (kilometer 23). Bali Duty Express, Jalan Cok Gede Rai, Peliatan (kilometer 24).

Libraries—Dewa House, Jalan Monkey Forest, Ubud Kelod. Hotel Menara, Jalan Raya, Ubud.

Pharmacy—Apotik, Jalan Coke Gede Rai, Peliatan (opposite roundabout).

Post Office—Corner Jalan Raya/Jalan Pos, Ubud.

Postal Agent—Nomad's, Jalan Raya, Ubud.

Tourist Info—Bina Wisata, Jalan Raya, Ubud.

7

Candi Dasa and Lovina (Bali's East and North Coasts)

1. The General Picture

EAST BALI

The southeastern coast of Bali is the cradle of a civilization that blossomed after the Majapahit Kingdom fled from Java in the fourteenth century. Klungkung was the seat of the first and still premier royal family in Bali. The other royal families are said to have been members of the king's family who moved away from Klungkung to set up in their own right. In later centuries they waged war with each other.

The road from Denpasar to Klungkung passes through the town of Celuk, which specializes in silverware, and the large market town of Gianyar. The second half of the 50-mile (80 kilometers) journey is much more scenic. Padangbai, the port for ferries crossing the strait to Lombok, is a couple of kilometers off the main road. Eight miles (13 kilometers) before Karangasem, at Candi Dasa, the road meets the coast and there are plenty of accommodations. (Nusa Penida, which is visible off the coast, was once used as a penal colony by the Balinese kings, but you probably won't be staying there.)

Half a mile (1 kilometer) before the town of *Karangasem* there is a road to the left which skirts the east of Mount Agung, winding its way around the cliffs and across rivers on the slopes of the highest mountain

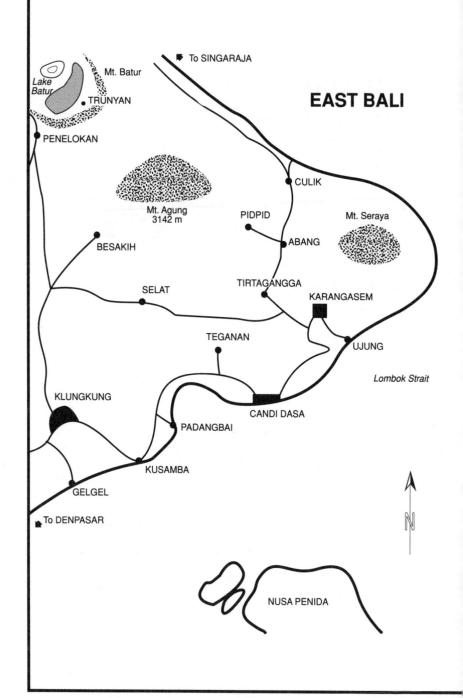

Fishing prahus at Candi Dasa

in Bali. **Tirtagangga Water Palace** is situated some 4 miles (6 kilometers) along this road. There are budget rooms next to the Water Palace, including the **Taman Dhangan Inn**, which overlooks the tranquil pools. There are a number of budget *losmen* in the town of Karangasem, but the nicest place to stay is *Candi Dasa*, where restaurants, bungalows, and *losmen* overlook a narrow sandy beach. Candi Dasa grew very quickly during the 1980s, and reminds many of Kuta in the 1960s and 70s. Fortunately its distance from entry points to Bali will help it retain its character.

There are many interesting places to visit in the area that are within easy reach of Candi Dasa, the main tourist area. A couple of these are **Teganan Village** and **Goa Lawa Temple and Bat Cave**. You can even have a go at climbing **Mount Agung** or **scuba diving** at Ballina with Bali Pro.

A new community for Westerners has recently popped up amongst the coconut palms at *Candi Dasa*, which is named after a temple overlooking the tidal lagoon and is 8 miles (13 kilometers) from Karangasem and 48 miles (67 kilometers) from Denpasar. Candi Dasa is in a very pretty setting. The main street is shaded by overhanging Kapok and coconut trees, and most of the accommodations are set amongst coconut plantations, so the whole area is cool and breezy. The view from the beach sweeps from Nusa Penida island to the inlet of Padangbai, with a lighthouse on the headland. On the landward side, there are rolling hills which are difficult to climb, but offer fantastic views once you get to the top.

West of the lagoon the beach is 15 yards wide at low tide and you can walk 50 yards out on the rock shelf with the coral gatherers. Wear shoes so as not to cut your feet. The shelf extends along the whole length of Candi Dasa beach except for a small section where the fishing boats enter. At high tide waves crash against the retaining walls. East of the lagoon the beach is rockier, but that hasn't stopped the spread of accommodation to this beach also. On the eastern headland the locals cultivate seaweed on rope suspended between stakes.

Candi Dasa is an ideal place to make your base if you want to keep away from the southern resorts. You can stay at the beach and go sightseeing without having to brave Denpasar traffic every day. However, there is very little in the way of night life—yet.

NORTH BALI

The port of *Buleleng*, situated at the mouth of the river of the same name, was for many years the center of Dutch influence in Bali. Stone warehouses on the waterfront handle cargo from as far away as

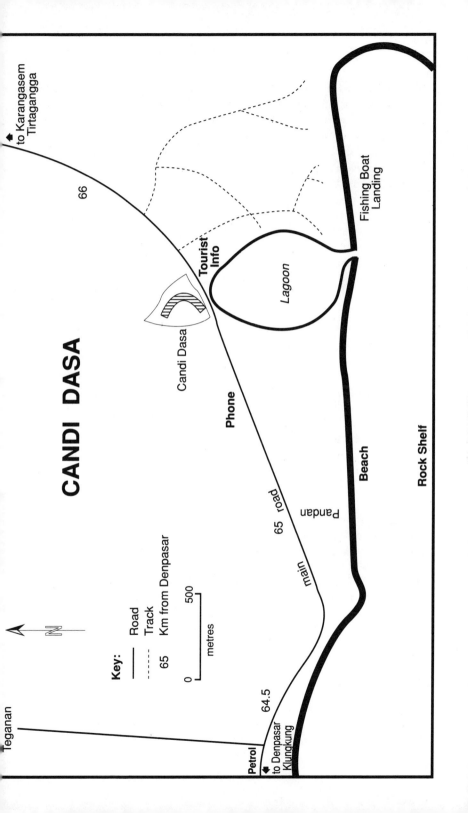

CANDI DASA

Key:
- Road
- Track
- 65 Km from Denpasar

0 [____] 500
metres

N

Teganan

to Denpasar
Klungkung

Petrol

64.5

main

65 road

Pandan

Phone

Candi Dasa

Tourist Info

Lagoon

66

to Karangasem
Tirtagangga

Fishing Boat
Landing

Beach

Rock Shelf

Singapore and Hong Kong, and interisland vessels anchor offshore. Walking along the shore one can imagine the former bustling port of entry. The present reality is that the old anchorage has long silted up, and, except for in the wet season, the river is too shallow and full of reeds and rubbish for travel.

Singaraja is a half mile (1 kilometer) away from the coast in the cooler suburbs towards Bedugul. The government offices are on the corner of Jalan Veteran and Jalan Ngurah Rai, and all road distances are measured from this point. Opposite is the Tourist Information Center. Two hundred yards away is the Gedong Kertya Historical Library, which is in the compound of the former royal palace, and the Sasana Budaya Art Center. Nearby on Jalan Gajah Mada, which leads from the Post Office towards Denpasar and Bedugul, are the royal temples, Pura Dalem and Pura Desa Bale Agung.

Lovina Beach is actually a number of beaches and villages spread out along 5 miles (8 kilometers) of coastline to the west of Singaraja. Lovina proper, which is at Kalibukbuk village, is 11 kilometers from Singaraja and offers a wide range of accommodations, restaurants, and other facilities. The other grouping of places to stay and eat is centered on *Anturan village* at the 8-kilometer post. The first place out of Singaraja, Baruna Cottages, is only 2 to 3 miles (3 to 4 kilometers) from the Banyuasri Bus Terminal and gas station.

The easiest way to get to Lovina from Singaraja or Buleleng is by *bemo* from the Banyuasri Bus Terminal. If you arrive from Kintamani or Karangasem, you have to transfer to Jalan Ahmed Yani or Banyuasri itself. Keep an eye on the kilometer posts for the distance back to Singaraja.

The original Lovina was the name of a restaurant built in 1954 when Singaraja was still the capital of Bali. After the capital was moved to Denpasar in 1960, business fell off and the restaurant was demolished. Permata Cottages now stands on the site. The few *losmen* that existed in the early 1970s were in turn flattened in the 1976 earthquake.

Anturan village is quieter than Kalibukbuk, not having hawkers selling on the beach. However, there is less variety of accommodation, bars, and cafes.

Being 62 miles (100 kilometers) from Denpasar, Lovina offers a more relaxed holiday than Kuta or Sanur. There is plenty to do there, such as snorkeling on the reef 500 yards offshore, trekking in the foothills or farther afield in the central mountains, visiting the many local temples, soaking oneself in the hot sulfur pools, or just lazing around on the gray sand beach where the sun sets behind the towering peaks of Java.

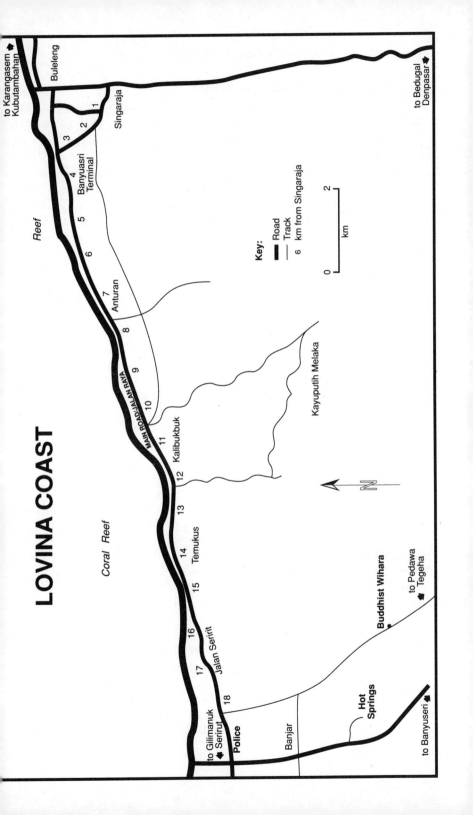

2. Long-Distance Transportation

There are no **airports** in east or north Bali, so you have to enter and leave from the airport near Kuta. To confirm your ticket be sure to phone Garuda or the airport yourself. Otherwise you mightn't get on your plane.

The port of Padangbai near Candi Dasa is the **ferry** terminal for Lombok Island. By island hopping and roughing it you can get as far as Timor and Indonesian New Guinea. Ferries leave daily but departure time varies. The northern port of Bululeng was a hub for interisland and Southeast Asian trade, but silting up of the river has reduced the flow of ships to a trickle.

Buses to the east coast leave from the Kereneng Bus Terminal in Denpasar. Ask for the bus or *bemo* going to Karangasem or Klungkung. At Klungkung you will change to another *bemo* to Karangasem. Candi Dasa is 13 kilometers before Karangasem. The bus that leaves every hour is cheaper than the *bemo*, but it takes longer as it stops to pick up rural produce on the way. However, it is certainly more interesting, especially on market day when goods and animals are piled high on the roof and in the aisles.

To get to Kereneng Terminal from Kuta or Nusa Dua, catch a *bemo* to Tegal Terminal in Denpasar. Then catch a 3-wheel suburban *bemo* to Kereneng. From Sanur there are *bemos* direct to Kereneng.

Buses to the north coast generally leave from Kereneng Bus Terminal and go via Granyar and Penelokan/Kintamani to Singaraja. Another option is to take a bus from Ubung Bus Terminal in Denpasar to Singaraja via Bedugul/Lake Bratan. The route via Bedugul is shorter and less hair-raising, as there are fewer dangerous curves on this road. Buses are bigger, with more passengers, so you may feel less vulnerable on the bus than on an 8- to 10-seater *bemo* minibus.

To go cross-country from Lovina to Candi Dasa by bus, catch a *bemo* from Lovina into Banyuasri Terminal in Singaraja and change to another *bemo* for the Bululeng Terminal, which is on the other side of town. Eighteen-seater buses leave from here at 8 to 9 A.M. each morning and irregularly later in the day. The trip that follows the eastern coastline takes 2 1/2 hours. It's one of the best drives in Bali. The blue sea and Lombok Island are out the east side. Overshadowing the west side is the awesome Mount Agung, the mother mountain of Bali which also happens to be a highly active volcano. When you arrive at Karangasem Terminal, change to any bus or *bemo* heading for Denpasar or Klungkung. Candi Dasa is 13 kilometers from Karangasem.

To go to Ubud from Lovina, first take a bus or *bemo* to Denpasar from

Banyuasri Bus Terminal in Singaraja. This bus is best if it goes via Bedugul. From Kereneng Bus Terminal in Denpasar, catch a *bemo* straight to Ubud. Some hotels in Lovina organize minibuses for guests direct to Ubud. This is certainly the easier way and is not much more expensive, as you have to change several times by public transport.

If you're going to East Java from Lovina, buses from Singaraja leave for the Gilimannk ferry terminal every day. At Banyuwangi a **train** goes to Surabaya and buses to Surabaya and Malang. Get off at Probolinggo for the famed Bromo Sunrise (see Chapter 8). From Surabaya and Malang continue on to Jogya or Jakarta.

There is an agent for bus tickets at Jalan Ahmed Yani 3, in Singaraja.

Driving an **automobile** around these parts of Bali is not for the uninitiated and can be quite tiring because you must concentrate all the time. Look at the scenery and you could hit something, or be hit *by* something. Some people hire a car and driver for a day and cover both the east and north coast in one go. If you do plan to drive yourself, I recommend you take the Bedugul road, as the other road from Kintamani to Singaraja is really hairy. Local buses and trucks cut every corner, even when there is zero visibility. The local drivers make offerings at small roadside altars so that the gods/spirits will see them over the mountain safely. Once you've seen the driving, you may do the same.

Gas stations are a very scarce commodity in Bali once you move away from the south, so fill up whenever you can. There is a Pertamina gas station about one mile before the river on the edge of Karangasem, and a petrol kiosk at the turnoff to Teganan. In the north, the main Pertamina petrol station is opposite the Banyuasri Bus Terminal, on the western side of Singaraja.

3. Local Transportation

In eastern Bali, **local buses** run between Denpasar and Karangasem (also known as Amlapura) to a set timetable of once an hour from 5A.M. until dusk. Minibuses (called *bemo*) leave when full or about 2 to 3 times an hour during busy times of the day. Minibuses usually change at Klungkung, halfway between the two towns. The minibuses stop more often and for a longer time while local villagers load and unload produce, chickens and all.

Bemo fares in 1990 were:

Candi Dasa to Karangasem	Rp250
Candi Dasa to Klungkung	Rp500
Karangasem to Tirtagangga	Rp250

| Candi Dasa to Denpasar | Rp1,200 |
| Karangasem to Singaraja | Rp1,700 |

The Friendship Shop at Candi Dasa operates an **airport shuttle service**. It's certainly a lot easier than all the changes needed to get there by public transportation, and much quicker, too.

In *northern Bali*, the large town of Singaraja is the center of the transportation network. There are **two bus and minibus terminals** in Singaraja—Banyuasri on the west side of town, and Bululeng near the old port.

If you're coming via Kintamani or Karangasem, your bus stops at Buleleng Terminal and you have to get across to Banyuasri Terminal in a tiny minibus. This costs about Rp150. You can also wait along Jalan Ahmed Yani on the way to Banyuasri, a mile from the Post Office, where the minibus (*colt*) or bus from Denpasar or Ubud via Bedugul stops at Banyuasri Terminal. At Banyuasri you can change to another *bemo* going west to Lovina or cross the street outside the terminal and catch a *bemo* coming from town. Most of the bungalows and budget *losmen* are around the 8 kilometer and 11 kilometer posts. Between kilometer 8 and 9.5 is the village of Anturan. Kalibukbuk village extends from kilometers 10.5 to 11.5, (Kilometers from Singaraja, that is.).

Bemo and bus fares in 1990 were:

Buleleng to Banyuasri	Rp150
Singaraja to Kalibukbuk	Rp300
Kalibukbuk to Banjar Market	Rp250
Banjar to Buddhist Wihara	Rp250
Kalibukbuk to Pulaki	Rp1,200
Singaraja to Git Git Waterfall	Rp600
Singaraja to Bedugal	Rp600
Singaraja to Air Sanih	Rp600
Singaraja to Denpasar via Bedugul	Rp1,750
Singaraja to Karangasem	Rp1,750

Distances between towns in north Bali in kilometers are:

Singaraja to Denpasar via Kintamani	120 km
Singaraja to Denpasar via Bedugul	78 km
Singaraja to Karangasem via coast	137 km
Singaraja to Air Sanih	18 km
Singaraja to Kubutambahan	12 km
Singaraja to Gilimanuk	85 km
Kalibukbuk to Singaraja	11 km

Kalibukbuk to Gilimanuk   74 km
Kalibukbuk to Denpasar via Bedugul   89 km

4. Hotels and Lodging

There are no expensive, first-class accommodations at Candi Dasa or Lovina. At Candi Dasa the dearest are only $50.00 per night, and at Lovina it's even less. When booking, you should check whether or not your room will have air-conditioning and hot water. Even some of these moderately priced rooms may not have them.

MODERATELY PRICED ROOMS

Right in the center of the village, facing the beach, are the **Candi Dasa Beach Bungalows (Inn) II** (Tel. (361) 35536-7). These two-story traditional-style buildings have thatched roofs and a real Balinese feel about them. Overlooking the beach is one of the best restaurants and cocktail bars in this part of Bali. Rooms with air-conditioning, a private bathroom, and either a balcony or a verandah will set you back less than $30 per night for a single room. Book through Garuda Airlines or write directly to Candi Dasa Beach Bungalows II, Candi Dasa, Karangasem, Bali, Indonesia.

Rama Ocean View Bungalows (Tel. c/o (361) 51864) and **Candi Cottages** (Tel. c/o (361) 51711-4) are positioned outside the main village. Both are quite new, with air-conditioned rooms and a swimming pool. Rama has its own restaurant and bar. Candi Cottages has a shuttle bus to get you to the village center where most of the restaurants are. Another new place to stay is **The Watergarden** (Tel. (361) 51093,35540) (Fax: (62) (361) 35540). While not directly facing the beach, the complex's gardens are beautiful, with lily ponds between the rooms. These last three hotels can be booked through Garuda Airlines or direct to each hotel, Candi Dasa, Karangasem, Bali, Indonesia.

On the Lovina coast, the two best places to stay are **Simon's Seaside Cottages** (Tel. (362) 41183) at the village of Anturan, and **Aditya Bungalows** (Tel. (362) 41059) at Kalibukbuk village. These two villages are two miles apart. Prices here for an air-conditioned room facing the quiet black-sand beach are less than $30 a night per single. Both places have restaurants, and Simon's has a laid-back bar, too. Both of these hotels can be booked through Garuda Airlines or write at Simon's Seaside Cottages, Anturan, Singaraja, Bali, Indonesia; and Aditya Bungalows, Kalibukbuk, Singaraja, Bali, Indonesia.

BUDGET-PRICED ROOMS AND BUNGALOWS

This group of cottages in the middle of Candi Dasa were built in the early 1980s, and at that time were a big jump in the level of accommodations available in the area. Before that it was strictly back-packers only. The following three are nestled between the main road and the beach, and each has a restaurant, bar, or cafe looking over the beach: **Pondok Bamboo** (Tel. (361) 35534); **Puri Pandan Beach Inn** (Tel. (361) 35534); and the **Candi Dasa Beach Bungalows (Inn) I** (Tel. (361) 35538). Single rooms are $20 to $25 a night. There are another twenty to thirty budget cottages spread out along the beach at Candi Dasa that cost from $5 to $10 a night. Some of the best are **Pandawa, Puri Pudak, Srikandi, Amarta, Ida**, and **Kelapa Mas**. Conditions in these are clean but a little primitive.

In the north, Kalibukbuk village at Lovina has more than ten budget/backpacker places to stay. The best of these are **Nirwana Seaside Cottages** (Tel. (362) 41288), **Permata Cottages**, and **Angsoka Bungalows**. At Anturan village between kilometer posts 6.5 and 9.5 are the **Baruna Beach Cottages, Banyualit Beach Inn**, and **Mandira Cottages**. All of these cost less than $20 a night. If, for some reason, you want to stay in Singaraja overnight, the best are the **Hotel Garuda** at Jalan Ahmed Yani 74, and the **Duta Karya Hotel** at Jalan Ahmed Yani 55. These two are cheap, Javanese-style hotels. Other reasonable cheapies near the beach are **Manggala Homestay** at kilometer post number 4, and at kilometer 9.4 a road leads to the **John Dive Inn** and **Kalibukbuk Beach Inn**.

5. Restaurants and Dining

The north and east coasts may lack night life, but they don't lack restaurants and cafes. You will notice a similarity in the menus, most having a mix of Western, Indonesian, and Chinese meals. Prices for a main course run from around US$5 to US$10. Outside the tourist areas of Candi Dasa and Lovina, however, you'll find few places to eat other than Balinese *warung* food stalls.

At Candi Dasa, three recommended restaurants serve good food and drinks with views over the beach of Nusa Penida Island. **Pandan**, the first true restaurant in Candi Dasa, has been open over ten years. The others are at the **Candi Dasa Beach Bungalows**, numbers I and II. **T.J.'s** at The Watergarden makes up for its lack of water views with an interesting menu and good food in a garden setting. **Amarta** and **Camplung** are two budget-priced favorites in central Candi Dasa. If you fancy a stroll before you eat, head off for the **Rama Beach Cottages**, half a mile along

Candi Dasa bungalow

the beach. **Depot Sumber** serves local Balinese dishes in the *warung* style. Eating out in other parts of eastern Bali means going local, whether at street-side *warung* stalls or the occasional Chinese restaurant in one of the towns. For cheap food in Karangasem there is **Lenny's** seafood and Chinese restaurant on Jalan Gajah Mada 30, as well as **Rumah Makan Bali**, which is in the bus terminal, strangely enough.

The Lovina coast in north Bali has restaurants and cafes strung out for three miles. Leaving Singaraja the first is the **Baruna Restaurant** at kilometer 6.5, followed by the **Harmoni** and **Perama** restaurants at kilometer 8. Also at Anturan village, but facing the beach, are **Lila Cita** and **Banyualit Seafood**. Further on at the village of Kalibukbuk near kilometer 11 are **Manggala II**, **Dayana Seafood**, and **Cafe Lovina** (on the site of the original Lovina Restaurant).

A couple of hundred yards away is the **Singa Italian**, serving pizza and spaghetti, and **Superman's** (for backpackers).

At the end of Lovina is the **Samudra Restaurant**, serving seafood and Chinese dishes. As well as these there are another twenty small, cafe-style eating places catering to backpackers and other budget travelers.

6. Sightseeing

EAST BALI

There are many interesting places to visit along Bali's eastern and northern coastlines, but you'll need to do a bit of walking to see them all.

You might start by walking around landscaped swimming pools fed by a **hot sulfur spring** at Air Sanih, or the village of **Tegenan**, where the people still follow the old *Bali Aga* ways. **Temples** are everywhere, dotting the villages and countryside and begging exploration. Guided tours are available to most of the places in east Bali, although such tours may only come from Kuta, Sanur, or Nusa Dua. You can hire a car at Candi Dasa from **Pandawa Tour** on the main street, or charter a *bemo* with a driver for the day (or half day) through your accommodations at Lovina.

The two largest towns in the vicinity of Candi Dasa are both former royal capitals that competed with each other for control of the surrounding territory of fertile rice fields and coconut plantations. **Klungkung** was where the royal families of Java settled when they fled the onslaught of Islam in the fifteenth century. The ancient **Kerta Gosa** law courts and gardens are on the main street.

The last king of Klungkung was Ida Dewa Agung Geg. He died in 1964, having married some 40 wives and fathered over 100 children. In town there is a bank, post office, pharmacy, and doctor, as well as a variety of handicraft shops. The paintings that these shops sell come

Pandan Restaurant, Candi Dasa

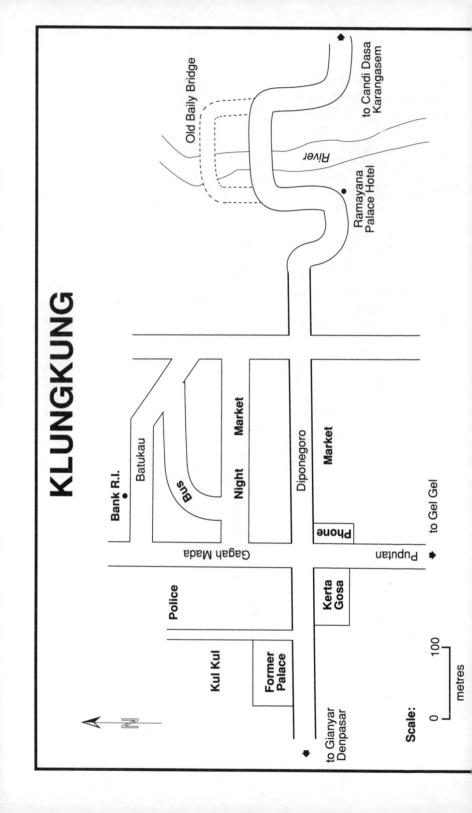

from the village of Kamasen and are based on the paintings on the ceiling of Kerta Gosa meeting hall. The only authentic antiques are wooden doors from the Singaraja area, or the traditional sashes called *songket*, which are very rare now. Klungkung is 41 kilometers from Denpasar. Candi Dasa is 24 kilometers further east. If traveling by *colt* minibus, you may have to change here.

Karangasem is the easternmost town in Bali. Before the 1968 eruption of Mt. Agung, it was known as Amlapura. That was before the western side of the town was destroyed by a river of lava. The Royal Palace still stands and is open to tourists.

Karangasem district is famous for its two water palaces at Tirtagangga and Ujung. These water palaces are a series of some six olympic-size pools that are fed by spring water from the nearby volcano Mt. Agung. Most of the buildings and statues have been destroyed by volcanic activity, and the pools have cracked walls, but some of the pools have been restored, especially at Tirtagangga. Built by the local royal family of Karangasem, they are called palaces and are considered to be holy connections with the mother mountain of Bali, Mt. Agung.

The **Ujung Water Palace** is four kilometers from town past the bus terminal. The area is well known for its fresh fruit. On the way to Karangasem from Candi Dasa, the road traverses a rift valley near the village of **Bug Bug**. The scenery is spectacular.

If you are looking to avoid the noise and dust of the market towns and prefer quieter spots, try the tranquil **Tirtagangga Water Palace**. Earthquakes have caused repeated damage at Tirtagangga, which is situated on the slopes of Mt. Agung. Fortunately the local people and government are engaged in a continual restoration program. Stay at Taman Ayu and eat at the **Dhangan Taman Inn** which overlooks the pools. The water in the pools is so clear, fresh, and cool that you can easily spend half the day basking in the sun and cultivating a tan. To get there, take the turnoff just before the Karangasem bridge towards Singaraja.

High up on the slopes of Mt. Agung are the small settlements of **Putung and Selat**. If you're driving, turn off at Subangan at kilometer 78 and get ready for a rough road and spectacular views.

Close by Candi Dasa is the village of **Teganan**. This village of the *Bali Aga* people provides one with an insight into Balinese life before the fifteenth century. Teganan is at the end of a narrow valley less than one hour's easy walk from Candi Dasa. The villagers live in brick and mortar houses in the form of longhouses, set in three rows. **Gerinsing** weaving is a famous handicraft from here.

Between Candi Dasa and Klungkung are the ports of **Padangbai** and **Kusamba**. These are ferry terminals to the islands off East Bali. From

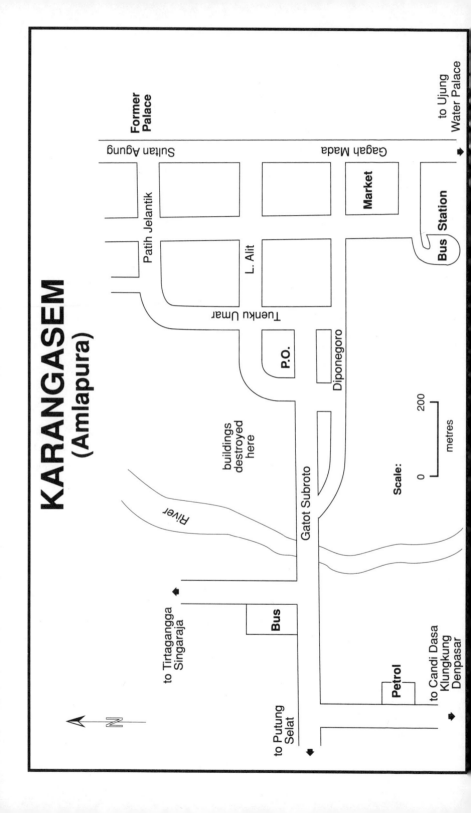

Padangbai Beach

Padangbai ferries cross to Lombok, where you can connect to Irian Jaya. There is a beautiful beach next to the ferry terminal, and a few cheap but dirty *losmen*. The best place to stay is the **Padangbai Beach Inn**. Kusamba is a much smaller port where the ferry crosses to Nusa Penida, just 100 yards off the main road.

There are two major **temples** on the main road between Candi Dasa and Klungkung. **Goa Lawah** bat cave and temple is at the Desa Pesinggahan village, 30 miles (50 kilometers) from Denpasar. **Pura Sekidu** is 62.7 kilometers from Denpasar.

NORTH BALI

I have divided the northern coastline into two sections: east of the town of Singaraja and west of Lovina Beach.

To the East of Singaraja

North Bali between Singaraja and Air Sanih is more similar in looks to Java than Bali. The town of Kubutambahan, 11 kilometers east of Singaraja, was once the center of a great kingdom. A number of large temples are reminders of its former glory.

Pura Maduwe Karang at Kubutambahan is the biggest temple in north Bali. Nearby on the corner of the Kintamani road is **Pura Bale Agung** and 200 meters away is **Pura Dalem**.

Pura Beji at Sangsit is 7 kilometers from Singaraja. It is dedicated to the rice crop.

Pura Jagaraja is on the road into the hills from Sangsit. At Sawan is a village of gong-smiths.

Pura Desa at Tamblang is 5 kilometers from Kubutambahan.

Pura Ponjok Batu is a smaller temple 10 kilometers from Kubutambahan on a cliff over the sea where the Karangasem road leaves the coast.

As well as temples, the **Air Sanih** area offers beautiful coastal views near the Air Sanih swimming pools. The pools are fed by fresh spring water. There are bungalows and a restaurant in the complex. For 3 kilometers past Air Sanih the road overhangs the cliff, passing sandy coves that shelter fishing boats. The resort is 15 kilometers from Singaraja.

The **Git Git Waterfall** is 9.5 kilometers from Singaraja on the road to Bedugal. You'll have to walk 1 kilometer through the ricefields.

South into the mountains, there is an orchid market and botanical gardens at **Bedugul**. The **Pura Ulu Danu** temple was flooded by the rising level of **Lake Bratan** in the 1970s but has since been reclaimed. The lake is good for waterskiing and the **Bali Handara** Golf Club is

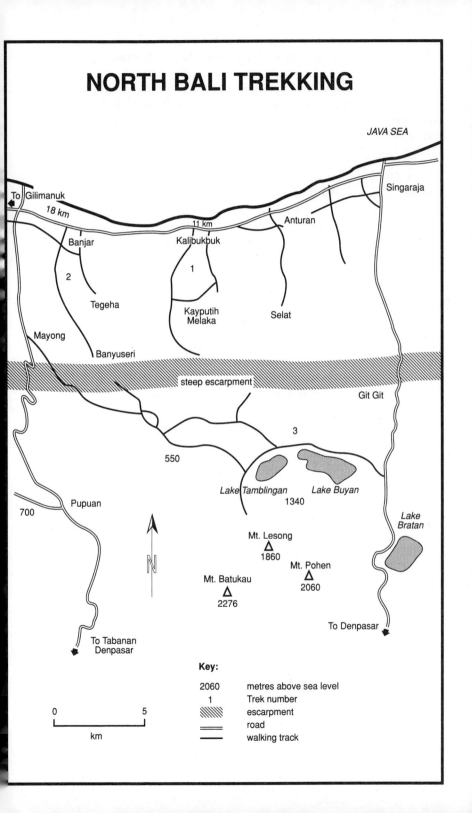

nearby at Panca Sari. There are budget accommodations around the lake, bungalows in the forest, a hotel on the edge of the escarpment 2 kilometers towards Denpasar, and luxury villas at the Bali Handara. The area is very cold at night.

To the West of Lovina

In 1985 the **Banjar Hot Springs** were redeveloped to include a swimming pool and showers, a restaurant, and a bar. The source of the hot water for the pool is behind the restaurant. Another smaller hot spring is one hundred yards upstream from the main pool. Here, amongst the foliage, the rock has been cut away to form a small bath with the hot water gushing from a spout overhead. Alternate between a quick dip in the river and a long soak in the pool. The best time to visit the hot springs is in the cool of the afternoon or early evening.

How to Get There:

—Near the 18 kilometer post turn towards the hills
—One mile towards the hills is the Banjar morning market
—50 yards on the left past the market is a sign to the hot springs
—Walk up this road, passing the temple on your right
—300 yards past this temple are the hot springs
—Catch a *bemo* from your hotel to the intersection
—Catch a *dokar* or *ojak* from the intersection to the market
    (*dokar* = horse and cart; *ojak* = lift on motor bike)

The hillside **Buddhist Wihara monastery** is reached by turning left at the intersection in the middle of the Banjar market. Then follow the road upwards and to the right for two miles.

At the 14.5 kilometer mark, you can follow a dirt road about 500 yards to the **Sing-Sing weir**. The weir itself, a six-foot concrete barrier across the river, is not much, but follow the stream a few hundred yards farther and turn left into the fields to the waterfall. This is the real attraction. Swimming in the weir is not advisable due to dirty water. The waterfall has cleaner water, but the rocks are slippery.

Desa Kali-Anget is a typical North Balinese village 1 kilometer to the west of the Banjar market. The name means "hot river." The village temple is a good place to witness Balinese culture. The elders of the temple are friendly.

Situated 3 miles (5 kilometers) towards Gilimanuk from Lovina, **Desa Labuan-Haji** is typical of the towns in north Bali which have been populated by Javanese migrants. It's quite dusty and sterile, but an interesting comparison if you don't plan to cross the strait to Java.

SINGARAJA

JAVA SEA

Surapati

Buleleng Bus

To Kintamani
Karangasem
Kubutambahan

Diponegoro

P.O.

Gagah Mada

Buleleng River

Ahmed Yani

Dewi Sartika

Kartini

Banyuasri Bus

Seririt

To Lovina
Gilimanuk

Sudirman

Banyumala River

Ngurah Rai

Pahlawan

Veteran

Tourist Info

Denpasar

N

0   250
metres

A traditional harbor for luggers trading with Kalimantan is **Celukan-bawang**. It is 12 miles (20 kilometers) west of Kalibukbuk.

A monkey forest surrounds the old **Pulaki temple** 28 miles (45 kilometers) to the west of Lovina on the way to Gilimanuk. The temple is one mile off the main road on a cliff above the beach. Tours are organized from Lovina to attend ceremonies.

Possibly the best place for scuba diving and snorkeling in Bali, **Pulau Menjangan** is part of the Teluk Terima National Aquatic Park. A permit from the ranger is needed to enter. Boats to Manjangan Island leave from Teluk Terima Harbour. Very basic accommodations are available 3 miles from the main road opposite the island. Take your own diving gear with you. Situated 30 miles (50 kilometers) west of Kalibukbuk or 12 miles (20 kilometers) before Gilimanuk.

In Singaraja town you can visit the **Gedong Tirta Historical Library** and the **Sasana Budaya Art Center**, both on Jalan Veteran. On the road towards Bedugul is the **Bratan** gold and silver craft village. The mouth of the Buleleng River and the old colonial warehouses are on Jalan Surapati. The main **Hindu temples** around town are **Pura Dalem** and **Pura Desa Bale Agung** on Jalan Gajah Mada and **Pura Segera** on Jalan Surapati near the old harbour.

7. Guided Tours and Going It Alone

Getting to some of the places listed in the previous section may not be easy without your own transportation. There are tours into the area but they often originate from Kuta or Sanur, so the best way is to rent a car, with or without a driver, or "charter" a *bemo*. The other alternative is to catch local buses and do a lot of walking. For the more adventurous at heart, two treks are included in section 9—one to the peak of Mt. Agung and the other through the villages and lakes of northern Bali's highlands.

Local tour operators are **Pandawa Tour** on Jalan Raya in Candi Dasa and the travel office at **Aditya Bungalows** on the Lovina stretch at kilometer post 12.1.

8. Water Sports

There's plenty of beautiful coral in the sea, but unfortunately little is organized locally to take advantage of it. Most of the **diving** places listed in section 8 of Chapter 5 are in this part of Bali, so we won't cover that again. If you don't carry your own snorkel and goggles, you'll be able to rent some at Candi Dasa or Lovina. Then set a price with one of the local sailboat owners and head off for a beautiful day's swimming. Most hotels and bungalows in this part of the island *don't have swimming pools*. You should also note that the beach at Candi Dasa disappears at high tide, so when you see the sand, head for it.

9. Other Sports

At this stage there are no organized spectator or participator sports in this part of Bali. What this area does have to offer is wild terrain for adventurers. Near Candi Dasa you can **climb Mt. Agung**, a very active volcano.

One proven climbing route is via the village of Selat. Be sure to take a jacket, flashlight, and enough food and water to last two days, as none will be available after Selat. Inform the police at Selat of your plans and see them again upon descent. Your route from Selat takes you 5 kilometers along a rocky road of lava to Sebudi and on to Sangkawasa. Stay the night with the priest of Pasar Agung temple, and pay for offerings for a safe journey before you go. Leave *early* the next morning (2 to 3A.M.— the earlier the start the better, to get home before evening) for an easy hour's walk through a pine forest and another hour to a small glacial valley of stones with a permanent spring. At 6,000 feet the trees thin out. At about 8A.M. you should reach the 3,142-meter peak (nearly 10,000 feet) and the crater full of sand and sulfur. The descent to Sangkawasa takes six hours. Don't forget to report to the police at Selat.

Each of the following **treks** take you into the high country behind Lovina, where you have fantastic views over the coast. They are all in loop form. If you get tired or dusk falls, head back the way you came rather than continuing on. Take food and water for emergencies.

1.) **Kayu Putih Malaka (2-3 hours)** Take the asphalt road opposite the Ayodya Hotel at kilometer post 10.5 into the hills. At Desa Kayu Putih, follow the road to the right/west until you meet another road heading downhill back to the coast.

2.) **Banyuseri & Pendawa (8-10 hours)** Follow the main road through Banjar market into the hills. It's quite a steep climb to the Banyuseri village at the 5 kilometer post. Stop for refreshments at a small *warung* at the 4 kilometer peg before the final climb to the plateau. Continuing through the ricefields, the road climbs towards your left and is passable only to hikers and off-road vehicles for the next 3 miles (5 kilometers). The road skirts the ridge and emerges at the village of Banjar Tegeha. Public transportation back to Banjar exists in the form of an *ojak* (lift on motor bike). A fee of Rp600 should get you back to the Banjar market. If there is a local truck going down, hitch a ride! Stop off at the Buddhist Wihara on the way down.

Should you wish to do the 14-mile (22 kilometers) trek in the opposite direction, turn left at the crossroad at the Banjar market. The road climbs steeply for about 1.5 miles (3 kilometers) to the Buddhist Wihara, and then climbs 4 miles (7 kilometers) to Desa Pedawa, where the asphalt road ends. Turn right at the *T*-junction in Desa Pedawa, then take the right fork past the public bathing place and follow the track 3 miles (5 kilometers) to Desa Banyuseri on the plateau. From here descend to Banjar.

Whichever way you go, call in for a soothing soak in the hot springs on the way back.

3.) **Lake Tamblingan (2-3 days)** This is a much longer trek that goes in a similar but longer arc. Start at the town of Pengastulan, 7.5 miles (12 kilometers) west of Kalibukbuk. Take the road heading south to Pupuan, Antosari, and Denpasar. Stop at Mayong, approximately 6 miles (10 kilometers) into the mountains, and head east towards Kayuputih, Mudak, or Goblek. From Kayuputih it is possible to get back to Banjar/Lovina. After Mundak the road is not passable in the rainy season. Check to see whether it is raining in the mountains (or Ubud) before you leave, because it rarely rains at Lovina. The track skirts the old crater rim, with views over Lake Tamblingam and Lake Buyan. The track meets the Denpasar-Singaraja road 6 miles (10 kilometers) north of Bedugul and Lake Bratan, 12 miles (20 kilometers) from Singaraja.

10. Shopping

Teganan village is the largest of the few remaining villages of the *Bali Aga* people, and is the main producer of their traditional arts and crafts. **Gerinsing** woven cloth is unique to this area. You can buy it at the shop at Teganan and at the gerinsing shop at Candi Dasa. **Paintings** (usually watercolor) that are based on the stories on the ceiling of the Kerta Gosa courthouse in Klungkung can be bought in the *antique shops* that line Klungkung's main street. "Antiques" here may be new or old, but they are still made by Balinese craftsmen. Carved **doorways** are brought down from the Singaraja region and sold in Klungkung. This would have to be one of the best-looking commercial streets in Bali. I remember when it was all under construction in the late 1970s and tradesmen were carving traditional bas reliefs into the building frontages.

At Candi Dasa itself, there are a few **general stores** that sell toiletries, drinks, and t-shirts. These are *Eddy Shop*, *Friendship Shop*, and *Sanjaya General Store*. Kepala Mas has a small clothing boutique.

In the north there are not many established places for tourists to shop. Much business is done on the beach, where the ladies will display their selection of **batik**, t-shirts, shorts, tablecloths, and woven Balinese fabrics. These roving sellers usually come from the highland villages around Penelokan and travel around to the different tourist areas, such as Kuta, Ubud, and Lovina. Singaraja town has three **large markets**; *Anyer market* on Jalan Diponegoro, *Banyuasri market* on Jalan Ahmed Yani, and *Buleleng market* on Jalan Gajah Mada. The largest shopping complex is also on Jalan Diponegoro. Outside town on the way to Bedegul is the **Bratan Gold and Silver Village**, where locals produce and sell jewelry.

11. Night Life and Entertainment

As with Ubud and other country areas, the east and north coasts don't have much to offer in the way of Western-style night life. They have much less than Ubud, in fact—zero. The liveliest you'll find is a restaurant that serves cocktails. Even a performance of the traditional arts is hard to come by, so at Candi Dasa and Lovina it's a case of early to bed and early to rise, and get out into a relatively non-tourist oriented part of Bali.

Candi Dasa does occasionally have **dance and drama performances** at night at Pandan Harum, Amarta Homestay, and at the Arts Center next to the lagoon. All of these are on Candi Dasa's main street. Restaurants and cafes that overlook the beach at Candi Dasa, such as in the *Candi Dasa Beach Bungalows*, and the *Pandan Restaurant*, stay open till late, generally closing by 2 A.M., depending on when the last patron leaves. So does *T.J.'s*.

On the north coast, Singaraja and Buleleng are dead after dark. The beach is so spread out, it is hard to find more than a couple of restaurants together, which makes it quiet at night. *Kalibukbuk Village*, at kilometer 11, is a very mild exception. The restaurant at *Aditya Bungalows* stays open till late and there are a couple of Kuta-style open-air bars along the road beside the lagoon. Follow this road to the beach and turn right and you'll find the *Nirwana Cottages Restaurant* that stays open till late.

12. The East and North Coast Address List

Note: For this part of Bali, one may be better off contacting services in Chapter 5 or your local hotel manager. Local bookings and medical services may not be reliable or thorough, and English is spoken less in this region than in others.

CANDI DASA

Banks—Bank Rakyat Indonesia, Jalan Kesatian, Karangasem. Bank Rakyat Indonesia, Jalan Batukaru 7, Klungkung (Tel. (361) 21042).

Bookshop/Library—*Kelapa Mas* on Jalan Raya.

Consulates—the nearest American consulates are at Sanur (Tel. (361) 8478), Surabaya, or Jakarta. The nearest Canadian Consulate is at Jakarta.

Doctor—Dr. Seoronya Pamudji on Jalan Raya, next to the telephone office, or at Sanur.

Garuda Airlines—outside Pandawa restaurant on Jalan Raya. Also see Chapter 5, section 12.

Gasoline—at turnoff to Teganan village.

Money changers—Tri Ayu Graha on Jalan Raya near telephone office.

Postal service—*Sanjaya* store on Jalan Raya.

Post Office—in Karangasem town on the main road as you head into town after crossing the bridge.

Telephone office—on the main road, Jalan Raya.

Travel agent—*Friendship* shop on Jalan Raya.

NORTH BALI

American Consulate—the nearest consulate is at Sanur Beach (Tel. (361) 8478)

Banks—Bank Dagang Negara, Jalan Ahmed Yani 66, Singaraja. Bank Dagang Negara, Jalan Surapati, Singaraja. Bank Bumi Daya, Jalan Surapati, Singaraja. Bank B.N.I. 1946, Jalan Erlangga 14, Singaraja. Bank Dagang Negara, Jalan A. Yani 60, Singaraja. Bank Rakyat Indonesia, Jalan Ngurah Rai 14, Singaraja.

Doctor—there are a few doctors on the main road leading into Singaraja from Lovina, Jalan Ahmed Yani 75-95, or try at Sanur.

Garuda Airlines—Jalan Ahmed Yani, Singaraja. Also see Chapter 5, section 12.

Health clinic—Jalan Ahmed Yani, Singaraja.

Hospital—Jalan Ngurah Rai, Singaraja.

Money changer—Fernando, Jalan Seririt, Lovina (kilometer post 11.5). Harta, Jalan Seririt, Lovina (kilometer post 10).

Nitour Travel—Jalan Ahmed Yani 57, Singaraja.

Post Office—Jalan Diponegoro, Singaraja.

Postal agent—Aditya Bungalows, Lovina (kilometer post 12.1) (Tel. (362) 41059).

Postal agent—Permata Bungalows, Lovina (kilometer post 11.2).

Telephone Office—Jalan Ngurah Rai, Singaraja.

Telephone—Aditya Bungalows, Lovina (kilometer post 12.1) (Tel. (362) 41059).

Tourist information—Jalan Veteran, Singaraja.

Tourist information—Aditya Bungalows, Lovina (kilometer post 12.1) (Tel. (362) 41059).

8

East Java

1. The General Picture

Coming from Bali, the first province in Java is East Java, which is followed by Central and then West, so I have divided Java in thirds also, following the provincial boundaries. In East Java, the most interesting places are the highland city of *Malang*, *Mount Bromo*, and also the capital, *Surabaya*. East Java is the least developed province in Java, though it is rich in human and natural resources.

This has not always been the case. The last Hindu-Buddhist kingdom of Indonesia, and probably the greatest, was based here, leaving behind temples and artifacts around Malang and Trowulan village. In the early 1400s, the kingdom en masse moved to Bali to escape the spread of the Moslem religion, Islam.

Malang, with a cool climate and friendly people, is a convenient staging point for climbing Mount Bromo or Mount Sumeru. Bromo is 100 kilometers away to the northeast, and Sumeru can be seen from town in the dry season. Twenty kilometers away near the south coast is the Karangkates Dam on the Brantas River.

Another 30 kilometers past Karangkates, near the island called Pulau Sempu, is a beautiful and as yet undeveloped area with safe swimming and a natural **rainforest** with walking trails. There is no public transportation to the area and off-road vehicles are necessary. The Forestry

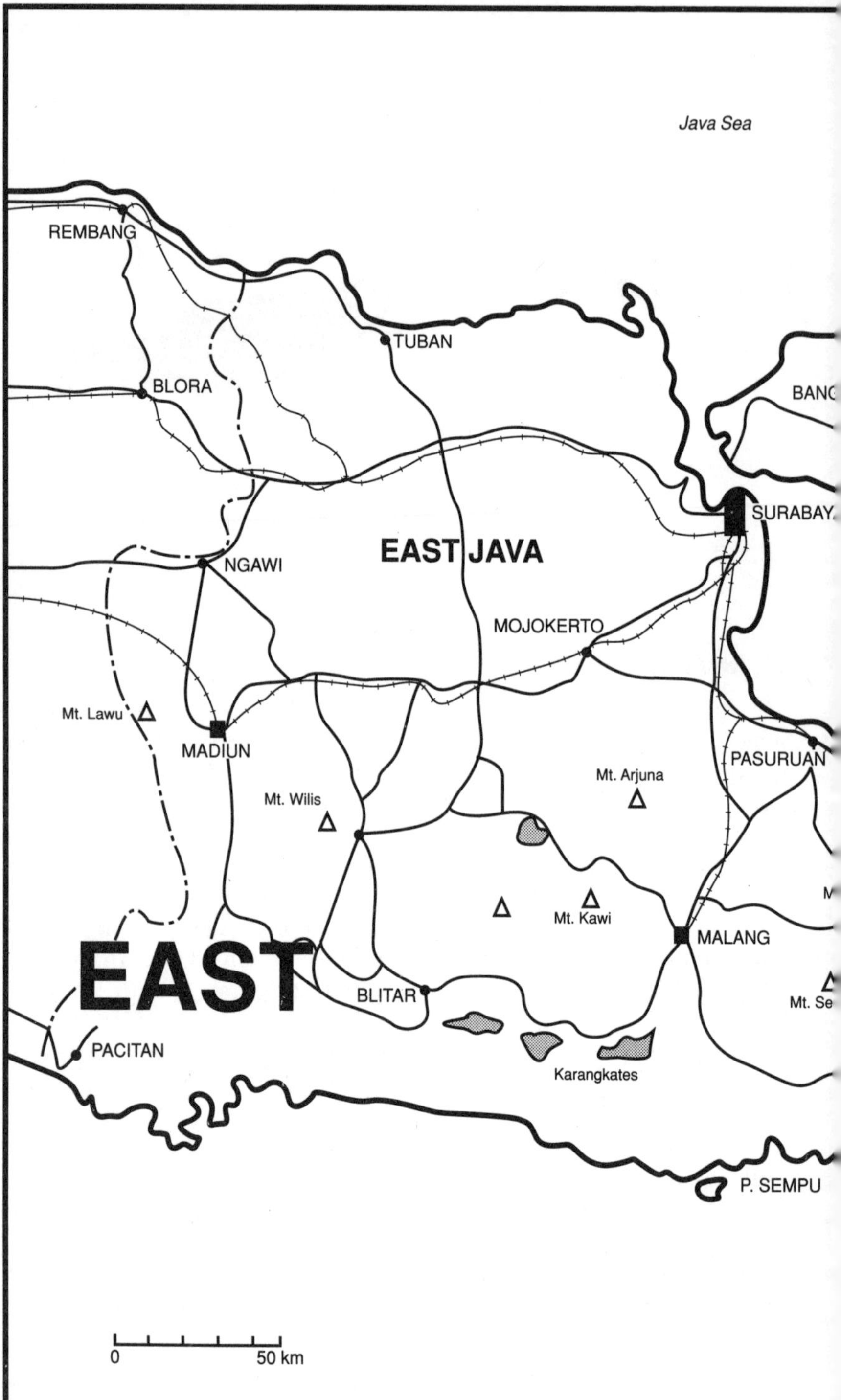

Java Sea
REMBANG
TUBAN
BLORA
BANG
SURABAY
EAST JAVA
NGAWI
MOJOKERTO
Mt. Lawu
MADIUN
PASURUAN
Mt. Arjuna
Mt. Wilis
Mt. Kawi
MALANG
EAST
BLITAR
Mt. Se
PACITAN
Karangkates
P. SEMPU
0
50 km

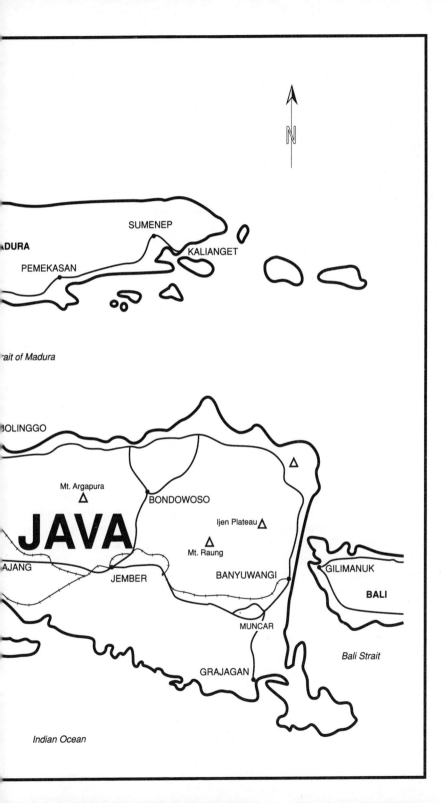

Department is still undecided whether to log the rainforest or not. Being one of the last areas of natural primary rainforest in Java, the long-term tourism potential is there to be developed. Hopefully the rainforest will remain. The nearest town to the area is Turen on the Karangkates-Lumajang road.

The mountain resort of **Selecta** is a pleasant day's outing. Stop off at the Candi Singosari temple on the way. Southwest of Malang, near the town of Blitar, is an extensive temple complex, Candi Panataran. On the road to the temple from Blitar is the mausoleum of the first president of Indonesia, Ir. Sukarno, who was born at Blitar. Indonesians from all walks of life come to pay homage to the man who did so much for the emerging Indonesian nation.

Mt. Bromo must be one of the most famous sunrises in the world. Often over a hundred people line the rim of Bromo's crater to watch the mist and sand-sea (the sand plain in the volcano's mouth) change colors as shafts of light reach into the valley. It is a spectacular and unique experience.

Leaving the hotel on the outside rim at 4 A.M., the dawn worshipers descend on horseback onto the icy sand-sea. Two kilometers away, some 200 steps lead up to Bromo itself, which pumps white sulfur smoke into the air. Most visitors are breathing or puffing strongly, as the top of the stairs up Bromo is 7,000 feet (2,300 meters) above sea level.

Surabaya, once the major port of colonial Indonesia, was left behind Jakarta in the growth of the 1970s and 1980s. There is still a big port, and plenty of industry, but the city has little to offer in the arts. However, the port is still the starting point for ship journeys to the outer islands. If you are planning to visit Sulawesi, Kalimantan, or any of the islands between Java and New Guinea, check at the Pelni Shipping Company office for scheduled departures. There are many other ships plying these routes and it is possible to arrange a berth or deck space on these at Tanjung Perak harbor. The staff of the Government Tourist Office at Jalan Pemuda 118 are very helpful and will be glad to show you how to occupy your time should you be waiting for a boat.

Check the program at *The People's Amusement Park*. There may be an interesting evening performance, such as traditional dance or a local rock group. While the most picturesque route to Java from Bali is via Malang, if a daytime stopover in Surabaya is necessary, be sure to visit the best *zoo* in Indonesia. Situated opposite the Joyoboyo bus station at the southern end of town, the zoo has a seemingly endless array of birds, an island community of monkeys and other apes, an old Komodo dragon, and an even older-looking Garuda eagle.

Surabaya is also known as the "City of Heroes," from the early days of independence when the British army tried to reintroduce colonial rule on behalf of the Dutch, following the Japanese surrender in 1945. Technically, the British army went there to disarm and repatriate the remnants of the Japanese occupation forces, but this had already been done by the Indonesian army. Then the Indonesians tried to resist the incoming British forces, and what amounted to war broke out. Indonesian resistance in the city was fierce but short-lived, and the defenders left the city to carry out guerrilla warfare in the countryside. Heroes' Day is commemorated on November tenth each year.

2. Long-Distance Transportation

East Java is well connected to Bali and the rest of Java by regular plane, train, and bus services. There are also taxi/rental cars that come with a driver for trips to Semarang and Jakarta. If you were thinking of driving around Java yourself, you will need to go to Jakarta to pick up your car. Getting to Mt. Bromo is included in this section.

If you're planning on **flying**, Garuda, Merpati, and Bouraq Airlines fly between Surabaya's Juanda Airport and Bali, the major cities of Java, such as Jakarta, Semarang, Jogya, and Bandung, and other islands of Indonesia. As usual, *Garuda* (Tel. (031) 44082, 40460) is my recommended airline. The Surabaya ticketing office is at Jalan Tunjungan 29. Garuda flies to Denpasar three times each day, at 7 A.M., 2 P.M.., and 5 P.M., and has other afternoon flights at varying times.

There are nine flights each day to Jakarta, starting at 6 A.M. and finishing at 9 P.M. To Semarang there are two flights a day—at 11:45 A.M. and 5:20 P.M. There are four connections a day for Singapore via Jakarta, from 6 A.M. to 2 P.M. To Jogya there is one afternoon flight a day at 4 P.M., and to Bandung one daily flight at 9 A.M. One-way, full-adult fares from Surabaya are US$88 to Jakarta, $44 to Denpasar, and $30 to Jogyakarta. Flying time to Denpasar or Jogya is 15 minutes, and to Jakarta half an hour. The flights are on Fokker F28 jets.

Merpati Nusantara Airlines (Tel. (31) 45870, 40648) has three flights a day to Jakarta, two a day to Bali, and one a day to Jogya.

Bouraq Indonesia Airlines (Tel. (31) 42383, 470621) flies to Denpasar and Jakarta daily. For both airlines the fare to Jakarta is $65, to Jogya $55, and to Bali $30 (all one-way). Merpati and Bouraq both fly only prop-driven aircraft, though this may change in the early 1990s.

Surabaya is the main **train** terminus in East Java, and is home to the *Bima Express* and *Mutiara Express*. These are the overnight express trains that run between Surabaya and Jakarta. The *Bima Express* heads southwards via Madiun, Solo, Jogya, Banjar, Tasikmalaya, and Bandung. It departs from Surabaya's main station, Gubeng (which is at the end of Jalan Pemuda), at 4 p.m. each day. The one-way fare with a sleeper (*klas utama*) to Jakarta is $20. The *Mutiara Utara Express* follows the north coast (*utara* means "north") via Semarang, Pekelongan, and Cirebon. This train is not to be confused with the *Mutiara Selatan* (*selatan* means "south") which goes via Jogya to Bandung, as sleepers are not available on the *Mutiara Selatan*.

The *Mutiara Express* (Utara) also leaves at 4 p.m. each day but from the Pasar Turi Railway Station, which is on Jalan Semarang. The fare to Jakarta is the same as on the *Bima*: $20 (*klas utama*). The *Mutiara Selatan* to Bandung costs $12 each way and leaves from Gubeng Station at 5:40 p.m. each day. In the first-class section (*klas utama*) you should have assigned seating, unlike economy class, which is overcrowded and has with open seating. Avoid the *Purbaya* morning train to Purwokerto via Jogya and Solo, as it is economy only, and a very hot day train. To Semarang there is the *Cepat Siang* (literally "daytime express"), which leaves from Pasar Turi Station each day at 1:30 p.m. The fare is $3 one way.

Heading eastwards to Bali and Mt. Bromo, there is the economy-class *Mutiara Timur* (literally "east"), which leaves at 9:40 a.m. and 10 p.m. from Gubeng station. The evening train connects with a bus to Denpasar after you have crossed the Bali Strait by ferry.

To Mt. Bromo, you can travel second class on the morning train, *Mutiara Timur Siang*, as far as Probolinggo, which is the staging point for the drive into the mountains. There is a train from Surabaya to Malang and Blitar but these are economy only, and I recommend against them. It's better to take the bus to Malang.

The following few paragraphs refer to overnight express buses for long-distance travel. Day buses are not recommended for more than 50 to 100 miles in Java. They are extremely hot and slow, due to continual stopping. *Colt* minibuses are no better.

Surabaya's intercity bus terminal is Joyoboyo Terminal on Jalan Wonokromo, to the south of the city center. Coming from Bali, you may need to connect to another bus to continue your trip to Jogya or Jakarta.

Overnight express buses (said "*bis malam cepat*") leave each afternoon or early evening for destinations in Java and Bali. You can buy your ticket from the kiosks manned by each company at Joyoboyo Terminal. Before holidays however, this can be a problem because Indonesians tend not to line up; they prefer to all push at once to get to the ticket window. In that case you would be better off going to one of the travel agents suggested in section seven.

Bus companies that run to *Denpasar* are Bali Indah (Tel. (31) 470846) at Jalan Ahmed Jais 102; Cakrawala (Tel. (31)43067) at Jalan Kacapiring

14; and Gitabali (Tel. (31) 471984) at the Hotel Bali on Jalan Makam Peneleh. There are several other bus companies on Jalan Makam Peneleh that run to *Denpasar* or *Singaraja* (in North Bali). To *Jogyakarta* there is Adam Express (Tel. (31) 472393) at Jalan Basuki Rakhmat 64 and Jawa Indah (Tel. (31) 44765) at Jalan Gembong Asih II. Jawa Indah also operates to *Jakarta*, as does Continental (Tel. (31) 40618) at Jalan Arjuna 22, and Mawar Express (Tel. (31) 45698) at Jalan Mawar 26.

Malang is a relatively small town, so it is easy to get to each bus company's ticket office and buy your ticket direct. **Overnight express buses** from Malang go as far as *Denpasar, Jogya,* and *Semarang,* where you connect to *Jakarta.* The fare to *Bali* or *Jogya* is pretty much the same, at $4 (Rp8,000) for non-air-conditioned, older buses, or $6 (Rp12,000) in more modern and air-conditioned coaches. The better bus companies in Malang are Malang Indah at Jalan Aries Munander 62, which operates to *Bali, Jogya* and *Magelang*; Pemudi Express at Jalan Basuki Rakhmat I, which operates to *Bali, Jogya* and *Semarang*; Anugerah/Agung at Jalan I.A. Suryani 16, which also goes to *Bali, Jogya* and *Semarang*; and Bali Indah at Jalan Basuki Rakhmat II, which only runs to *Bali.*

Surabaya is an important port for Pelni, the government-owned **passenger ship** line. Most of the boats have roll on/roll off facilities for cars, trucks, and buses. Sleeping is in cabins or on deck, something like in the Mediterranean. The best place to get up-to-date information on Pelni shipping schedules is at their harbor office on Jalan Tanjung Perak. You could also hear about cabins available on cargo ships, which are preferable because they aren't so overcrowded. The same goes for unscheduled Pelni sailings. For scheduled passenger services operated by Pelni, you can also book tickets at the travel agents named in section seven.

The quick and easy way to get to *Mt. Bromo* is by **plane** to *Surabaya,* then **taxi** to the Bromo Permai I Hotel at *Ngadisari* in the mountains. Check into the hotel, with another room for the driver, and return to Surabaya in the morning. It's a four-hour drive each way.

You could book into a hotel in Surabaya if you don't want to spend two days on the go. It is possible to pre-book this side-trip through Garuda Airlines, or make your own arrangements as you go. From Bali, this round trip actually takes only twenty-four hours, leaving and arriving back at 3 P.M. The cost is around $120 per person if two or three people share the taxi. When you land at *Surabaya* airport, you can get a taxi to Bromo through the Mirama Hotel, which has an office in the airport restaurant. The airport taxi will be much more expensive and the driver may not want to stay overnight. At Bromo, you will be unlikely to find a vacant taxi to bring you back to Surabaya.

Coming from Bali on an **overnight bus**, you will arrive at *Probolinggo* at around midnight. From *Jogya* you will arrive around 10 P.M. Buses from *Surabaya* run all through the day, part of the way along a toll road. Get off your bus at the Hotel Bromo Permai II, which is on the main street (Jalan Sudirman) next to the railway line (opposite the bus terminal), or at the Victoria Hotel, one-half mile (1 kilometer) along Jalan Sudirman towards Surabaya. From these hotels there is transportation to *Bromo* during the day and in the evenings until 2 A.M.

To *Ngadisari* village it takes around 1.5 hours by *colt* minibus, and then it's another minibus for one and a half miles (2 kilometers) to the Bromo Permai I Hotel, which is situated on the outside rim overlooking the black sand-sea and Bromo itself. There are budget-priced *losmen* guest houses in Ngadisari village.

When sunrise is over, it is time to head back down the mountain. There is a constant stream of minibuses going to *Probolinggo* in the early morning, so you can arrive at Probolinggo town between 9 and 10 A.M. The next leg of your trip will be quite tiring if traveling by bus, as it is at least 7 hours by day-bus to *Denpasar* or *Jogya*, both of which are 200 to 250 miles away (300 to 400 kilometers). If you are heading towards *Bali* and don't want to travel through the heat of the day, you can catch a bus to *Surabaya* (2.5 hours) and then fly to *Bali*. The Garuda flight leaves at 1:30 P.M. and costs Rp50,000. Take a bus that does **not** go on the new toll road (*jangan lewat tol*), get off at Aloha, and then charter a *bemo* the 3 miles to the airport for around Rp2,500. If you are heading west it is recommended to go to *Malang*, 60 miles (100 kilometers) away. From Malang there are overnight buses to *Jogya* or *Jakarta*.

It should be noted that some tours coming from Surabaya leave Surabaya hotels at 2 A.M. and drive to Tosari village, where they observe the sunrise "over Bromo," not "from Bromo." Visually this is much less spectacular, though travelling time is not as long as to Ngadisari. To get to the Hotel Bromo Permai you must go via the town of Probolinggo and the village of Ngadisari.

3. Local Transportation

Surabaya has a reasonable **taxi** service, operating at all hours with the fare taken from the meter. This is a spread-out city, so a taxi is definitely the preferred way to get from airport to hotel and to other places around town. A taxi service to Mount Bromo (3 to 4 hours' drive) operates from the Mirama Hotel at Jalan Raya Darmo 68-76 (Tel. (031) 69501-9). *Malang* doesn't have a regular taxi service for crosstown traffic. The locals would be more likely to travel by the traditional taxi—the pedal-powered *becak*. There is a taxi service for travel from Malang to *Probolinggo* or *Mount Bromo*. One operator is the Mujur Surya travel agent at Jalan Bromo 33a, Malang (Tel. (034) 24652, 24533). You can often find a taxi in the carpark of Malang's better hotels for crosstown travel, or hire one by the hour (fix the rate in advance).

Surabaya's main **bus** routes run from north to south—from Tanjung Perak harbor and Jembatan Merah (Chinatown) to Joyoboyo Intercity Terminal and Aloha (near Juando Airport). The *Joyoboyo to Jembatan Merah* route goes along Jalan Raya Darmo, Jalan Basuki Rakhmat, Jalan Embong Malang, Jalan Blauran, Jalan Bubutan, and Jalan Veteran to Jalan Jambatan Merah; it returns (north to south) via Jalan Veteran, Jalan Gemblongan, Jalan Tunjungan, Jalan Pemuda, Jalan P. Sudirman, Jalan Urip Sumoharjo, and Jalan Raya Darmo to Joyoboyo.

The *Joyoboyo to Tanjung Perak Harbor* route turns off at Jalan Bubutan to the harbor. Otherwise it's the same as the above.

Buses from Bali or other towns in Java stop at the Joyoboyo Terminal. There are buses to the city center via the above routes, or you can walk outside the terminal to Jalan Raya Wonokromo for buses that follow the same route.

Malang has three main **bus** terminals. Dinoyo on Jalan M.T. Haryono is for buses going to Selecta, Madium, and Kediri. Terminal Patimura on Jalan Patimura is for buses going to Bali, Surabaya, and Probolinggo. Gadang Terminal to the south of town is for buses to Karangkates dam and Blitar.

The *bemos* in Malang follow a set route and are an easy way to get to the temples that dot the countryside around the city.

To get to *Candi Singosari Temple* you first need to get to Patimura Terminal, then catch a *bemo* to Blimbing, then change to one to Singosari. The fare from Malang to Blimbing is Rp200, and from Blimbing to Singosari costs Rp250.

To *Candi Jago* or *Candi Kidal* (*candi* is Javanese for "temple"), you also take the bemo from Patimura Terminal to Blimbing (Rp200), then change to a minibus to Tumpang (Rp350). The temple is one half mile (1 kilometer) away.

To *Candi Panataran* temple, catch a *bemo* or bus from Gadang Terminal to Blitar town (Rp600), then squeeze into an old station wagon (*opelet*) for the ride to the temple (Rp500).

To *Selecta* hill resort, take a minibus from Dinoyo Terminal to Batu town (Rp400), then change to another minibus to Selecta (Rp400).

After you have caught the *bemo* to *Singosari* village or *Tumpang* village, you still need to cover half to one mile to the temples. Near where the *bemo* stops you will see a man with a horse and cart. He is your transportation to the temple sites. You will need to beat him down on a price before you get onto the carriage. He may start at a crazy price of a few thousand rupiah. You should be able to get the *dokar* for Rp500 to *Candi Singosari* and under Rp1,000 to *Candi Jago*. *Dokar* are a great way to travel, especially during the heat of the day.

4. Hotels and Lodging

EXPENSIVE HOTELS

East Java has two international-class hotels and they are both in Surabaya. The **Hyatt Bumi Surabaya** (Tel. (31) 511234) is a new hotel aimed at the business traveler. Rooms are spacious; each has three telephones and a color TV that includes CNN, CBS, five other channels, and in-house movies. Single rooms start at $US140 a night and suites go up to US$350. Book through your local Hyatt hotel, your travel agent, or write direct to: Hyatt Bumi Surabaya, Jalan Basuki Rakhmat 124, Surabaya Indonesia (Fax: (62) (31) 470508).

The **Garden Palace Hotel** (Tel. (31) 470001, 479251) is a well-appointed high-rise addition to the older **Garden Hotel**, which is around the corner on Jalan Pemuda. This is also a business-oriented hotel that is fine for travelers, too. Some rooms have views across the river to the harbor. Single-room rates are US$90 and the average suite is $200 per night. Late checkout at a 50% surcharge is available until 6 P.M. For reservations, contact Golden Tulip Worldwide Hotels, Garuda, your travel agent, or book direct at: Garden Palace Hotel, Jalan Yos Sudarso 11, Surabaya, Indonesia (Fax: (62) (31) 516111, 516138).

MEDIUM-PRICED HOTELS

This group of hotels in East Java are good value for the money. Single rooms go for US$50 to US$65 per night in Surabaya and $30 to $50 at Malang. Rooms are generally spacious and well appointed, with shower and air-conditioning or fans in cool Malang. Sometimes the hotel layout or architecture can be quite interesting, such as at the Splendid Inn in Malang or the colonial-era Majapahit Hotel in Surabaya.

Surabaya

Hotel Mirama (Tel. (31) 69501) has satellite TV, a twenty-four-hour coffee shop, twenty-four-hour room service, a lobby bar, and two restaurants—one serving European, Chinese, and Indonesian meals and the other Japanese/Korean. There is a travel agent, drugstore, and money changer in the hotel shopping arcade. Book direct at the hotel, Hotel Mirama, Jalan Darmo 68-76, Surabaya, Indonesia. If you want to save yourself 30 percent off the room rate, make your booking through the hotel's booth at the Surabaya airport restaurant.

The Garden Hotel (Tel. (31) 470001) was one of the first modern hotels catering to the needs of the foreign tourist. The hotel's facilities are now a bit plain and outdated, but it does have everything you need, and is on a quiet, wide street.

For reservations, contact your travel agent, Golden Tulip World wide Hotels, Garuda Airlines, or book direct at the Garden Hotel, Jalan Pemuda 21, Surabaya, Indonesia.

The Majapahit Hotel (Tel. (31) 43351) was built during the colonial era and was originally called the Orange Hotel. This hotel has plenty of charm and Old-Worldliness, and is on Surabaya's main commercial street. Book direct at the Hotel Majapahit, Jalan Tunjungan 65, Surabaya, Indonesia. Other hotels in Surabaya are the Elmi Hotel (Tel. (31) 471571) at Jalan Sudirman 42; the Hotel **Simpang Natour** (Tel. (31) 42151) at Jalan Pemuda 1-3; and **Patrajasa Hotel** (Tel. (31) 68681) at Jalan Gunungsari.

Malang

Malang has the **Montana Hotel** (Tel. (341) 22751), recently rebuilt on the site of the original hotel at Jalan Kahuripan 9, and the **Hotel Pelangi** (Tel. (341) 27456-7), with plenty of facilities, such as twenty-four-hour room service to the seventy-four rooms. This hotel looks rather like a motel, and is conveniently located opposite the central square at Jalan Merdeka Selatan 3, Malang.

More like a comfortable, homey guesthouse is the **Splendid Inn** (Tel. (341) 66860, 28169), which has a highly recommended restaurant and a quiet cocktail bar. The Splendid Inn is just a short walk from the shopping district at Jalan Majapahit. The newest hotel in Malang is the **Malang Regent's Park Hotel** (Tel. (341) 28311 15). It has standard rooms, suites, a Chinese restaurant, a coffee shop, a pool, and all the modern services. A ten-minute walk to the Basuki Rakhmat commercial district, the Regent's Park is at Jalan Jaksa Agung Suprapto 12-16, Malang, East Java, Indonesia (Fax: (62) (341) 61408).

BUDGET HOTELS

Single-room rates for this group vary from $15 to $30. Most rooms have a bathroom and a fan. Air-conditioning may be available in some rooms, and is worth the extra in Surabaya, a very hot city. You may be able to get coffee or cool drinks in your hotel, but you'll have to go out to eat.

Surabaya

Try the **Olympic Hotel** (Tel. (31) 43215) at Jalan Urip Sumoharjo 65. This is halfway between Jalan Tunjungan and the zoo and is handy to taxis, buses, shops, and restaurants. The **Brantas Hotel** (Tel. (31) 45247) at Jalan Kayon 76-78 is at the lower end of this price bracket. It is only a short ride from the Gubeng railway station by the local taxi, a pedal-power *becak*. One arm of the Mas River runs by the hotel, so you can go for a cooling stroll in the afternoon and watch the locals at play.

The **Bamboo Den** (Tel. (31) 40333) is firmly entrenched on the back-packer circuit. It's quite overcrowded, with rooms or dormitory beds. The advantage is you can walk there from the Gubeng railway station. Also known as **Transito Inn**, The Bamboo Den costs $5 or so a night, and is located at Jalan Pemuda 19, next to the high-rise Pemuda Hotel. Other budget Indonesian-style hotels or *losmen* in Surabaya are **Hotel Carmen** at Jalan Pemuda 112, **Wisma Ganesa** on Jalan Sumatra, and **Hotel Sentosa** on Jalan Embong Kenongo. All are handy to the railway station. These cheapies are hot, with shared Indonesian-style cold-water bathrooms, but the sheets are clean and they only put you back $3 a night.

Malang

Hotel Riche is one of the better Indonesian-style hotels in Malang. The rooms are clean, and have shared cold-water bathrooms. The grounds are quite spacious, the central square is opposite, eating houses are nearby, and a ticket office for buses to Bali and Jogya is next door. At $10 a night, it's not a bad place to experience an Indonesian *losmen*. Other cheap but rougher *losmen* are the **Hotel Santosa** at Jalan Agus Salim 24 and the **Malinda Hotel** at Jalan Zainal Ariffin 39. The last two are in the busy central market area and cost $5 a night.

5. Restaurants and Dining

Surabaya

Surabaya is very much a Chinese city, and this is reflected in the preponderance of Chinese restaurants serving *yum cha* or *bubur ayam* for breakfast. The first is steamed dumpling brought to the table on a trolley and served out of bamboo boxes. *Bubur ayum* is a chicken/rice gruel served warm. Later in the day such restaurants revert to what we consider more normal Chinese cooking. Upmarket Javanese restaurants are not easy to find, although there are some clean and cheap Indonesian cafes on Jalan Kawi, a short way out of the city center, which are open from 7 A.M. to 10 P.M.

WESTERN

American fast food is represented by **Kentucky Fried Chicken** (Tel. (31) 471695) in the complex at Jalan Basuki Rakhmat 16-18. K.F.C. is open from 10 A.M. to 10 P.M. Another American franchise holder has two outlets called **Texas Fried Chicken** at the lower ground floor of Tunjungan Plaza (Tel. (31) 511081), which is on Jalan Basuki Rakhmat, and at the Delta Plaza (Tel. 515088—Ext: 3459), at Jalan Pemuda 37. **Swensen's Ice Cream** (Tel. (31) 471695) is open from 10 A.M. to 10 P.M. daily at Jalan Basuki Rakhmat 16-18, with the rich tradition of old San Francisco (Surabaya style). **Gandy Steakhouse** (Tel. (31) 40609, 471898), at Jalan Sumatra 51-53, should come up with a good steak at a fair price if it's anything like the Jakarta restaurant. **Cafe Venezia** (Tel. (31) 43091) serves steak and also specializes in Italian ice cream in what tries to be a European setting at Jalan Ambengan 16. Steaks and hamburgers are on the menu at the **24-hour coffee shop** at the Elmi Hotel (Tel. (31) 471571), Jalan P. Sundirman 42-44. The **Arumanis Terrace Cafe and Restaurant** (Tel. (31) 511234) at the Hyatt Bumi Hotel is a typical Hyatt coffeeshop during the day, but converts to a buffet/smorgasborg devoted to a different country's cuisine each night of the week. Other **coffee shops** are at the Mirama Hotel and the Grand Palace Hotel. The **Orchid Restaurant** (Tel. (31) 470001) at the Garden Hotel at Jalan Pemuda 21 serves European as well as Indonesian food.

CHINESE/JAPANESE

Chinese/seafood is a very common combination in Indonesia, and a highly recommended one at that. The *Golden Lotus Restaurant* (Tel. (31) 43942) is one such place, with a singer and band to croon to you in Chinese while you eat. The Golden Lotus is in the Andhika Plaza Building at Jalan Simpang Dukuh 38-40. For Hong Kong-style food, there is the **Hong Kong Palace** (Tel. (31) 46970-4), which is on the third floor of the Surabaya Indah building at Jalan Embong Malang 33-37. For more authentic local (and cheaper) Chinese food, head for Chinatown along Jalan Jembatan Merah, Jalan Veteran, and Jalan Pahlawan.

Upscale Japanese and Korean cuisine is served from 10 A.M. to 10 P.M. at the **New Nam San Restaurant** (Tel. (31) 69501-9), which is inside the Mirama Hotel. Also at the Mirama Hotel is the 24-hour **Ken Dedes Restaurant** (Tel. (31) 69501-9). Prices here are reasonable and the menu follows that local mix of Chinese, Indonesian, and European dishes. **Orient Express**, on Jalan Basuki Rakhmat, has a moderately priced buffet menu with Chinese, Indonesian, Indian, and other Asian selections. Another local favorite is the **Oasis Restaurant** (Tel. (31) 43187) in the Hotel Simpang Natour at Jalan Pemuda 1. In each of the high-rise department stores, you will find at least two Chinese or Indonesian eating places.

INDONESIAN

Fried chicken, quite different from the Kentucky or Texas versions, is a highly recommended local dish throughout the whole of Java. *Ayam goreng* is the sign to watch out for. Order the side dishes of steamed rice (*nasi putih*) and the green vegetable salad and you'll have a tasty, well-balanced meal. **Jakarta Ayam Goreng** (Tel. (31) 40936) is at Jalan Kusuma Bangsa 85, not far from the Gubeng railway station. **Kendungdoro Ayam Goreng** (Tel. (31) 45756) is at Jalan Kedungdoro 26A.

Sumatran buffet-style brought-to-your-table cuisine is best represented in the harbor area. The **Minang Riya Rumah Makan** (Tel. (31) 291443) is at Jalan Perak Timur 590, and the **Pancaran Minang Rumah Makan** (Tel. (31) 293648) is close by at Jalan Perak Timur 606. Minang food is economical as long as you finish each bowl that you start. You may have up to ten dishes in front of you on the table, so if you have only a little of each, make sure it's from the dishes that are easily divided and counted, such as pieces of chicken, fish, lungs, or eggs. Vegetables or curries are usually paid for by the whole dish.

Back near the station at Jalan Kusuma Bangsa 128 is the **Pengambon Rumah Makan** (Tel. (31) 46311). *Rumah makan* means, literally, "eating house".

Rijsttafel is the Dutch name for an assortment of Indonesian dishes laid out in buffet style. The **Warung Kopi Coffee Shop** (Tel. (31) 470001) at the Garden Palace Hotel on Jalan Yos Sudarso serves *rijsttafel* from 6 P.M. to 10 P.M. most nights, for a very reasonable $3.50 (Rp6,500).

Backpackers in Surabaya tend to congregate in the area between Jalan Sudirman and the Gubeng railway station. One of the attractions of this area is the cheap eating houses, especially roadside stalls and traditional cafes. **Depot 3** at Jalan Sudirman 4 serves Indonesian and Chinese meals for US$1, as well as freshly made fruit juices. Close by is a yogurt stall on the corner of Jalan Sudirman and Jalan Trengguli. Opposite the cinema on Jalan Pemuda is **Ayam Goreng Pemuda**, serving Javanese fried chicken, and next to the same cinema is a reasonably priced seafood restaurant. Crossing the river to the east, there are many traditional **food stalls** (*warungs*) in front of the Gubeng railway station that specialize in dishes such as soup (*soto Madura*), *nasi campur* (steamed rice with side dishes of meat, fish, soy cakes, and assorted vegetables), and *sate* (barbequed meat skewers with either beef, goat, or chicken), and that stay open until two in the morning. Be warned that *warung* food stalls are only for those with strong stomachs, due to the lack of refrigeration facilities and the need to compensate with chili. Stay away from shrimp (*udang*) and other seafood just to be sure. There is no point in having to run to the toilet every half hour for the next two or three days. A safer bet is the **Boncafe** at Jalan Raya Gubeng, also opposite the station.

Malang

Malang has a wide range of eating places, and none of them are expensive. The new shopping plazas on Jalan Agus Salim near the central market have outlets serving Western, Indonesian, and Chinese food, often in air-conditioned comfort. For cheap and clean Indonesian food, try the group of restaurants on Jalan Kawi, half a mile from the town square. Jalan Basuki Rakhmat, the main street, has the greatest number of restaurants. Some of these I have recommended below. I was not able to obtain phone numbers, but you won't need to make reservations anyway.

WESTERN

The best-known Western/European restaurant in town is the **Oen Restaurant** at Jalan Basuki Rakhmat 17, having been around from Dutch times. Another favorite is the restaurant inside the **Splendid Inn**, on the corner of Jalan Majapahit and the Tugu Roundabout. Both of these serve moderately priced meals in relaxed surroundings. **Amsterdam Steak** is a newer establishment inside the Gajah Mada Plaza on Jalan Agus Salim. **Kentucky Fried Chicken** has its local outlet next door in the Malang Plaza. Snacks are available from the **Hawaii Bakery** at Jalan Basuki Rakhmat 80.

Probably the most upscale place in town is the **Lavenda Restaurant** on Jalan Sumeru, which calls itself an international restaurant. Personally, I prefer the Oen and Splendid Inn.

CHINESE

Malang, unlike Surabaya, is not an overly Chinese town, so naturally enough there aren't a lot of Chinese restaurants. Try some Chinese fast food (usually noodles) in the **department stores** on Jalan Agus Salim and Jalan Basuki Rakhmat. For a more formal Chinese meal, there are the **Dragon Phoenix** on Jalan Ahmed Dahlan; **New Hong Kong** at Jalan A. Hakim 5; and the **Canton Restaurant** at Jalan Gatot Subroto 17.

INDONESIAN

Some of the better Indonesian restaurants are on Jalan Basuki Rakhmat, such as **Cafe Aneka Rasa** at number 7. Sumatran Padang

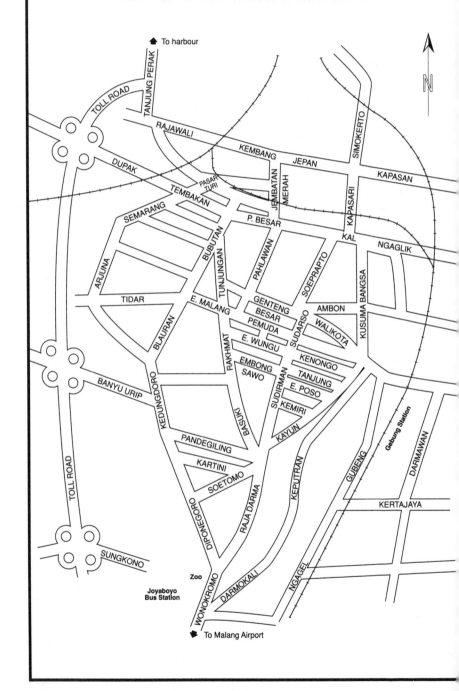

cuisine is served at **Minang Agung** at number 30, and also **Minang Jaya** at number 111. Nearby, on the corner of Jalan Sumeru and Jalan Bromo, is **Ayam Pemuda**, which specializes in tasty Javanese fried chicken. Budget-priced Javanese and other Indonesian food is available in the area near the central market and the cheap accommodations. On Jalan Agus Salim, try **Duta Rasa** in the Gajah Mada Plaza; **Depot Agung** opposite the Mitra Department Store; and **Depot Remaja** at number 20. Nearby is **Depot Murni** at Jalan Zainal Ariffin 39; and the **Cairo Restaurant** at Jalan Kapten Tendean 1. On the western side of town along Jalan Kawi, there are budget places to eat, such as **Pondok Bamboo** on the corner of Jalan Ijen. Cheaper still are food stalls at the **Pasar Senggol** evening market, which is off Jalan Majapahit, though I wouldn't eat there myself. You could try a cup of coffee maybe, but I have doubts about their cleanliness.

6. Sightseeing

Surabaya's one place not to miss is its **zoo**. Situated opposite the Joyoboyo Bus Terminal at the corner of Jalan Diponegoro and Jalan Raya Darmo, this zoo is notable for its **Komodo dragon**. This is an iguana-type lizard measuring six to ten feet in length. Komodo is an island halfway along the Indonesian island chain, between Bali and New Guinea. The variety and size of the bird enclosures are the best in Indonesia. You can watch the monkeys and other primates swing across to their own island in the center of the zoo.

Museum MPU Tantular is an ethnographic museum situated across the road from the entrance to the zoo. There are exhibits from Majapahit, Chinese ceramics, *wayang* figures, old photographs of Surabaya, and early *batik*-making implements. There is also an exhibition of early European mechanical items.

Old buildings around town include the **Hotel Majapahit** on Jalan Tunjungan. The first Indonesian flag after independence was flown here. The hotel has undergone many name changes, starting life as the Hotel Orange. The Japanese occupiers called it the Yamato Hotel, which then changed to the L.M.S., after a later owner, and thence to Mojopahit (an older version of Majapahit). **Grahadi** was the former Dutch governor's residence on Jalan Pemuda. It is now the official residence of the governor of East Java. In a garden is the statue of an earlier governor, killed during the communist uprising of 1948. At the rear of the park is a statue of Buddha dating from 1326, a product of the Singosari kingdom.

Chinatown in Surabaya is at Jembaton Merah (literally "red bridge"),

MALANG

To Jogya
To Surabaya Bali

N

SLAMET RIADI
SUPRAPTO
AGUNG
DR. CIPTO
KARTINI
SUTONO
PATIMURA
SUDIRMAN

SUMERU
IJEN
BROMO
ARJUNA
JAKSA
RAKHMAT
KAHURIPAN

SUROPATI
Bus
COKROAMINOTO
Railway Station

KAWI

TUGU
KERTA
GAGAH
MAD
MAJAPAHIT
BASUKI

Phone
MERDEKA
ARIS MANANDAR
TRUNJOYO
GATOT SUBROTO

ASHARI
HASYIM
KAUMAN
BARAT
AGUS SALIM
ARIFIN

KATAMSO
HASYIM
WIRJO
PRONOT
Shopping Centre
A. DAHLAN
MARTADINATA

JULIUS USMAN
SULTAN SYAHRIR
PASAR BESAR
Market

KYAI
TAMIN

To Blitar

site of the fiercest battle on Java during the independence struggle. The streets towards the east are the earliest Chinese buildings. Jambatan Merah is the busiest commercial district in Surabaya.

The **Arab Quarter** is the area around Ampel Mosque (Mesjid Ampel) which is east of Jalan K.H. Mas Mansur. The mosque was built by one of the nine Javanese great wise men (the *wali songo*), Sultan Ampel. The sultan, who died in 1481, is buried on the grounds of the mosque. The narrow alleys and buildings certainly create a Middle-eastern feel.

Generally, Surabaya looks very plain, but don't be put off. It's a very old city with modern, comfortable hotels which can be used as a base while exploring the rest of East Java.

Tanjung Perak Harbor (literally "Silver Point") is Indonesia's second biggest port after Jakarta and is the major transit point for Javanese passengers and merchandise heading for the other islands, especially Kalimantan (Borneo), Sulawesi (Celebes) and Irian Jaya (Dutch New Guinea). The anchorage for traditional sailing boats, called *prahu* is on the right as you enter the harbor precinct.

Out of town, 33 miles (55 kilometers) to the south, is the hill resort of **Tretes**. This is the place where locals escape the heat of Surabaya on weekends. Surabaya was an important center for the Dutch, and many houses in the area have a European feel.

Malang is the other large city in East Java, and is set on a cool plateau dotted with **temples** from Java's Hindu-Buddhist past. If you are interested in temple spotting, allow a couple of days on your itinerary for Malang.

The closest temple to Malang is **Candi Singosari**, named after the Hindu dynasty of the same name. Built in 1300 just after the death of the Singosari dynasty's last king, Kertonegara, the temple has decorations on the lower levels that were never completed. Nearby are two huge, bulbous statues that are half human, half animal guardians to the temple and possibly the whole Singosari kingdom. To get to the temple, take a *bemo* to Blimbing and Singosari town. At the end of town, take a left at the cinema (Bioskop). The first guardian is 600 yards away.

Two smaller temples are near the village of Tumpang, east of Malang past Blimbing. **Candi Jago** is up a road to the left 100 yards before the Tumpang market. This temple has five levels of stories carved into the temple and its retaining walls. The stories start at the top and work down counterclockwise. Ask the caretaker to explain to you the tales of love and war from the Indian epics, the *Ramayana* and *Mahabarata*. Candi Jago was built between 1270 and 1340.

Candi Kidal is 3 miles (5 kilometers) of pretty countryside but bumpy road to the northeast of Tumpang. This is one of the smallest of the

Candi Kidal, Malang

Singosari temples, but it makes up for it with intricate reliefs and arched doorways.

South of Malang near the town of Blitar is **Candi Panataran**, an extensive temple complex built between 1200 and 1450. Most of the buildings that have survived to the present are from the middle of the fourteenth century, such as the tall, thin "Dated Temple," A.D. 1369. When it was built, there would have been wood and thatch structures that blended in with the terraces.

A short way down the road from Blitar towards the Panataran temple is the mausoleum of Indonesia's first president, **Sukarno**. For many years this unmarked grave was a very humble affair, belying Sukarno's role in securing Indonesia's independence from Holland. Sukarno was buried here in 1970, next to his mother's grave.

Selecta is the locals' favorite hill resort, nestled on the slopes of Mount Arjuna 12 miles (20 kilometers) west of Malang. Take your swimsuit for a dip in one of the cool, clear pools. In the area are apple orchards, so try some tasty local fruit during your stay in Malang. Further up the slopes of Mount Arjuna is the source of the mighty Brantas River, which winds its way through East Java, past Malang and other towns to the north coast near Surabaya.

The town of Malang is a pretty place, though with few places in particular to visit. The beauty is in the buildings, the attitude of the people, and the Brantas River, whose curves influence the layout of the town. The **night market** (*pasar senggol*) doesn't have much to buy, but there are cheap eating places.

Mt. Bromo is the singularly most impressive place to visit in East Java. The Bromo experience involves getting up at 3:30 A.M., having a quick coffee, crossing a sea of gray sand, climbing a few hundred steps up to the volcano's rim, and watching the sun rise over the eastern rim of the main crater. The ridges and rivulets change colors as the sun rises. Some mornings, over one hundred people of all ages and means make the trip. Going to Bromo was the highlight of one of my trips to Indonesia and I recommend it to everyone of sound health. This unfortunately does not include asthmatics, who may find the rarefied air and sulfur fumes a problem. On the way across the sand-sea (a literal translation of the local name. It is the large, flat area of gray sand inside the volcano) is the symmetrical brown cone of Mt. Batok. In the distance, to the right, from the rim of Mt. Bromo you can see the top of Mt. Semeru, puffing white smoke.

The entry point to Mt. Bromo is 1.5 miles (2 kilometers) from the town of Probolinggo (on the Surabaya side). Probolinggo is 62 miles (100 kilometers) from Surabaya, or 56 miles (90 kilometers) from Malang on

Mount Bromo on the left, puffing smoke, and the sand-sea

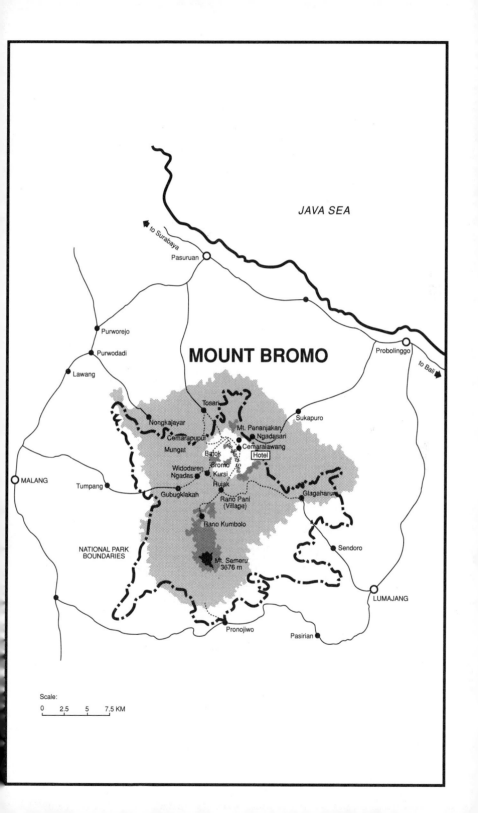

the north coast road leading towards Bali. Turn off the main road and head towards the mountains. The road climbs steadily for 12 miles (20 kilometers), then steeply for 3 miles (5 kilometers) to the town of **Sukapura.**

Another steep, winding 11 miles (18 kilometers) leads to the Tengger village of **Ngadisari.** The Tengger villagers are among the last people in Java who follow the Hindu religion, and when I asked some locals if the people of Sukapura are Hindu too, the answer was "No, they are Moslem. The Hindu people from there have gone to Bali." What is likely is that Ngadisari and the surrounding hills were so hard to reach before the road was built that Moslem missionaries were never able to penetrate the area.

Just over a mile (2 kilometers) past Ngadisari is the Bromo Permai Hotel. At night the large restaurant of the hotel buzzes with excitement in anticipation of what the early morning will bring. In October, for example, sunrise is at 5:15 A.M., so it's best to wake up at 3:45 A.M., have some coffee, and start your ride on horseback the 30 minutes and 2 kilometers to the steps. You then climb the steps up to the rim and watch the colors change as dawn approaches. Once up on the rim, walk around towards the east (left) for a better view and to avoid the sulfur fumes. The climb up the steps literally takes your breath away, probably due to the altitude. Following sunrise, some people prefer to walk back across the sand-sea. However, the steep road at the end of the sand up to the hotel is quite exhausting.

By 7:30 A.M. most people are back at the hotel, ready for breakfast and the descent back down to the coast.

7. Guided Tours and Going It Alone

Minibus tours run to all of the places mentioned in the previous section. You can book these tours through your hotel or a travel agent in Surabaya or Malang. If you plan to stay in the hotel at Bromo, you should be able to book it through Garuda or your local agent. In Surabaya try **Nitour** at Jalan Urip Sumoharjo 63, (Tel. (31) 45309); **Pacto** at Jalan Raya Darmo 70 (Tel. (31) 472706); **Pasopati** at Jalan Urip Sumoharjo 21 (Tel. (31) 44001), or **Tunas Indonesia** at Jalan Pemuda 1-3 (Tel. (31) 46898).

Private taxis can be hired from these agents in Surabaya or through the Mirama Hotel. When I went to Mt. Bromo, I hired a taxi for the one-way drive from Malang to Probolinggo, where I caught a *bemo* from the Victoria Hotel to the summit. The taxi was from **Mujur Surya Tours** at Jalan Bromo 33A, Malang (Tel. (341) 24652, 27957, 24433), who also offer other travel and ticketing services. For the Mt. Bromo experience, you would be advised to take a taxi to the top and keep it for the return trip. If you're staying overnight, that means paying for your driver's room, too. At Bromo or Probolinggo, it would be difficult to find a vacant taxi in the morning. You might be lucky at the Bromo Permai I Hotel or the *bemo* terminal at Ngadisari. At Probolinggo, try the Victoria Hotel or the Bromo Permai II Hotel, both on the main street, Jalan Sudirman, for a taxi. Taxi fares between Bromo and Probolinggo are very negotiable, depending on the time of day and where the driver lives. As in other parts of Java or Bali, you can "charter" a *bemo* minibus so that it operates as a taxi without picking up other passengers. It will be much quicker to do this than wait for a regular taxi.

8. Water Sports

Water sports are not something that East Java is remembered for, though there are plenty of **swimming pools** to cool off in. In *Surabaya* there are swimming pools at the Bumi Hyatt, Mirama, and Elmi Hotels. If you are not staying at the hotel, you will need to pay a few dollars to get in. Selecta, outside of *Malang*, has swimming pools filled with cold, mountain water. To the south of Malang is the Karangkates Dam and hydroelectric scheme on the Brantas River, where **water-skiing** facilities are available. At this time, however, I am a bit sketchy on details, so you should check with your hotel or a local travel agent before you drive the 12 miles (20 kilometers) from Malang to Karangkates.

9. Other Sports

I don't know of any spectator or participation sport venues in East Java. Surabaya may have a tennis court or two, but I haven't found them yet.

The Hyatt Bumi Hotel does have the Club Olympia, an aptly named **fitness center** with a gym and sauna. The Elmi Hotel has a similar set-up.

What East Java *does* have is Mt. Semeru, Java's highest mountain at 11,400 feet (3,676 meters). **Climbing Mt. Semeru** is a lot more physically demanding than going to Bromo. You will need to carry food, water, sleeping bags, and a tent, as you will sleep out for two to three nights. For safety reasons, go in a group of at least three or four people, so that two can go for help if necessary. Mt. Semeru is normally approached from the town of *Lumajang* to the east.

Leaving Lumajang on foot, you pass through forest that gradually thins out as you get higher. By the second day the way is strewn with gravel from previous eruptions that makes the going slow. Here the mountain is so steep that for every two steps you advance, you slide back one. You should reach the ash-covered summit on the second day, and may choose to spend the night near the peak to watch the sunrise. From here, Mt. Bromo is not far away to the north. Please note that because I have not climbed the mountain myself, I am not able to give more specific details, though I do know that Semeru is climbed on a regular basis.

10. Shopping

Surabaya's long history as a trading port makes it a good place to pick up a variety of genuine early European and Chinese porcelain and Indian brass statues, as well as woven blankets from the eastern Indonesian islands of Sumba, Roti and Timor. Most of the self-named "Art Shops," which sell antiques, art, and carvings, are found along Jalan Basuki Rakhmat, such as **Wing On Art Shop** at Jalan Basuki Rakhmat 5; **Sudi Mampir Art Shop** at Jalan Basuki Rakhmat 122; **Bali Art Shop** at Jalan Basuki Rakhmat 144; **Purnama Art Shop** at Jalan Basuki Rakhmat 146; **Rais Art Shop** at Jalan Basuki Rakhmat 146A; **Kartika Art Shop** at Jalan Basuki Rakhmat 148; **Elyta Art Shop** at Jalan Basuki Rakhmat 160A; and **Royal Art Shop** at Jalan Basuki Rakhmat 160B.

Others are the **Penguin Art and Flower Shop** at Jalan Nasuton 45; **Bangun Art Shop** at Jalan Raya Darmos, and **Hasan Art Shop** at Jalan Urip Sumoharjo 22A. All of these are worth visiting. You never know what you may find.

Surabaya's most accessible **traditional markets** are Pasar Turi on Jalan Pasar Turi and Pasar Tunjungan Surya on Jalan Tunjungan.

East Java's main commercial strip is along Surabaya's Jalan Tunjungan, which extends into Jalan Basuki Rahmat, and the offshoot, Jalan Embong Malang. This area has Surabaya's largest department stores and bookshops. **Chinatown** has a multitude of small retail outlets selling kitchen appliances, stationery, foodstuffs, and fabrics. Just as numerous are wholesalers and international traders, tailors, and mechanics. This is the real engine room of the city—a hive of activity 24 hours a day between Jalan Jembatan Merah and Jalan Bubutan.

Surabaya's five biggest department stores, in alphabetical order, are Embong Malang Permai on Jalan Embong Malang; NAM on Jalan Embong Malang; Surabaya Delta Plaza on Jalan Pemuda; Toserba Indo Plaza on Jalan Semutkali; and Tunjungan Plaza on Jalan Basuki Rakhmat.

All of Java is well endowed with **bookshops** (*toko buku*). Arguably the best chain is called **Gramedia**, which has its Surabaya branch on Jalan Basuki Rakhmat near the Hyatt Bumi Hotel. Jalan Tunjungan has a few along its length, such as **Toko Buku Indira**, Toko Buku Pelangi, and **Toko Buku Sari Agung**, in order heading away from the Hyatt. At the end of Jalan Tunjungan turn left and you will find **Toko Buku Karya Anda** on Jalan Praban, opposite the Wijaya Shopping Center. Across the river from Jalan Tunjungan, there is a group of smaller bookshops on Jalan Penelah.

The main problem with bookshops in Surabaya is that they don't cater to an English-speaking market, so it is hard to find a good paperback to read. What English-language books there are tend to be more business and technical oriented. You should be able to find current international magazines, however, as well as books dealing with Indonesia's history and people.

Elsewhere in East Java, you can buy *batik* cloth at **Malang's central market**, but more than likely the cloth comes from Central Java so you may be better off shopping for *batik* there. Old Dutch furniture pieces can be found throughout East Java because this was an important colonial plantation area for coffee and tobacco. Some Dutch families had been here for several generations before the Japanese arrived in 1942.

Java has lots of "**department stores**," which are often called "Plazas." Malang has a couple on Jalan Agus Salim, which is between the green central square and the central market. Each counter is owned and run by a different merchant, but there are no physical boundaries between the counters. Competition is stiff between the stores, so prices are reasonable, although high rents can mean prices are higher than in smaller shops. These are good places to buy toiletries.

In Malang the main traditional market is on Jalan Pasar Besar, one street away from the department stores if you're walking away from the central square. These markets are the cheapest place to buy fruit, vegetables, and *batik* cloth.

In regards to books and magazines, you're likely to have much better luck in Surabaya. The pickings are a little slim in Malang. You might try the newsagents at the bigger hotels if you're desperate for news.

East Java's plantations have produced **coffee** for hundreds of years. They were all nationalized by the Indonesian government in 1957. Try the local version, *kopi tubruk*, where the thick grounds are left in the cup or glass. It's a bit like Turkish or Greek style, and is beautiful in the morning.

Apples are grown in the highlands at Selecta near Malang. The temperate climate in most of East Java also allows a wide variety of **European vegetables** to be grown, so try some vegetable soup or chew on them raw.

11. Night Life and Entertainment

Nearly all East Java's sophisticated entertainment is at Surabaya's high-rise hotels, such as the Bumi Hyatt, Elmi, and Mirama Hotels and along Jalan Embong Malang in the city center, but we'll get to them in a minute.

In *Malang* there are **cinemas** in the department stores on Jalan Agus Salim. While the movies shown are mostly Indonesian and Chinese language, you can find some English-language movies, and some possibly with subtitles. So far, I have been able to find few **drinking holes** in Malang, other than the **Mandala Pub** in the Malang Plaza on Jalan Agus Salim (which is not a pub as we know it), the bar/restaurant at the **Pelangi Hotel** on Jalan Merdeka Selatan, and the **Regent Park Hotel**. Otherwise, you can buy a beer at the restaurants in the other better hotels, or at Chinese or Western restaurants that have been mentioned already is section 5. That's all for Malang, so the rest are in *Surabaya*.

The **Hyatt Bumi Hotel** (Tel. (31) 470875) has the two best bars in town. One of them, the Harbor Tavern, has a live band which was an all-Filipino group when I was there. Late in the evening this turns into a disco. The other, the Atrium Lounge, is a cocktail bar in the evenings, with live background music that includes jazz, piano, classical European, and a traditional Javanese *gamelan* xylophone ensemble. The **Mirama Hotel** (Tel. (31) 69501) has a sunken **lobby bar** where you can relax to live jazz. The **Elmi Hotel** (Tel. (31) 471751) also has a bar, which they call a pub.

At the Harbor Tavern at the **Bumi Hyatt** and the pub at the **Elmi Hotel**, later in the evening you will notice a change in lighting and tempo of the music as these locales change into discos. Another disco in Surabaya is the **Top Ten Club** in the Tunjungan Plaza Building on Jalan Basuki Rakhmat. This nightspot jumps from 10:30 P.M. to 3:00 A.M. most nights. I've also heard of the **Atum Disco** at the Atum Shopping Plaza, but I haven't been there yet.

More subdued entertainment, Chinese style, is the **Golden Park Restaurant and Supper Club** (Tel. (31) 270004-8), which stays open until 11:00 P.M. and has Taiwanese or local Chinese singers. The Golden Park is in the New Grand Park Hotel at Jalan Sudirman 3-5.

The more modern **cinemas** in town are in the central commercial district. Be sure to check that the English dialogues haven't been dubbed over with Indonesian for the session you're paying for. Two cinemas are on Jalan Embong Malang, namely the **President Theater** and the **Arjuna Theater**. Another is the **Ria Theater** on Jalan Duryat (which is off Jalan Basuki Rakhmat near the Hyatt Bumi Hotel).

Lastly, there is a **roller-skating rink**, called **Go-Skate**, at Jalan Embong Malang 33-37 on the fourth floor. On the daily program are figure-skating classes and the Paradise roller-disco. Join in, don't be shy. Not so many years ago, the only entertainment in Surabaya was the **T.H.R. (People's Amusement Park)** on Jalan Kusuma Bangsa. Open from 6 P.M. till 11 P.M. each day, it has performances of traditional Javanese dance-drama, jazz, and Indo-rock as well as arts and craft exhibitions. Check the program for details. Next door is the **Taman Remaja playground**, with carousels and other motorized rides.

12. The East Java Address List

Note that Jalan Basuki Rakhmat is a major street in both Surabaya and Malang.

Banks—Bank Bumi Daya, Jalan Basuki Rakhmat 2-4, Surabaya (Tel. (31) 41275). Bank Bumi Daya, Jalan Merdeka Barat 1, Malang (Tel. (341) 22451). Bank Central Asia, Jalan Tunjungan 51, Surabaya (Tel. (31) 41493). Bank Central Asia, Jalan Veteran 26, Surabaya (Tel. (31) 26101). Bank Central Asia, Jalan Basuki Rakhmat 72, Malang (Tel. (341) 27701). B.N.I. 1946, Jalan Pemuda 36, Surabaya (Tel. (31) 41351). B.N.I. 1946, Jalan Basuki Rakhmat, Malang. Bank Dagang Negara, Jalan Tunjungan 39, Surabaya (Tel. (31) 40710). Bank Rakyat Indonesia, Jalan Basuki Rakhmat 42-44, Surabaya. Bank Rakyat Indonesia, Jalan Basuki Rakhmat 26A, Malang.

Embassies and Consulates—The American Embassy is in Jakarta on Jalan Medan Merdeka Selatan, Jakarta (Tel. (21) 360 360). The American Consulate is in Surabaya at Jalan Raya Sutomo 33 (Tel. (31) 69 2878). The Canadian Embassy is in Jakarta on the 5th floor of the Wisma Metropolitan Building, Jalan Jendral Sudirman, (Tel. (21) 510709).

Garuda Airlines—Jalan Tunjungan 29, Surabaya (Tel. (31) 40460, 40480).

Hospitals (*rumah sakit*)—R.S. Dr. Sutomo, Jalan Dharma Husada 6-8, Surabaya (Tel. (31) 40061). R.S. Darmo, Jalan Raya Darmo 90, Surabaya (Tel. (31) 66253). R.S. Saiphul Anwar, Jalan Agung Suprapto, Malang.

Immigration office—Jalan Kayon 50, Surabaya (Tel. (31) 40707). Jalan Agung Suprapto, Malang.

Pharmacies—Drug store, Mirama Hotel Shopping Arcade, Jalan Raya Darmo 68-72, Surabaya. Apotik, Tunjungan Plaza, Jalan Basuki Rakhmat, Surabaya. Apotik Matahari, Jalan Basuki Rakhmat 3, Malang. Apotik Kabupaten, Jalan Basuki Rakhmat 11, Malang.

Post office—Jalan Pemuda, Surabaya. Jalan Merdeka Selatan 1, Malang.
Telephone office—Jalan Embong Malang, Surabaya. Jalan Basuki
Rakhmat 9, Malang.
Tourist information—Jalan Pemuda 118, Surabaya. Jalan Semeru (Webb
English Course), Malang. Corner Jalan Tugu and Jalan Majapahit,
Malang.

9

Central Java

1. The General Picture

Central Java (*Jawa Tengah*) is the real Java. The acknowledged originator of *batik*, the Javanese language, dance, and possibly the *wayang* shadow play, this part of Java was building great stone Hindu-Buddhist monuments one thousand three hundred years ago. Some of these still stand. Many, having been toppled by earthquakes, have been accurately reconstructed and are a draw for both foreign and local tourists and religious pilgrims. The two most important towns in Central Java, from a cultural and artistic point of view, are Jogyakarta (Jogya) and Surakarta (Solo), so I will be concentrating on them. Thirty-seven miles (60 kilometers) separate these two towns, which are approximately halfway between Bali and Jakarta.

Shopping for *batik* cloth or *batik* paintings and watching the *wayang* dance-drama are the highlights of many visitors' stay in Java. Jogya and Solo offer the best of both.

Jogyakarta was the traditional seat of the Mataram Empire, which built the temples of Borobudur and Prambanan and ruled Java for hundreds of years. Better known as Jogya, this town is considered by many to be the cultural heart of Indonesia. *Batik*, traditional dance, the *wayang* puppet play, the *wayang* dance-drama, and the *gamelan* orchestra evolved over the centuries at the palaces of Jogya and Solo. Especially formative

211

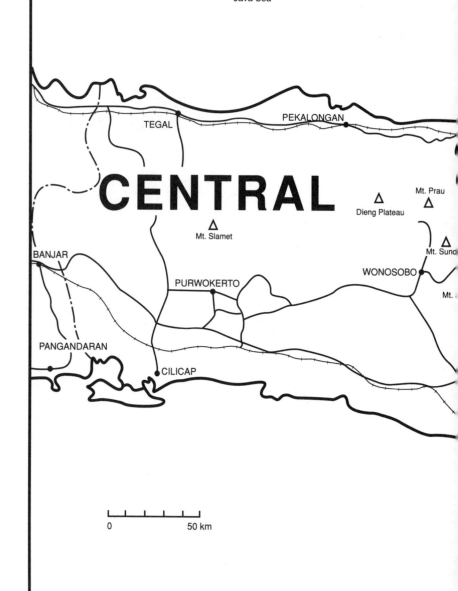

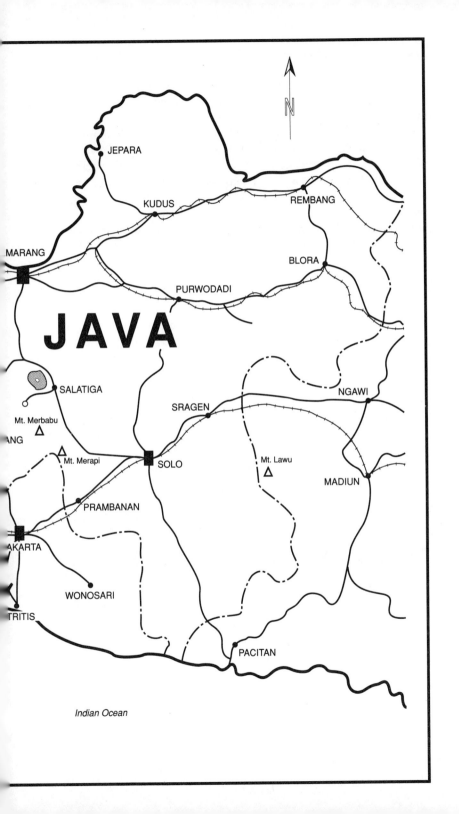

were the years of Dutch control, when the warring rulers were deprived of absolute power. This led them to channel their energies into developing the performing arts and *batik* designs.

The most interesting places to visit in Jogya are the Sultan's Palace and the adjoining Water Castle, which was the former rulers' playground and now houses many *batik* painting studios. For *batik* cloth, there are factories that follow traditional methods on Jalan Tirtodipuran and the *batik* museum on Jalan Sultan Agung. Farther afield, there are carved stone monuments spread out across the Prambanan Plain between Jogya and Solo and into the highlands at Dieng, and mountains to climb.

With so much to see and do, Central Java is understandably a magnet for tourists and most use Jogya as their base. Jogya is also a student town. The slow lifestyle and low living costs attract Indonesians to Gajah Mada University, and foreigners to the studios and schools that teach the local arts already mentioned.

Jogya has a special place in Indonesia's fight for independence from Holland. One of the first rebellions was by Prince Diponegoro in the eighteenth century. The last was when the Dutch tried to reclaim their former colony, but the republican forces, led by Sukarno and General Nasuton, resisted. After their own "long march" from Jakarta, the Indonesians made Jogya their last stronghold, in a war of attrition they were eventually able to win.

Solo or Surakarta, the town that surrounds the Kraton Surakarta Hadiningrat, retains much of the feel of old Java. After independence, the sultan of Surakarta was stripped of his official title. However, the social hierarchy, of which he is currently the head, still permeates Solo society. Within the brick walls of the greater *Kraton* (palace) there now live more commoners than blue-bloods, and most of the detached buildings have been taken over by the government to be used as schools. The large, wooden doors near the high, white tower open into a private world that goes back fourteen generations. A *gamelan* adjoins the waiting area, and close family friends are permitted to join the family when they play. From a raised tile floor, the rhythms of the *gamelan* ring through the pillars and out into the night.

Because fewer Westerners come here, Solo is probably a better place to buy *batik* than Jogya. Browsing is more relaxed, though at the larger markets things can get a bit hectic. Pasar Klewer, which is at the western entrance to the Alun-Alun, is one of the largest wholesale *batik* markets in Indonesia. To get to the central market, Pasar Gede, go out of the front (north) gate of the Alun-Alun and continue straight ahead past the Post Office until you come to a bridge on the right. Cross the bridge and

Goatherders near Solo

the market is opposite. Behind the market stretches the old Chinese quarter.

Kraton Surakarta Hadinigrat is a palace which rivals the palace of Jogya in size and splendor. It was built in 1745 by Susunan Pakubuwana II following the fall of the other older *Kraton* at Kartasura to rebels in 1743. The rebels managed to hold the *Kraton* for over one year until they were overthrown with the help of the Dutch.

The history of this period is full of rebellions by wayward princes, and was followed by the eventual division of the Greater Prambanan Plain into two large kingdoms. Later, two smaller fiefdoms were ceded to relatives of the rulers in order to quell the continual warfare that had taken such a heavy toll on the Javanese people. This division made the job of the Dutch much easier. Their initial aim was purely to trade, but they gradually became deeply involved in court intrigue. As in other European colonies, unfriendly rulers were deposed and more flexible ones put in their places.

Much of Solo has come a long way in the past 200 years, whilst some parts of town take one back as though in a time machine. The young of Solo are a sign of its modernity, the lanes through the town and the *Kraton* the key to its past. Solo is best explored on foot or by *becak*, giving one a chance to see and feel the pace of life in what is perhaps the most relaxed town in Indonesia. Without the overexposed air of nearby Jogya, the atmosphere of Solo soothes the mind. Artistically, Solo has as much to offer as Jogya, but you have to dig a little deeper to find it. Commercialism in its worst forms hasn't yet come to Solo. Let us hope it never does.

2. Long-Distance Transportation

Jogya and Solo are pretty close to halfway on your trip from Bali to Jakarta. Jakarta is 375 miles (600 kilometers) to the west and Bali is 435 miles (700 kilometers) to the east, so unless you want to spend 14 to 18 hours on the bus or train, you would be advised to fly.

Garuda (Tel. (274) 4400, 5184) is the most reliable airline, operating morning and afternoon jet flights from Jogyakarta to *Jakarta, Surabaya*, and *Bali*. Flying time to each destination is around half an hour in conditions that are often bumpy due to the mountains that you fly over. The economy airfare from Jogya to Bali is US$58, to Jakarta $63, and to Surabaya $30.

Garuda flies to *Jakarta* four times a day during the week and five times on weekends, starting at 8 A.M., and the last at 5 P.M.; to *Denpasar* there are three flights a day, from 5:50 A.M. until 4:10 P.M.; to *Surabaya* at 5:15

A.M. seven days a week; and to *Bandung* twice each morning, 8 A.M. and 9:30 A.M. For international travelers, there are two connections a day to *Singapore*, at 9:30 A.M. and 12 noon. Garuda Airlines' Jogya office is at Jalan Mangkubumi 56, and the airport is out of town going towards the Prambanan temple complex.

From Solo, Garuda flies daily at 8:40 A.M. to *Denpasar*, daily to *Surabaya* at 7:05 A.M., and twice daily to *Jakarta* at 8:40 A.M. and 4:05 P.M. Garuda's Solo office (Tel. (271) 6846) is at the Kusuma Sahid Prince Hotel, at Jalan Suryopranoto 22. The airport is called Adisumarno and is 9 miles to the west of the town.

From Semarang, Garuda flies twice daily to *Denpasar* via *Surabaya* at 7 A.M. and 3:25 P.M., and eight times daily to *Jakarta* between 6:25 A.M. and 5:10 P.M.. The Garuda office in Semarang is at Jalan Gajah Mada 11, (Tel. (24) 20178, 20910, 23317).

You should have no trouble connecting to an international flight from Bali's Ngurah Rai Airport or Sukarno-Hatta Airport at Cengkarang on the western edge of Jakarta. At the time of this writing, a new domestic airline had been given permission to set up using jet aircraft, thus breaking the Garuda monopoly. More precise details are not yet available, though when you get to Indonesia, the new airline may be in the air.

Bouraq (Tel. (274) 86664) and **Merpati** (Tel. (274) 4272) are two long-standing domestic airlines that have traditionally been restricted to operating prop-driven aircraft. That restriction may be lifted soon. At present, Bouraq and Merpati offer cheaper fares for longer flying time. Both have morning and afternoon flights to *Jakarta*, *Surabaya*, and *Bali*, as well as most of the other major cities in Indonesia. Bouraq's ticketing office is at Jalan Sudirman 37; Merpati is down the road at Jalan Sudirman 7. Airport tax is applicable to international flights and should be able to be purchased in advance. Domestic fares also have a tax, but it is automatically included in the price.

Taking the **day train** out of Jogya or Solo really gives you a perspective on what Central Java is all about. You look across the flat rice fields to the mountains, the tiled brick houses whizzing by in the foreground. To *Jakarta* take the air-conditioned *Fajar Utama*, which leaves at 7 A.M. and arrives in Jakarta at 3:30 P.M. An executive-class ticket costs $14 (Rp27,000). The **night train** is the quickest to *Jakarta*; the *Bima Express* with sleepers leaves at 9:10 P.M. and arrives at 6 A.M. Single fares range from US$17 to $22 one way. The *Bima Express* going in the other direction (to Surabaya) passes through Jogya at around midnight. Because both of these trains have been en route for several hours already, you may find someone in your seat or sleeper. Don't be afraid to call the conductor and have them removed.

To *Bali* you catch the *Bima Express* or another train to Surabaya and connect to *Banyuwangi*. From Banyuwangi you need to get to the **ferry** terminal and catch a bus from *Gilimanuk* to *Denpasar*, as there are no trains on Bali. This is not the only way to get to Bali. Another option is to take the train to *Surabaya* and change to an overnight express bus direct to *Denpasar*. These buses leave Surabaya each afternoon from the Joyoboyo bus terminal and arrive first thing in the morning. Each leg of this trip, whether by train or bus, is 6 to 8 hours, so you may choose to spend the day in Surabaya.

To *Bandung* in the highlands of West Java there is the *Mutiara*, which has a first-class section costing $8; or very slow, hot, and cheap day trains.

If you're going from *Jogya*, there are no daytime, non-stop **coaches or buses** that run between Jogyakarta and *Bali, Jakarta,* or *Surabaya*. Indonesians prefer to travel longer distances during the cool of the night, and I generally follow their lead.

Overnight express buses always have a schedule that allows them to arrive at their destination early in the morning. The *Jakarta* buses leave at 4 P.M. and arrive at 6 A.M. The longer trip to *Bali* leaves at 3:30 P.M. and arrives at *Denpasar* at 8 A.M. The fare to Jakarta or Bali is $13 (Rp25,000) for an air-conditioned coach or $10 for an older bus without air-conditioning. *Bandung* is half that price, as the buses aren't so modern. Reliable bus companies include **Cakrawala, Muncul, Bhayangkara, Bali Indah,** and **Bali Cepat.**

Travel agents that specialize in bus ticketing are on Jalan Sastrowidjayan in the Pasar Kembang backpacker part of town. Try **Kartika Travel** at Jalan Sastrowijayan 10; and **Panorama Travel** at number 21. The main bus terminal for intercity (including overnight express) buses is on Jalan Supeno near Kota Gede. Find out which buses leave earlier from outside the travel agent or have a shuttle bus so you don't have to worry about getting to the terminal.

In *Solo*, the bus companies are found near the main market (*Pasar Gede*). To *Jakarta* the better companies are **Bhayangkara** on Jalan Pasar Gede and **Cakrawala** on Jalan Urip Sumarjo (corner Jalan Widuran). The fare is $4.50 (Rp8,500) for air-conditioning or $3 for non-air-conditioning. Departure time is 3 P.M. each day. **Bandung Express**, at Jalan Kepatihan 22, departs Solo daily. Last time I was there, there were no coaches with air-conditioning. The non-A/C fare to *Bandung* was $3 (Rp5,500).

Heading east, **Agung Express**, at Jalan Urip Sumoharjo 171, has buses departing for *Malang* and *Surabaya* at 9:30 P.M. Non-air-conditioned buses cost $2.60 (Rp5,000). To *Denpasar* or *Bali*, the **Cakrawala** bus company, on Jalan Urip Sumoharjo (corner Jalan

Widuran) has a new air-conditioned coach leaving at 3 P.M. for $5 (Rp9,500).

Buses leaving from Jogya and heading for *Malang, Surabaya, and Bali* pass through *Solo* but don't always pass through the intercity terminal on Jalan Kapten Tendean. Also, book early, because they may not have any good seats left. During 1980-81 when I was living in Jakarta, I often went to Solo by overnight bus. Bhayangkara was my favorite bus line, because I felt the most secure with their drivers. The drivers didn't take risks on the country roads, the buses were comfortable, and they rarely broke down. I usually booked my ticket a day in advance so that I had my choice of seat—an aisle seat near the front, where there is more leg room and fewer bumps. These are very important considerations when the trip to *Jakarta* takes 14 hours and to *Denpasar* 18 hours.

I don't know of any **car rental** companies in Central Java that come without drivers. Taxis are a good way to see the temples and sights of Central Java, but are not a feasible way of getting to West or East Java. Full information on taxi companies and fares is given in the next section.

3. Local Transportation

There is public transportation to all the major attractions in Central Java located outside of Jogyakarta, as well as a most delightful way to get around town called the *becak* (pronounced BET-chuck). This pedal-powered, 3-wheeled vehicle resembles a bicycle with a very large wheel-chair attached to the front forks. You sit in the covered front section and catch the cooling breeze as you glide along Jogya's or Solo's streets. You can hire them by the hour or from point to point. If you're going sight-seeing for a morning, for example, you're better off paying Rp1,000 (50 cents) an hour and having him wait than hassling around looking for another one. Pick one up outside your hotel if you're staying near the center of town, or from Jalan Marlioboro if you're out near the Am-barukmo Palace Hotel.

The *becak* is Java's suburban taxi and one of Indonesia's great joys. Just remember to fix a price before you sit down. You can even use a *becak* to travel around the temple complexes of Borobodur and Pram-banan. Do your bargaining where the *becak* drivers are assembled next to the bus stop. The same rate applies in Solo as in Jogya—Rp1,000 an hour or Rp1,000 per kilometer (half mile) should be the maximum paid.

Jogya also has more conventional four-wheel **taxis** to take you around town or out of town, by distance or by the hour. The main taxi lineup (Tel. (274) 2731) is at Jalan Senopati, next to the General Post Office. The average rate is Rp7,500 ($4) per hour, with a minimum of two hours around town. Out of town, one-way fares are set by the taxi co-operative. Ask to see the current schedule. Prices in January of 1991 for one-way/round-trip journeys in rupiah (US$1 = Rp2,000) were:

Borobudur	Rp 28,250/37,500
Prambanan	Rp 20,900/27,750
Parangtritis	Rp 31,000/41,250
Imogiri	Rp 22,150/29,500
Solo	Rp 47,750/63,750
Sukuh Temple	Rp 78,750/105,000
Magelang	Rp 28,150/37,500
Wonosobo	Rp 81,500/108,750
Dieng	Rp 103,750/137,500
Semarang	Rp 84,400/112,500

Waiting time is charged at $4 (Rp7,500) an hour. Some taxi companies in Jogya are **Indra Kelana** (Tel. (274) 2112) at Jalan Mangkubumi 56; **Airlangga Guest House** (Tel. (274) 3344) at Jalan Prawirotaman 4; **ASA** (Tel. (274) 88018) at Jalan Kaliurang; **Centris** (Tel. (274) 2548, 4877) at Jalan Diponeforo 64; **J.A.S.** (Tel. (274) 61717) at Jalan Kapten Tendean 39; and **Rajawali** (Tel. (274) 2144) at Bandara Adisucipto airport.

Solo is 37 miles (60 kilometers) to the northeast of Jogya, so fares to the sights will vary—sometimes more and sometimes less. The **taxi** terminal in Solo is on the corner of Jalan Kratonan and Jalan Veteran.

Minibuses, called *bemo* in Bali and Java, are also called *colt* in Java, from the name of the Japanese Mitsubishi model. These ten-seater buses with a side door operate according to two different systems. One is more like a bus, following a set route, taking up and setting down passengers on the way. *Colt* minibuses crisscross Jogya in virtually all directions, the attendant of each bus calling out the destination. I don't recommend *colts* for travel around town; the *becak* is much more pleasurable. However, outside Jogya to smaller towns where buses don't operate, *colts* are sometimes the only local transportation.

PAPSA, also known as *"colt* travel," is more of a taxi service, leaving from a depot at set regular intervals and dropping you off at your hotel, home, or that town's PAPSA depot. A slight drawback is that PAPSA sometimes spends time driving around the suburbs picking up and dropping off passengers. Anyway, this gives you a chance to see how the locals live. The advantage is that you can plan your trip in advance without the expense of going by taxi, in which you really have to pay for the taxi going home empty. *Colt* travel, or PAPSA, is a very convenient form of moving between the larger towns of Central Java, such as Jogya, Solo, Magelang, and Semarang (one- to two-hour trips).

PAPSA is not recommended for longer distances outside of Central Java because it only operates during the day. Being stuck all day in a cramped minibus without air-conditioning is not a pleasant experience. An overnight bus or train are better alternatives.

Minibus companies in *Jogya* are at the northern end of town, mostly past the railway line. In Solo, many are together on Jalan Yos Sudarso (formerly Jalan Nonongan), which is midway between the *Kraton* and Puro Mangkunegaran. Leaving from *Jogya to Solo* try **S.A.A.** at Jalan Diponegoro 9A, **Trisula** at Jalan Wahidin 50, **Ksatrya** at Jalan Katamso 8, or **Anugrah** at Jalan Katamso 11. From *Jogya to Semarang* try **Wijaya** at Jalan Diponegoro 35 or **Rahaju** at Jalan Diponegoro 15. Rahaju also goes to *Magelang*. **A.B.C.** at Jalan Mangkubumi 58 goes to *Kediri*. Wijaya also goes west to *Cilicap* port, an overland transit point on the way to Pangandaran Beach, just over the border in West Java. One-way fares to all these places are only one or two dollars—to *Solo* Rp2,000; to *Semarang* Rp3,000; to *Magelang* Rp1,500, and to *Cilicap* Rp5,000. *Colt* travel and PAPSA leave every 30 minutes between *Jogya* and *Solo*. You should book at least 45 minutes in advance.

Jogya has a **city bus service** that goes all over town, but I don't recommend it as a way of getting around town. These orange, medium-size buses are very crowded and hot, with latecomers hanging out the door as it takes off. City buses leave from the terminal on Jalan Supeno and follow eight routes, all of which are one-directional. You will be able to pick up a bus route map from the Tourist Information Office on Jalan Marlioboro, next to the Mutiara high-rise hotel. There is only one fare to be paid for one ride, Rp100 (US 5 cents).

Intercity express buses are a good option for travel between the large towns in Central Java. Seating is relatively comfortable and all passengers must be seated. Look for the sign *cepat,* meaning "express." On each route there are a set number of stops at smaller towns or crossroads on the way, which means that few local villagers use them. *Cepat* buses are used more by white-collar workers to travel to and from work. I used them often when travelling from Solo or Jogya to Semarang. The best place to get on one is at a bus terminal, because they always stop there.

Normal intercity buses leave the bus terminal regularly, but their problem is that there is no limit to the number of times a bus can stop to take on or let off passengers, nor to the total number of passengers squeezed into the bus, nor to the amount of rural produce (including live animals) that can be taken inside the bus or stacked up on the bus's roof. This is an interesting way to travel if you've got some spare time and you like to see the locals close-up.

The **train** is not recommended for travel around Central Java, as most

Dokar carriage in Central Java

of the routes cater to travel to West or East Java. Stick to the bus or minibus for moving within the province.

The *andong* horse and carriage setup works on a similar system to the *becak*, only it is larger. Standing ten feet high and fifteen feet long, they are frequently used by women market traders to cart produce from the central markets back to their own shop. Other *andong* are kept clean and used by family groups to go visiting around town. Another horse-drawn carriage is the *dokar*, much smaller than the *andong*, and so a bit cheaper. Both are more expensive than a *becak* but less than a taxi. Haggle hard before you get in, otherwise you'll have an argument at the other end.

Rent a **bicycle** for a day or two and you'll get a good feeling for *Jogya's* rhythm. Many locals travel by bicycle, and tourists do too, so you won't be out of place. Be sure to check that the horn and brakes work before you go, or bring it back and exchange it if you're not happy with the one that you've been given. Several hotels in the Pasar Kembang backpackers' area near the railway station rent out bicycles at a daily rate of around Rp1,500 (US 75 cents). Try the *Asiatic Hotel* at Jalan Sastrowijayan 4, or the *Indonesia Hotel* across the road at number 9. There is also a rental office on Gang Sastrowijayan II.

In *Solo, The Westerners* guesthouse for backpackers has bicycles to rent, but only to guests who are staying there. This situation may have changed since I was there last. *The Westerners* is on a lane called Jalan Kamlayan Kidul, which runs off Jalan Yos Sudarso near the *batik* Keris showroom. If you don't have any luck there, try some small hotels in the Keprambon area.

Jogya has some six **motorbike** rental companies along the street outside the railway station, Jalan Pasar Kembang. However, unless you're there on business or are an experienced motorbiker, I wouldn't recommend a motorbike as a viable way to see Jogya. What's the point when you can go everywhere by *becak*? I must admit, though, that I found the motorbike ride to Parangtritis and back very enjoyable. The current daily rental rate is near Rp10,000 ($5.00), plus insurance. Helmets are compulsory, and an international driver's license is recommended to save on hassles. A gas station (*Pertamina*) is on the corner of Jalan Suropati and Jalan Katamso, and be sure to fill up before you leave town.

4. Hotels and Lodging

Two of the best places to stay in *Jogya* are the new wings of the Garuda and Mutiara Hotels, both of which are on the main street, Jalan Marlioboro. From these, many of Jogya's cultural sites, as well as restaurants and shops, are within walking distance. The *Kraton* (palace) is a ten-minute *becak* ride away. For those who want to be closer to the palace or are on a limited budget, Jalan Prawirotaman is a quiet street with eight guesthouses. Most of these have air-conditioning and swimming pools. Nearby are cafes, boutiques, and *batik* factories. The rest of the up-market hotels are some 4 miles out of town on Jalan Adisucipto, going towards the airport and Solo. Best known among these are the **Ambarrukmo Palace Hotel** and the **Sahid Garden Hotel**. Good facilities they may have, but they're a bit far out of town for my liking. Backpackers tend to congregate around Pasar Kembang near the railway station, especially Jalan Sastrowijayan and Gang (lane) I and II, which run between this road and Jalan Pasar Kembang. This area is very basic and single rooms cost less than $3 a day. Another budget area is Jalan Dagen, which runs off Jalan Marlioboro opposite the tourist information office.

In *Solo*, the **Mangkunegaran Palace Hotel** is attached to the smaller palace and the **Kusuma Sahid Hotel** has as its foyer an old Javanese building. The Keprambon area has mostly budget accommodation along Jalan A. Dahlan and Jalan Ronggowasito. Other towns in Central Java have mostly moderately and budget priced rooms, such as *Semarang, Magelang, Dieng, Salatiga,* and *Parangtritis.* Single room rates run from $5 to $20 a night.

EXPENSIVE HOTELS

One of the attractions of Central Java is its low cost of living, and this filters through to hotel rates. The end result is there are no hotels that you would call expensive. Single rooms are generally under $100 a night, so we'll start with moderately priced hotels.

MEDIUM-PRICED HOTELS

Jogya

The **Garuda Hotel** (Tel. (274) 86353) dates from the colonial era, and what remains of the older buildings is now the foyer. The first main extensions were built in the 1980s; the latest 120-room additions are planned to open in early 1991. All rooms are air-conditioned, have modern bathrooms, and a balcony. The Garuda Hotel is centrally located at Jalan Marlioboro 60, close to shops, restaurants, transportation, and many cultural attractions. Single rooms go for around $100 a night. In Indonesia, book through the Natour group. In North America book through Garuda Airlines or write direct to Hotel Garuda, Jalan Marlioboro 60, Jogyakarta, Indonesia. (Fax: (62) 274 4074).

Not far along Jalan Marlioboro, next to the tourist information office, is the **Mutiara Hotel** (Tel. (274) 4531, 5173), with some 140 centrally air-conditioned rooms, 24-hour room service, and a pool. The rooms and service are quite acceptable, as are the two bars and two restaurants. At night the disco in the basement gets going, or you can step out the door onto Jalan Marlioboro to find numerous cafes and restaurants. Single rooms at the Mutiara (meaning "pearl") are $60 a night; suites start at $100. Book through the Intan Group, Garuda Airlines, your travel agent, or write to the Hotel Mutiara, Jalan Marlioboro 18, Jogyakarta, Indonesia (Fax: (62) 21 87240).

A few miles out of town is the other group of moderately priced hotels. For many years the **Ambarrukmo Palace Hotel** (Tel. (274) 88488) reigned as Jogya's premier hotel, set in lush gardens and offering all the average tourist wanted in terms of room facilities. It has several bars and restaurants, a night club, tennis court, golf course, and a nightly cultural show. Nearby, there are a few restaurants or you can walk to the *Kota Baru* (new town) shopping area or catch a cab down to Jalan Marlioboro. Single rooms are under $100 a night, suites up to $300. In the U.S. you can book via Los Angeles (Tel. (213) 857 5551) or San Francisco (Tel. (415) 362 2540); Garuda Airlines; or direct at Ambarrukmo Palace Hotel, Jalan L. Adisucipto, Jogyakarta, Indonesia. (Fax: (62) 274 88933).

In the same general area on the Solo side of Jogya is the **Sahid Garden Hotel** (Tel. (272) 3697). It has cottages in six and a half acres of land, a 24-hour coffee shop and room service, pool, shopping arcade, and a free shuttle bus service into town. Room rates are similar to the Ambarrukmo. Book through the Sahid chain, Garuda Airlines, or write direct to the Sahid Garden Hotel, Jalan Babarsari, Tambakbayan, Jogyakarta, Indonesia.

Solo

The **Mangkunegaran Palace Hotel** (Tel. (271) 5683) is owned by His Highness, Prince Mangkunegoro and is situated adjacent to the walls of Solo's second palace, after which it is named. The hotel's 50 rooms are air-conditioned, with 24-hour room service, a pool, and coffee shop. Book through your travel agent or write direct to Mangkunegaran Palace Hotel, Istana Mangkunegaran, Solo, Indonesia.

Close by is the **Kusuma Sahid Prince Hotel** (Tel. (271) 6356, 7022). It is built around a former royal residence, which now forms the main entrance and foyer. This place dates from 1909 and is full of charm, with its teak beams and high ceilings. There are over 100 air-conditioned rooms with 24-hour room service, and a restaurant open from 6 A.M. to 11 P.M., a swimming pool, and a shopping arcade. Book through the Sahid Group, Garuda Airlines, or write direct to Kusuma Sahid Prince Hotel, Jalan Sugiyopranoto 22, Solo, Indonesia. Room rates for these Solo hotels are $60 for a single room and up to $100 for suites.

BUDGET-PRICED ROOMS

This group is quite acceptable for those who want to stay in *Jogya* in a Western-style hotel in the same areas as the better hotels already mentioned. Prices run about $35 to $50 a night for a single room. Comfortable accommodations at an even cheaper price can be found in the guesthouses along Jalan Prawirotaman, which is on the southern side of Jogya's *Kraton* (palace).

Of the hotels, the **Hotel Arjuna Plaza** (Tel. (274) 3063, 86862) is centrally located near the Garuda Hotel, a short walk over the railway tracks to Jalan Marlioboro. The Arjuna Plaza's rooms and suites are all air-conditioned, with hot showers, TV, and 24-hour room service. There are *wayang* cultural shows three nights a week held in the French Grill Restaurant. You can grab a snack or breakfast at the coffee shop. Book through Garuda Airlines or communicate directly at Hotel Arjuna Plaza, Jalan Mangkubumi 48, Jogyakarta, Indonesia.

Next door, at Jalan Mangkubumi 46, is the **Batik Palace Hotel** (Tel. (274) 2149), which offers similar services, as well as a swimming pool. Included in the *batik* Palace's rate is a Continental buffet breakfast and afternoon tea after you have returned from sightseeing.

Out of town near the Ambarrukmo Palace Hotel is **Puri Artha** (Tel. (274) 5934-5), which has Balinese-style bungalows combined with Dutch decor. These are all air-conditioned, with private shower and verandah. Book through Garuda or write direct to Puri Artha, Jalan Cendrawasih 9, Jogyakarta, Indonesia.

Also on that side of town at Jalan Sumoharjo 63 is the **Srimanganti Hotel** (Tel. (274) 2881). This hotel has Indonesian-style decor and a *gamelan* orchestra plays in the foyer from 7 P.M. to 10 P.M. each Saturday. There is also a bar and restaurant.

Jalan Prawirotaman is a pleasant, tree-lined suburban street on the southern side of Jogya close to the *Kraton* palace, *batik* factories, and other cultural sites. It is not within easy walking distance of Jalan Marlioboro, so a *becak* is the best way to get there. Jalan Prawirotaman also has some cafes and small restaurants, so you won't need to go too far to eat. All of the **guesthouses** recommended have a private bathroom. Some are cooled by air-conditioning, while others are cooled only by fan, which isn't very effective in a hot town like Jogya. Some also have a swimming pool. Four of the better ones, in alphabetical order, are: **Airlangga Guest House** (Tel. (274) 3344) at Jalan Prawirotaman 4; **Kirana Guest House** (Tel. (274) 3200) at Jalan Prawirotaman 30; **Sriwijaya Guest House** (Tel. (274) 2387) at Jalan Prawirotaman 7; and **Sumaryo Guest House** (Tel. (274) 2852) at Jalan Prawirotaman 18A.

If you don't mind roughing it, which means sharing an Indonesian-style bath and toilet, and no fan or hot water for $3 to 5$ a night, there are backpacker accommodations in the area near the Jogya railway station. The better of these are **Asia Africa Hotel** at Jalan Pasar Kembang 25; **Batik Palace Hotel** at Jalan Pasar Kembang 29; **Indonesia Hotel** at Jalan Sastrowijayan 9; or the **Blue Safir Hotel** at Jalan Dagen 34. As well as these, there are dozens of other places to stay of all grades in Jogya.

In *Solo*, budget accommodations are mainly in the Keprambon area near Jalan A. Dahlan, but most are Indonesian-style *losmen* with shared bathrooms and no hot water or fan for $2 to $3 a night. On Solo's main street, there is the reasonable **Cakra Hotel** (Tel. (271) 5847) at Jalan Slamat Rihyadi 171, which has rooms with air-conditioning and private bathroom for $20 a night. **The Westerners** (Tel. (271) 3196) is a budget homestay attached to the residence of Mr. Mawardi Moeslich at Jalan Kamlayan Kidul 11, which is a lane that runs off Jalan Yos Sudurso near the Batik Keris shop. Rooms here are very basic, and go for $2 a night. The attraction is the friendly atmosphere of the household, as well as their bicycles for rent (to guests only).

5. Restaurants and Dining

Jogya

Jogya has a good selection of places to eat that serve Western food, ranging from steakhouses and French grills to 24-hour coffee shops and ice-cream parlors. Asian food includes the Javanese specialties of fried chicken (*ayam goreng*) and *gudeg*, a combination of vegetables and meat served in buffet form. The better hotels, as usual, have coffee shops and Western and Asian restaurants. What I have listed here are Western, Javanese, Sumatran, and other Indonesian and Chinese eating houses. Main courses of Western meals average $2 to $5, and $1 to $3 for Asian. Jogya is recognized as one of the cheapest places to eat in Indonesia, and while the quality of the meals may vary, at least they are invariably wholesome.

The **Legian Restaurant** (Tel. (274) 87 9852) offers a mix of meals in a cool rooftop setting at Jalan Perwakilan 9 (corner Jalan Marlioboro). At Jalan Marlioboro 20 is the **Mira Steakhouse**. Other steakhouses are **Gita Buana** (Tel. (274) 4334) at Jalan Adisuapto 170 and **Sparta Steakhouse**, also on Jalan Adisuapto (kilometer 6). Nearby is a **Holland Bakery and Ice Cream** outlet. There are several of these through Java, something like coffee shops and all air-conditioned for a break from walking. In Jogya, other Holland Bakeries are at Jalan Sudirman 61 and in the Borobudur Plaza building on Jalan Magelang on the northwestern side

Home delivery noodles

Street vendor

of town. At Jalan Diponegoro 52, there is another **Gita Bujana** serving snacks and light meals. Farther along this strip at Jalan Urip Sumoharjo is the **One Plus One** coffee shop that stays open till 2 A.M. **Kentucky Fried Chicken** is at Jalan Adisucipto 165. Note that Diponegoro, Sudirman, Urip Sumoharjo, and Adisucipto are names applied to different sections of the same street. At the other end of town along Jalan Prawirotaman are the **Riki French Grill** at number 31, the **Hanoman Garden Restaurant** at number 9, the **Palm House** at number 56, and **Restaurant Gajah** at number 4.

Near the railway station on Gang Sastrowijayan I is the backpackers' favorite, **Superman's**.

INDONESIAN

As mentioned, Javanese fried chicken gives the Kentucky and Texas versions a run for their money. The best on Jogya is **Ayam Goreng Nyonya Sukardi** on Jalan Adisucipto (kilometer 7). Near the railway station on Jalan Pasar Kembang is **Ayam Goreng Pemuda**. **Mama Supribatin** opens an evening outdoor stall serving fried chicken on Jalan Pasar Kembang near the railway station. The other Javanese specialty is *gudeg* served at **Pak Wongso** on the corner of Jalan Marlioboro and Jalan Garuda. **Bu Titro** serves *gudeg* at Jalan Adisucipto near the 9 kikometer post.

Sumatran *Padang* food is very spicy, with liberal amounts of chili pieces. You are charged according to the number of small bowls that you eat from. Each dish is in a separate bowl, sometimes numbering up to twenty. **Bagindo** and **Mangkubumi** are next door to each other at Jalan Urip Sumoharjo 80, and serve good *Padang*. Heading towards the Ambarrukmo Palace Hotel are **A.C.C.** at Jalan Adisucipto 59 and **Ayan** at Jalan Adisucipto 178. For a selection of very basic Indonesian restaurants, go to Jalan Mangkubumi for **R.M. Rene** at number 57, **R.M. Sederhana** at number 61A, and **Warung Barjo Ronde** at number 61B.

Each evening, street-side food stalls serving Javanese specialties such as *gudeg, burung dada* (quail), *kepiting/kerang* (crabs and mussels), and *susu segar* (fresh, hot milk) are on Jalan Marlioboro near the Tourist Information Office. Stalls serving similar food are on Jalan Sudirman outside the Bethesda Hospital.

CHINESE

These restaurants serve the common mix of Chinese, seafood, and European dishes in clean surroundings. Their cheap prices make them a favorite of budget travelers. Most are concentrated on Jalan Marlioboro and Jalan Magelang near the Borobudur Plaza. Very popular are the

Colombo at Jalan Marlioboro 25, **Helen** at number 44, and **Shinta** at number 57. On Jalan Magelang these restaurants cater more to the locals, as there are no hotels nearby. Try **Sintawan, Warung Anda** and **Valentino.**

Solo

In Solo, the safest places to eat are the restaurant or coffee shop at the Mangkunegaran Palace Hotel and the Kusuma Sahid Hotel. There is also a group of restaurants serving Indonesian food, Chinese food, and fresh fruit on Jalan Diponegoro near the Pasar Triwindu flea market. Three miles (5 kilometers) out of town to the west (past the Sriwedari arts center) is **Ayam Goreng Matukoro**, serving Javanese fried chicken. Two Sumatran *Padang* restaurants are on Jalan S. Rihyadi. **R.M. Setia** is at number 96, and **R.M. Intan** is at number 160. In the evenings, there are *sate* (meat skewers) stalls on Jalan Yos Sudurso.

6. Sightseeing

Most visitors to Central Java use Jogyakarta (Jogya) as their base and from there visit Solo, Dieng and Parangtritis and the temples spread out across the Prambanan Plain such as Borobudur, Prambanan and Kalasan. Because there is so much to see and do in Central Java, I have divided sightseeing into four parts: 1) around town in Jogya; 2) around town in Solo; 3) temples and monuments out of town; and 4) side trips to the mountains or the beach.

AROUND JOGYA

The **Sultan's Palace (Kraton)** is the traditional center of this town; in fact the town grew up around the *Kraton*. Built in 1755 by Sultan Hamengkubuwono I, the main rendered (covered with a smooth cement mix) brick walls are each over half a mile in length. Inside there are many open-sided pavilions called *pendopo*, as well as private quarters for wives and children. Public entry to the *Kraton* is via Jalan Polowijayan on its western side from 9 A.M. to 1:30 P.M. daily, except on Friday, when it closes at 11 A.M.. Inside there is also a museum with many pieces from the *Kraton*, as well as pieces left by the Dutch. The former main entrance faces the town square (*alun-alun*), but this part of the *Kraton* is now associated with the local university.

Taman Sari Water Castle was once the pleasure garden of the sultan, sitting adjacent to the *Kraton*. Sultan Hamengkubuwono I built Taman Sari a few years after finishing the *Kraton* proper. Much of it is now in ruins and inhabited by locals and *batik* painting galleries, but when exploring its tunnels, pools, and towers you can easily imagine the serenity

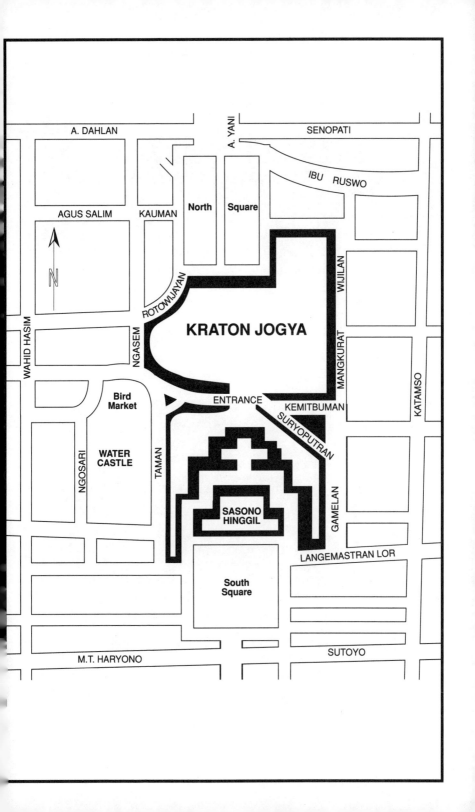

Borobudur

Temple wall motif

and beauty that existed. Taman Sari is also entered from Jalan Polowid-jayan, not far past the public entrance to the *Kraton*.

Bird Market (*pasar burung*) is on Jalan Ngasem, which is on the same side of the *Kraton* as the public entrance. Here are hundreds of beautiful birds in hanging cane cages and, while you won't be able to take a bird back home, you can take a cage.

Art Museum Sono Budoyo faces the main square on Jalan Alun-Alun Utara. As you enter the square from Jalan Marlioboro, turn to the right and it's fifty yards on your right.

The busiest part of town is **Jalan Marlioboro**, which runs (one way) away from the railway line and the Garuda Hotel, past the Mutiara Hotel and the tourist information office to the traditional main market, Pasar Beringharjo. At this point it changes its name to Jalan Ahmed Yani. On the right is the Dutch garrison built in 1765—**Fort Vreeburg**. Now a historical museum, it is open to the public on Saturdays and Sundays from 2 P.M. to 5 P.M. This foothold within the Sultan's domain contributed a great deal to securing the Dutch position and the suppression of many Jogyakarta rebels against colonial rule.

Next door is **Gedung Agung** (literally "state guesthouse"), a colonial mansion started in 1823 and finished 30 years later. It was the presidential palace from 1948 to 1950, during the war for independence. Set in expansive gardens, it's not open to the public. Another hundred yards on you will come to a main intersection with the original "Javasche Bank," built in 1914, on the right and the post office, built in 1910, on the left. Continue straight through the intersection between these buildings and you come to the main square (Alun-Alun Utara), an integral part of the *Kraton* complex, with its two mystical banyan trees. To get to the public entrance to the *Kraton* palace from Jalan Marlioboro, turn right at the General Post Office and bank into Jalan A. Dahlan. Two to three hundred yards farther on take a left into Jalan Ngasem. At the market turn left and you come to the entrance. To the right is the road leading into the Taman Sari water castle.

Back at the General Post Office, if you turn left (not straight to the square), and continue for some three hundred yards to Jalan Sultan Agung you come to the **G.K.B.I.** *Batik* **Research and Development Institute**, which is open to the public. Here there are displays on how *batik* manufacture has evolved and the many ways that it can now be produced. Also on the left side of Jalan Sultan Agung is the second palace of Jogya, **Puro Pukualaman**. The Pakualam Principality was established in 1813 by Sir Stamford Raffles, then governor of Java. It was hoped that this would add stability to a turbulent period of the royal court. The original palace was destroyed by earthquake in 1867 and restored a year

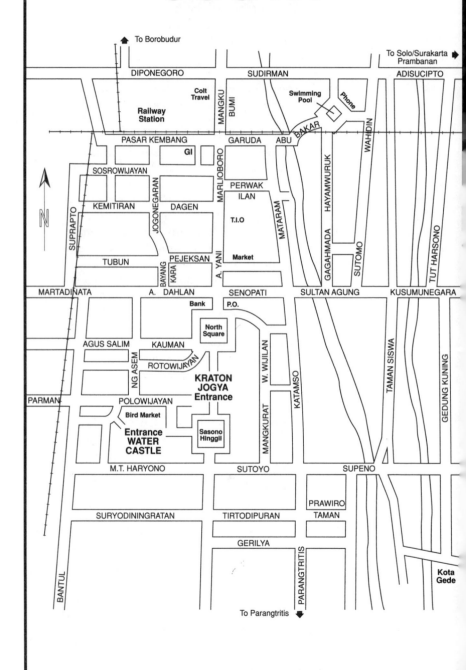

Candi Mendut Temple

later. The palace is not open to the public, but dance rehearsals by members of the royal family are held on Thursday evenings from 6:30 P.M. to 8:30 P.M.

From the G.K.B.I. *Batik* Institute, head for **Jalan Tirtodipuran** on the southern side of the *Kraton* to visit **traditional *batik* factories** that follow the production techniques of the last century.

AROUND SOLO

Solo (Surakarta) has much to offer the visitor in terms of architecture and the Arts. For me the attraction of Solo is that it is largely unaffected by the pressures of tourism, unlike Jogya.

The **Susunan's Palace** (*Kraton Hardiningrat*), of similar dimensions to *Kraton Jogya*, was built in 1750 by King Pakubuwono II. Later kings added the gate, tower, and mosque. As you enter the Alun-Alun northern square off Jalan Slamat Rihyadi or Jalan Coyudan, you come to the high-walled security entrance which funnels visitors towards the main entrance. In the old days, unwelcome visitors would have been attacked and repelled here before the impressive gates that now stand open. Inside the gates, you come to an open area the size of a small parking lot. Directly in front of you is the private entrance of the Susunan (Sultan). On your right is the **Sasono Mulyo** dance school, run by the palace and featuring many descendants of the royal family as well as talented commoners. The public is allowed to enter this compound and watch students rehearse in the open-sided building (*pendopo*).

As you pass through the main gates, if you turn to the left you will come to the **Kraton Museum and Art Gallery.** Exhibits include carriages, official regalia, portraits of former rulers, and archaeological finds. It was established in 1963 by the present Susunan Pakubuwono XII, and is open from 9 A.M. to 12:30 P.M. daily, except on Fridays. Another museum in Solo is the **Museum Radyapusaka** on Jalan Slamat Rihyadi, next to the Sriwedari entertainment complex on the western side of town.

Solo, like Jogya, has a major palace and a minor palace within the town proper. The **Pura Mangkunegaran** (or **Istana Mangkunegaran**) royal complex offers much to visitors, in that the inner sanctum (the *Dalem*) is open to the public. Here the *Dalem* has been turned into a museum "in situ," with glass cabinets displaying gold and bronze articles from the Hindu, Majapahit, and Mataram periods. This is a very highly regarded collection of archaeological pieces, put together by the late Mangkunegoro VII.

In front of the main building is the *pendopo*, an open-sided, raised platform measuring some 200 feet by 170 feet. Supporting the roof are

The Kraton Solo's south square

teak pillars over thirty feet high. The center of the ceiling was painted in 1937, inspired by traditional Javanese themes. The *gamelan* orchestra (xylophones and gongs) which is permanently placed on the *pendopo* comes to life each Wednesday to accompany traditional dance classes. Puro Mangkunegaran is entered via Jalan Kartini, and note that traffic flows around the walls of the palace in a clock-wise direction.

Markets in Solo are interesting places to visit, even if you don't plan to do any shopping. The wholesale *batik* market, **Pasar Klewer**, adjoins the main square on Jalan Coyudan; though being wholesale, it's not the best place to buy *batik* for yourself. **Pasar Gede**, the central market, is on Jalan Urip Sumoharjo. A very high roof with lots of glass keeps this market lighted and cooled, an unusual feat in this part of the world.

The side streets around Pasar Gede are Solo's **Chinatown**, an area of rice traders and clothing merchants and pot-holed streets. Another market is **Pasar Triwindu** antique market off Jalan Diponegoro. While many of the articles are newly made Dutch and Javanese "antiques," you can find original Dutch porcelain, old coins, hanging lamps, and *kris* daggers.

TEMPLES AND MONUMENTS

In recent years, many of the temples of Java have been fenced off to prevent vandalism and theft. Although this may detract from the setting, it has been necessary in a land where such temples no longer play a role in the people's normal religious life, and so are largely ignored. Fortunately, the value of these monuments and their art is now appreciated by the Indonesian government, and throughout Java restoration works are in progress. With continued cooperation between the Indonesians and the foreign agencies concerned, many more of the Hindu-Buddhist temples may rise out of the rice fields of Java.

Borobudur, 25 miles (40 kilometers) from Jogya near the town of Muntilan, is one of the world's greatest Buddhist monuments. Built in the early to mid-ninth century A.D. by the Sailendra Dynasty, pyramid-shaped Candi Borobudur is made up of terraces with statues and engraved reliefs that portray the life of the Buddha. To follow the story, start at the bottom and circle the temple in a clock-wise direction, approaching the summit one terrace at a time.

During the 1980s Candi Borobudur (*candi* means "temple") underwent a total restoration whereby every stone was given a computer number as it was taken apart. The central mound of earth, which the monument was originally constructed around, was encased in concrete and terraces were made on which the whole complex was reassembled, block by block. I went to Borobudur in 1983 during the restoration and in

SOLO

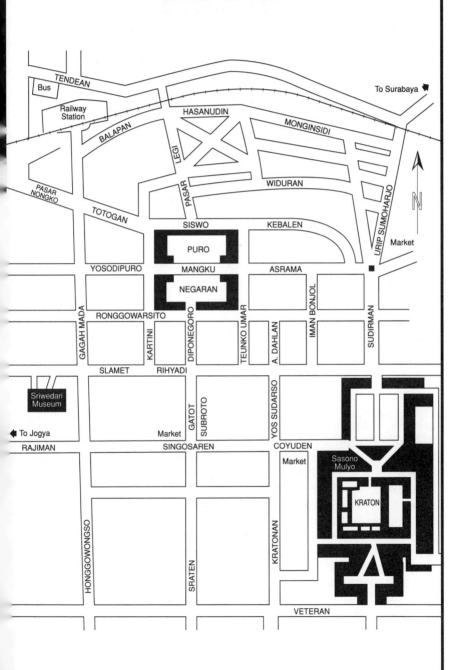

1987 after it had been completed. The United Nations body U.N.E.S.C.O. and the Indonesian government should be commended on the success of this project.

Borobudur's surroundings have also been improved, and are now more befitting such a grand monument. Prior to restoration, stalls and hawkers congregated at the base. Now the whole area has been cleared and replaced with landscaped gardens.

The Borobudur Study Centre opened in 1988. The monument itself is open every day from 6 A.M. to 6 P.M., except on public holidays.

Actually, this was not Borobudur's only restoration project. In 1815, Raffles visited the site and ordered that it be cleared of undergrowth and fully surveyed. Then, in 1907, Dr. Th. van Erp started on a massive 5-year restoration project. During this project it was found that Borobudur was built around a small hill. The problem was that rainwater seeped into the hill and the soil was shifting, pushing the terraces and walls out of line. The situation slowly deteriorated until it reached the stage that unless it was taken apart piece by piece and reassembled, the whole hill and temple would explode and be destroyed. Fortunately, that was avoided and the second restoration took place. All that the temple needs now is a few more rainy seasons and a growth of moss and lichen to look old again.

Within 2 miles (3 kilometers) of Borobudur are **Candi Pawon** and **Candi Mendut**, sister temples of Borobudur and built around the same time in the early ninth century. A beautifully relaxing way to travel between the three temples is by *becak*. From the bus terminal and parking lot, negotiate a return trip fare of around Rp6,000, or Rp4,000 for a one-way fare. From Mendut you can catch a local bus to Muntilan and another to Jogya.

Candi Pawon is a stupa (a stone monument some 20-30 feet high dedicated to an Indian god) one half mile (1 kilometer) from Borobudur. It is in a quiet, cool location off the main road. From Pawon you cross the Progo River over a Dutch-era bridge. In the wet season the water level can reach the road.

Another mile (2 kilometers) towards Muntilan is **Candi Mendut**. There is a Buddhist monastery opposite the temple, and inside Mendut is a 10-foot-high stone statue of the Buddha teaching two disciples of a similar size. Each year on the full moon in May, Javanese Buddhists conduct ceremonies here.

One hundred yards before Mendut is the Elo River. If you want to cool off, there is a swimming pool at the junction of the Mendut and the Borobudur/Muntilan road called Kolam Renang Taman Mendut.

In the **Prambanan complex**, the towering **Loro Jonggrang temple** stretches some 150 feet high. It was built by the Sanjaya Dynasty during the late ninth century A.D., and is dedicated to their Hindu god, Shiva. The main temple is located in the inner courtyard and is surrounded by several smaller temples in the outer courtyard. The temples are open from 6 A.M. to 6 P.M. daily, except on public holidays. As a result of recent restoration work, temples devoted to Brahma and Visnu reach skyward again next to the main temple. The main Prambanan temple provides the backdrop for open-air performances of the *Ramayana* dance-drama each year between May and October, during the dry season. For four nights each month at the time of the full moon, the *Ramayana* stories are played out again. One year I joined a busload of dancers from Kraton Solo on its way to Prambanan for a *Ramayana* performance. At the time I was staying at the prince's quarters in Solo and was able to join in many of their activities, so I feel that I can recommend the magic of this place to you with some authority.

The Prambanan complex also includes other, mainly Buddhist temples in the vicinity, such as **Kalasan, Sari, Sewu**, and **Plaosan**, as well as **King Boko's Palace** and **Sambi Sari temple**. These and other temples were damaged by the eruption of Mt. Merapi in A.D. 1006. Some temples collapsed, while others were covered in ash and other volcanic debris. All have undergone restoration work to varying degrees and this work is continuing. Generally speaking, these other temples don't have set opening times, though you may need to pay a donation to a restoration project via a caretaker.

In order of appearance when coming from Jogya along the Solo road, the Prambanan complex is made up of the following *candi*, or temples:

Candi Sambi Sari is 8 miles (12 kilometers) east of Jogya on the north (left) side of the main road. This is the only temple in the area which is set lower than the surrounding ground, probably due to build-up of volcanic material from Mt. Merapi and Mt. Merbabu.

Candi Kalasan is some 10 miles (16 kilometers) east of Jogya on the southern (right) side of the main road. This Buddhist temple was built in honor of a marriage between King Prancapana of the Sanjaya dynasty and a princess of the Sailendra dynasty. It has many finely carved lion heads and stands some 75 feet (24 meters) high, in the form of a Greek cross. The top of this impressive structure is made up of octagonal prisms, with stupas on the corners. Kalasan is dated A.D. 778, and forms a point of reference for dating the other Buddhist monuments.

Candi Sari is situated 600 yards northeast of Kalasan on the northern (left) side of the main road. Built at about the same time as Candi Kalasan, Candi Sari has three distinct vertical sections, each of which was formerly divided into upper and lower sections by wooden floorboards.

Even after a restoration in 1929-30, Sari is still in rather poor condition. Nonetheless, this former Buddhist sanctuary (*vihara*) is well worth visiting.

Candi Sewu is several hundred yards northeast of the main Prambanan temple. Sewu, an extensive Buddhist temple that once included 250 smaller temples, was probably built a bit later than Kalasan.

Candi Plaosan is another Buddhist temple one half mile (1 kilometer) east of Candi Sewu, consisting of two main temples standing side by side on terrace bases. The reliefs carved on the southern main temple depict man, on the northern, woman. The slender stupa is called its "Perwara" temple.

King Boko's Palace has beautiful views of Mt. Merapi and across to Candi Prambanan and Kalasan. Remains include the bathing pool for the princesses and the entrance to the auditorium. The palace is over a mile (2 kilometers) to the south of Prambanan so you would best be driven along the rough track.

Candi Banyu Nibo, dating from the twelfth century and with a curved roof and a stupa on top, is set in the fields an easy mile (2 kilometers) southeast of King Boko's Palace. Nearby is an anachronistic satellite earth station for Palapa.

Outside of Solo is a temple unlike other Hindu-Buddhist ruins in Central Java. It looks more like a Central American Mayan temple. **Candi Sukuh**, near the hill resort of Tawangmangu, is on the slopes of Mt. Lawu at an altitude of 2,900 feet. Candi Sukuh was closely linked with ancestor worship, an important belief in pre-Hindu Buddhist Java. As the Javanese often did, this ancestor worship was blended together with Hinduism.

There are reliefs of Garuda, the eagle and mythical carrier of Visnu; the king of birds, who was owned by Visnu; Durga; Bima; Semar; and other characters that are common in the *wayang* stories. The courtyard of Candi Sukuh consists of three terraces. Formerly, a person wishing to reach the *candi* had to climb many stairs from the plain to the shrine's courtyard. To enter the terrace you go through the *gapura*, or archway, which looks a bit Egyptian or Mexican when viewed from below. On the right and left of the entrance are reliefs that refer to the date of constructions, A.D. 1437, near the end of the Hindu-Buddhist period on Java. The temple is over a mile from the Solo to Tawangmangu road, 19 miles (30 kilometers) from Solo, so you would be best going with your own car and driver. Allow 3-4 hours for the return trip to Candi Sukuh and Tawangmangu.

The monuments on the **Dieng plateau**, a 6,000-foot-high valley, are among the oldest in Java. Inscriptions on these temples devoted to Shiva (which some say was a God-king cult) date from A.D. 809. Mist-shrouded Dieng has eight intact temples, namely the Arjuna group of **Arjuna, Semar, Srikando, Puntadewa**, and **Sembadra**, as well as **Bima, Darawati**, and **Gatotkaca**. Most of them are rather small buildings where the ruler or priest entered to commune with, or in fact become, God. The Dieng valley is around a mile long and half a mile wide at the northern end.

Candi Arjuna has a base 20 feet square with a projection to the west which supports a cubic body and a porch. The entrances and niches have *kala*-head (monster) carvings. The roof has three levels.

Candi Puntadewa is a little smaller than Arjuna, which has the most refined decorative engravings on Dieng. **Candi Bima** is a rectangular-shaped temple at the southern end of the plateau. The Dieng plateau has many other things to interest the visitor, such as geysers and colored lakes. There is budget-class accommodation at Dieng, but be sure that you are given lots of blankets and have warm clothing with you if you plan to stay the night. It can get icy cold.

Getting to Dieng by car or public transport, you will first need to go to Magelang, then to Wonosobo, before starting the climb to Dieng. The bus fare from Jogya to Wonosobo costs Rp1,200 and the connection to Dieng by old *opelet* wagon costs Rp800 each way. At *Wonosobo* you can eat at the **Dieng Restaurant** (Tel. (293) 266) on Jalan Kawedanan 29. In *Magelang*, the **Bhima Hotel** (Tel. (293) 233) at Jalan Achmed Yani has a restaurant and moderately priced rooms. The **City Hotel** (Tel. (293) 3347-8) at Jalan Daha 23 (formerly Jalan Tengkon), Magelang also has comfortable rooms and a restaurant.

OTHER PLACES TO VISIT

Apart from ancient stone monuments, Central Java also has its fair share of natural beauty spots, such as Parangtritis Beach on the south coast; the Mt. Merapi, Kaliurang, and Kopeng hill resorts in the mountain range, as well as Semarang and the other north coast towns. **Parangtritis** is the most mysterious of all the beaches on the south coast of Java. Legend has it that there is, or was, a tunnel leading from the Taman Sari Water Castle at Jogyakarta to a cave on the headland. After long meditation, the sultan traveled down the tunnel to meet the goddess of the South Seas, Nyai Loro Kidul. The tower at Kraton Solo is also to communicate with the goddess. She loves men in green, so don't wear green in or near the water, otherwise she may take you under.

There are hot springs half a mile (1 kilometer) before Parangtritis at the 27 kilometer post. Look for the sign *permandian* and wander around the **old baths**. The turbulent seas and the massive **sandhills** are the main attractions of Parangtritis these days. I recommend strongly against swimming in the sea, due to the strong and dangerous rip currents.

There is a **swimming pool** at Penginapan Parangdog, 200 yards past the 28 kilometer post. Leading from the bus stop at the 28 kilometer post towards the beach is a line of cafes and restaurants. These serve cool drinks, beer, and basic Indonesian meals. The only accommodation at Parangtritis is budget class. One of the best places to stay is **Penginapan Parangdog**, which has the swimming pool already mentioned.

There are two roads leading to Parangtritis from Jogya. One leaves town via Jalan Supeno and Jalan Pramuka, past the bus terminal and Kota Gede. On the way is the turnoff to Imogiri Royal Cemetery. This road goes into the center of Parangtritis to the 28 kilometer post. The other road leaves Jogya to the due south, along Jalan Parangtritis past the Jalan Prawirotaman accommodations area. The signs point to Kretek. The problem with this route is that the road stops on the wrong side of the river, so you need to ford the river on foot or by raft, and then walk over a mile (2 kilometers) to the center of Parangtritis.

Public transportation may be easier this way, as a minibus leaves from outside the post office, but the final leg is a bit strenuous. To get there by the first route, you need to get to the bus terminal on Jalan Supeno for the bus that goes direct to Parangtritis.

Imogiri Royal Cemetery is off this road, 12 miles (20 kilometers) from Jogya. Most of the former rulers of the palaces of Jogya and Solo are buried here. To get to the tombs from the road you need to climb 345 stone steps. A special time when people from all over Java come to Imogiri is the night of Thursday/*Kliwon*. (This is a combination of the Western and Javanese calendars.) Many Javanese believe that if you spend this night by the graves of powerful people you may be able to pick up some of their power.

The concept of power is very important to the Javanese. Those who have it are expected to use it. Those who don't have it respect those who use it wisely. The cemetery is open every day, but the buildings are only open on certain days. To enter these buildings you need to wear special Javanese clothing which is available for rental at the site.

Hill resorts offer a welcome change from the heat of the plains. The most popular ones in Central Java are Kaliurang and Kopeng. **Kaliurang** is 17 miles (27 kilometers) due north of Jogya on the slopes of Mt. Merapi. The peak of this active volcano can be seen in the early mornings, and even the Indian Ocean is visible in the distance on a clear day. Kaliurang has cottages for overnight accommodations and recreational facilities such as swimming pools and tennis courts. **Kopeng** is reached via the town of Salatiga, which is between Solo and Semarang. Salatiga itself is quite cool, but Kopeng, 14 kilometers to the west on the slopes of Mt. Merbabu, is some 4,600 feet (1,450 meters) above sea level, so you may need warm clothing in the evenings. For daytime leisure, there is a swimming pool, horseback riding, hiking along mountain trails, and tennis courts. There are plenty of cottages and restaurants for the visitor.

Semarang, on the northern Java Sea coastline, is the third large town (city) in Central Java, and is in fact the provincial capital. Its location away from the courts of Jogya and Solo, its sheltered port, and its easy access to Jakarta and Surabaya along the north coast road made it the preferred center of administration and trade. Semarang is thought to be the first place that Chinese landed in Java. Sam Po, an emissary from the Ming Court, came here in 1406 and 1416. The **Sam Po Temple** and cave, also known as Gedung Batu, is dedicated to his memory. To get to the Sam Po Temple, take the western road towards Kendal (Jalan Salaman over the bridge), and continue for a little over a mile (2 kilometers) to the large red and yellow building.

In town on Gang Lombok, which is off Jalan Pekojan, is the **Klinting Temple**, Semarang's largest. This beautiful temple with carved teak beams and a high ceiling was built in 1772. Many of Indonesia's wealthiest Chinese families trace their roots back to Semarang. Unfortunately, there are few Chinese houses left that still have their original ornate street frontages. Most were demolished during a "road-widening" program in the 1970s. Inside, however, solid teak beams and staircases are indicators of their former majesty.

In the streets around the bus terminal there are old Dutch warehouses. The provincial government building and the Christian church (1753) also date from colonial times.

Outside of downtown Semarang, heading southwards towards Ambarawa and Solo, is the cool, tree-lined suburb of Candi Baru. If you want to stay in Semarang, try the **Patra Jasa Hotel** (Tel. (24) 31 4441), which is perched on the side of the cliff overlooking the main business area and the Java Sea. The complex has restaurants, a coffee shop, a golf course, tennis courts, and a shopping arcade. The address is Jalan Sisingamangaraja, Semarang. (Fax: (62) (24) 31 4448).

Another hotel, this one in the downtown area opposite the central square, is the **Metro Grand Park Hotel** (Tel. (24) 27371). There are a number of mainly Chinese restaurants, a coffee shop, disco, and department store next door. The Metro Hotel is on Jalan Agus Salim 2-4, Semarang. (Fax: (62) (24) 28 9335).

7. Guided Tours and Going It Alone

Jogya has dozens of travel agents and tour operators to take you around the sights of Jogya, Solo, and the rest of Central Java. Most of the larger hotels, such as the Ambarrukmo, Garuda, and Mutiara, have travel agents on the premises. The Ambarrukmo alone has at least ten agents with offices there. Jogya's travel agents are usually open from 8 A.M. to 4 P.M. Monday to Friday; from 8 A.M. to 1 P.M. on Saturdays; but are closed on Sundays and public holidays. Downtown agents are **Intan Pelangi** (Biru) (Tel. (274) 4531, 62985) at Jalan Marlioboro outside the Mutiara Hotel, **Vista Express** (Tel. (274) 61353) at Jalan Marlioboro 72 on the ground floor of the Garuda Hotel; **Intrus Tour** (Tel. (274) 3611, 86972) at Jalan Marlioboro 177/183, and **Pacto** (Tel. (274) 2740) at Jalan Mangkubumi 51.

For the travel agents who have offices at the Ambarrukmo Palace Hotel, dial the hotel phone number ((274) 88488) and ask for the respective extension number. Some national tour operators and their extensions are: **Natrabu** (ext. 705), **Nitour** (ext. 137), **Pacto** (ext. 703), **Tunas Indonesia** (ext. 744), and **Vaya Tour** (ext. 121).

Going it alone is also possible, whether by *becak* around town and between some of the temples or taxi to the sights around Jogya and in the surrounding countryside. There are also buses and *colt* minibuses to the smaller towns and into the mountains. For more information see the section on local transportation.

8. Water Sports

Central Java is not an area noted for its water sports. The popular beach of Parangtritis on the south coast near Jogya is too dangerous for swimming. The northern coastline is muddy tidal flats, and there are no large lakes. That leaves **swimming pools**, which are situated in the grounds of the better hotels in each area. In *Jogya* the best pools open to the public are at the Ambarrukmo Palace Hotel (Tel. (274) 88488) and Sriwedari Hotel (Tel. (274) 2149) on Jalan Adisucipto; the New Batik Palace Hotel (Tel. (274) 2149) at Jalan Mangkubumi 46, and the Hotel Mutiara (Tel. (274) 3272) at Jalan Marlioboro 18. Most of the guesthouses on Jalan Prawirotaman are open to the public. Entry fees at the pools average $2 to $5 per person.

In *Solo*, the Kusuma Sahid Prince Hotel (Tel. (271) 6356, 7022) has a pool, as does the Mangkunegaran Palace Hotel (Tel. (271) 5683). Farther afield the hill resorts of **Kaliurang**, 17 miles north of Jogya, and **Kopeng**, which is some 65 miles north of Jogya via Solo and Salatiga, have outdoor swimming pools, kiosks, and extensive landscaped gardens that are just great for a picnic. Overlooking the north coast town of **Semarang**, some 70 miles from Jogya via Malegalang, is the Patra Jasa Hotel (Tel. (24) 314441), which has a more modest swimming pool.

9. Other Sports

There is about as much choice in this section as the last. Apart from **bushwalking** at Kaliurang, you can play **tennis** at the Ambarrukmo Palace Hotel (Tel. 9274 88488). You need to make your reservation one day in advance and take your own rackets and balls. The hotel also has a **golf course** which is well tended. Near the airport is the **Adisucipto Air Force Base Golf Course**, open from 6 A.M. to 6 P.M. To get to the clubhouse from the airport follow the road to the east from the civil air terminal.

Bicycling enthusiasts can rent gearless cycles at Jogya for sightseeing around town. Daily rental is under $1 from two budget hotels on Jalan Sastrowijayan, the Asiatic Hotel at number 14 and the Indonesia Hotel at number 9. Before setting out, make sure that the brakes and bell work properly.

10. Shopping

Batik is unquestionably your best buy in Central Java. For *batik* cloth there are many shops selling 10-foot lengths of *kain batik* on Jalan Ahmed Yani near Jogya's main market. This street is in fact an extension of Jalan Marlioboro. There shops also sell *batik* cloth made into clothing, especially shirts. For traditional *batik* cloth "(*kain batik*), try the Pasar Beringharjo market itself or the ladies near the entrance to Kraton Jogya Palace on Jalan Polowijayan. While these ladies (*Ibu*) who stack their *batik* under the shady trees like to charge tourists exhorbitant prices, you can also play one off against the other. If there are no other Western or local tourists around at the time, you can pick up good pieces for a reasonable price. Just devote an hour to sifting through the different patterns. The longer you take the lower the price you'll pay and what you get will probably be of better quality.

Most *batik* vendors tend to offer you poor-quality pieces first so they can make a good price. Try to hold the price while asking about *halus* (fine) pieces. The opposite of *halus* is *kasar*, meaning rough. This is a good bargaining ploy, whatever you're buying. Another place to look for *batik* cloth is the cottage industry *batik* factories on Jalan Tirtodipuran to the south of the Kraton palace.

Batik **painting** uses similar techniques of applying hot wax and immersing in dye, but with less geometric designs. Favorite subjects for *batik*

Jalan Marlioboro Street, Jogya

painting are the characters from the *wayang* and *Ramayana*, birds, landscapes, and abstract themes. The best place to buy *batik* paintings in Jogya is the Taman Sari Water Castle, where many artists work from the homes set among the ruins of a former sultan's pleasure gardens. For better quality *batik* paintings, try the more upmarket galleries and boutiques that are in the streets outside of the Water Palace, especially Jalan Ngasem and Jalan Ngosari. There are also studios down most lanes that lead off these two streets.

Solo, 65 kilometers from Jogya, is another good place to buy *batik cloth*, but only if you're going there already. Pasar Klewer is a major wholesale *batik* market on Jalan Coyudan, and the Pasar Gede central market also has a good range. Solo is the headquarters of some of Indonesia's largest *batik* companies, such as Batik Keris, Batik Semar, and Batik Danar Hadi. When buying shirts or linen stick to these brands and you can be sure of the quality. In Solo, **Batik Danar Hadi** is at Jalan Slamet Rihyadi 91 and Jalan Rajiman 8. **Batik Keris** is at Jalan Yos Sudarso 37 and **Batik Semar** is at Jalan Slamet Rihyadi 76 and Jalan Pasar Nongko 132.

Most of the best **silverworks** are located in the suburb of Kota Gede (big town), about 3 miles (5 kilometers) to the southeast of Jogya past the main bus terminal. Workshops are in the rear section and showrooms in the front, so you can buy direct after watching the craftsmen at work. Rings and other jewelry, filigree silver, and handicrafts are all made at Kota Gede. **Tom's Silver** (Tel. (274) 3070, 2818) at Jalan Kota Gede 3/1A and **M.D. Silverworks** (Tel. (274) 2063) at Keboan, Kota Gede are two long-established silverworks, M.D. being founded in 1936. Another is **Sri Moelj Silver** (Tel. (274) 88042) on Jalan Menteri Supeno.

For **antiques and souvenirs**, in *Jogya* the Jalan Marlioboro night market starts setting up along the sidewalk each afternoon. There you can pick up all sorts of **bronze statues** depicting Indian gods and *wayang kulit* figures, as well as the usual *batik* cloth and paintings. You can also buy small brass statues at Borobudur or Prambanan. Most of the pieces for sale are newly made and some are especially rough, but you can be lucky. In 1987 I found a 2-foot-high ornately carved bronze figure of Shiva being sold by a Javanese merchant. The smalltown people who had owned it had no further need for a Hindu god in a nominally Muslim province, so they put it up for sale. This is a typical pattern—you never know when you may come across an original piece. Just buy it when you have the chance, as tomorrow it may be gone. **Copper batik stamps** that were used to make "*cap*" (stamped) *batik* are also for sale . Measuring about eight inches square, they are used until their edges are burred. You can pick them up for a few thousand rupiah.

Solo has its own fair share of interesting pieces coming out of the woodwork, especially at **Pasar Triwindu** flea market. This market is tucked away down the lane off Jalan Diponegoro between Puro Mangkunegaroa palace and Jalan Slamet Rihyadi. There are stalls specializing in mystical Javanese **kris knives, Dutch ceramics and tiles, statues, hanging lamps,** and glass cabinets full of knickknacks. Close to 75 percent of the wares sold are newly made, but they're still worth taking home. There are some small shops and stalls along Jalan Singosaren that sell **Javanese ceramics.** Bigger stores are the **Bali Art Shop** inside the Sriwidari Arts Complex on Jalan Slamet Rihyadi and **Parto Art Shop** on Jalan Slamet Rihyadi opposite Hotel Kota. Another is on Jalan Urip Sumoharjo near the Agung Express bus office. For **brassware** try Pak Suliman at Jalan Dr. Wahidin 4. Solo's central market Pasar Gede and some of the surrounding small shops also should not be overlooked as sources of interesting pieces.

Jogya is a major center for tanning **leather** and turning it into bags and wallets, as well as *wayang kulit* figures. Most of the leather shops are near the railway station along Jalan Pasar Kembang and Jalan S. Parman. Stock from these shops also goes down to sidewalk stalls along Jalan Marlioboro for the night market.

Shops selling good-quality, copyright-approved **audiocassette tapes** are on Jalan Marlioboro, namely **Podomora** at number 30, **Sampurna** at number 43, and **Kota Mas** at number 187. **Setia Budi** at number 598 specializes in traditional *gamelan* and dance music. Jogya and Solo *gamelan* music is the most rhythmical and slow. Some *gamelan* is accompanied by singing and Javanese flute.

Shops and department stores on Jalan Urip Sumoharjo (formerly Jalan Solo) sell all kinds of imported goods, toiletries, photographic supplies, batteries, and most other things you may need. Or you can try Jalan Marlioboro, which has just about everything.

The wide thoroughfare known as Jalan Marlioboro is the most interesting place to go shopping, especially in the early evening around 7 P.M. All the shops have reopened after closing for an afternoon siesta and the locals and visitors alike are out in force. Heading slightly downhill towards the *Kraton* palace, there are sidewalk stalls selling clothing, leather, and other cheap souvenirs along its whole length from the railway line past the Garuda and Mutiara Hotels to the central Beringharjo Market. There are also several restaurants and cafes on the way, as well as cassette tape shops and bookshops.

Like most other towns in Java and Bali, the **Gramedia** and **Ayumas Agung bookshops** have the best English-language selection. Jogya has an important university—Universitas Gajah Mada—which publishes many works both in Indonesian and in English. Some of these cover Javanese culture and are worth buying. Gramedia is located at Jalan Sudirman 70, and Ayumas Agung is on the corner of Jalan Diponegoro and Jalan Mangkubumi. On Jalan Marlioboro is **Sari Ilmu** at number 119, and **Nirmala** at number 171. These last two also sell maps.

11. Night Life and Entertainment

In Jogya and Solo when thinking about entertainment, think **classical Javanese arts** and you'll have a feast. It's a bit like Ubud in Bali. Each night there is a performance of traditional dance or *wayang* plays in town. Should you be thinking of nightclubs or discos you may find Central Java a bit lacking. This type of entertainment is pretty much limited to the larger hotels, such as the **night club** at the Ambarrukmo Palace Hotel. Most of the other upmarket hotels have cocktail bars for a quiet drink, but that is about all.

So it looks like it's back to classical Javanese entertainment. Not to say there's anything wrong with seeing a few performances of this type while in Central Java; on the contrary, in this area these arts have maintained their high level of complexity. Background on these arts is given in Chapter 4, so here I'll concentrate on venues and times.

1. **Classical Javanese dance** is a product of *Kraton* culture, and fortunately the palaces of Jogya and Solo still promote dance and other arts. According to the experts there are certain differences between the styles of Jogya and Solo, but to most of us they look pretty much the same. What are most noticeable are the differences between Javanese (meaning central and eastern Java), Sundanese (West Java), and Balinese dance styles. The background stories are often the same, as are the instruments, costumes, and language. Differences that are more noticeable are the rhythm and tempo of the music and the dancers' movements.

The **Sultan's Palace of Jogyakarta** (*Kraton* Jogya), which is entered via Jalan Polowijayan on its western side, stages classical dance every Sunday morning from 10:30 A.M. to 12 noon. If you are in town mid-week, the **Asti Academy of Dance** on Jalan Colombo near the Jalan Urip Sumoharjo commercial area is worth a visit any morning except Sunday to watch the students practicing.

Another well-respected school is run by **Bagong K**. If you hear of a performance being put on by this man's group, it should be good. The **Bagong K School of Dance** is at Jalan Martadinata 9, Jogyakarta, which is an extension of Jalan A Dahlan/Jalan Senopati, which runs past the main bank and General Post Office.

At *Solo*, traditional dance is performed on Wednesdays at the **Pura Mangkunegaran Palace** to the accompaniment of the palace's *gamelan*

Gamelan orchestra, Solo

Wayang orang dance drama

orchestra. Dance as well as drama is practiced each afternoon Monday to Saturday at **Sasono Mulyo**, which is just inside the front gate of *Kraton* Hadiningrat Solo. Opposite is the private entrance of the *Susunan* (Sultan) and his family. The southern open square of this *Kraton* is called **Sasono Hinggil/Pagelaran**, which is another venue for dance and drama performances and practice.

2. **Gamelan** orchestra usually accompanies classical dance but also performs alone. The **Sultan's Kraton Palace of Jogya** is once again an ideal place to listen to *gamelan* music. The main components of a *gamelan* orchestra are xylophones and gongs, following a beat set by a small hand drum. *Gamelan* performances are held Monday and Wednesday mornings from 10:30 A.M. to 12 noon. Enter via Jalan Polowijayan. In *Solo*, the *gamelan* accompanies the classical dance on Wednesdays at **Puro Mangkunegaran palace**. At **SMKI** (a specialist high school) on Jalan Tambaksegaran, *gamelan* (also known as *karawitan*) is performed on a special night of the Javanese calendar each month on *malam Selasa/Kliwon*.

3. **Wayang kulit** is perhaps the best known of the traditional Javanese arts. Carved flat leather puppets that cast a silhouette onto a white sheet tell stories of old India. Sometimes these performances start around 9 or 10 P.M. and go until dawn. The puppeteer is thought to have mystical powers, as he brings the *wayang kulit* puppets to life, narrates, and sings for the whole duration of the performance. In *Jogya*, *wayang kulit* is performed each day (except Saturday) at the **Agastya Art Institute** (school for narrators) located at Jalan Gedong Kiwo MD II/237. The show goes from 3 P.M. to 5 P.M. Also in Jogya, at the south square (*Sasono Hinggil*) of the main *Kraton* or sultan's palace, there are *wayang kulit* shadow puppet play performances on the second Saturday of each month of the Western calendar. The whole story runs from 9 P.M. to 5 A.M., but you can leave at any time you like, and possibly come back later. This is what the locals tend to do.

In *Solo*, *wayang kulit* performances are held at the studios of **Radio Republik Indonesia (RRI)**, the government radio station, opposite the railway station. These are not quite so long, going from 8 P.M. to midnight on the third Tuesday and third Saturday of each month. Another *wayang kulit* venue in Solo is the home of Mr. Pak Suroto at Jalan Notodiningratan 100. Scheduling follows the Javanese calendar, namely on *malam Selasa/Legi*.

4. **Wayang golek** is similar in many ways to *wayang kulit*, except that the figures are more like puppets as we know them. In fact, *golek* literally means "puppet." The **Agastya Art Institute** in Jogya is the main venue. The time is Saturdays from 3 to 9 P.M., at Jalan Gedong Kiwo MD II/237.

5. **Wayang wong** dance-drama features people on stage rather than

puppets. The stories are again based on the Indian epics, the *Ramayana* and the *Mahabarata*, which tell tales of love and war between the Pandawas and the Karawas (goodies and baddies), Rama and Sita, rescue by the white monkey king, and other stories. In Jogya, *wayang wong* is performed at **Dalem Pujokusuman** (also known as **Bintaran Kidul**) on Monday, Wednesday, and Friday evenings from 8 to 10 P.M. *Wayang* performances are also staged at the **Arjuna Plaza Hotel** on Jalan Mangkubumi and at the **Ambarrukmo Palace Hotel** on Jalan Adisucipto.

In *Solo*, the **Sriwedari Cultural Center** on Jalan Slamet Rihyadi stages *wayang wong* dance drama each evening. The theater has beautiful backdrops that change with each scene. From Mondays to Saturdays the show goes from 8 P.M. to 12 midnight. On Sunday it starts and finishes an hour later. **RRI** also stages *wayang wong* on the second Tuesday of each month. RRI is situated opposite the railway station.

6. **Ramayana ballet** is one of the highlights of the artistic calendar each year. On four consecutive nights at the time of the full moon, this epic drama is staged under the stars at the Prambanan temple complex. The floodlit Loro Jonggrang temple serves as the background as up to sixty singers and hundreds of dancers play out the scenes of monkey armies, battles, and love. Acrobatics, giant kings on stilts, and fire are all part of the action on the stone stage. The *Ramayana* is only held at Prambanan during the dry season, which extends from June through October. At other times of the year there could be no guarantee on the weather. Jogya gets busier at *Ramayana* time, as visitors from all over Indonesia and the world target the *Ramayana* performance as part of their visit. If you're on a tight schedule you could book your *Ramayana* ticketing in advance through your hotel.

If for some reason you are not able to make it to Prambanan to see the *Ramayana* ballet, in Jogya every night of the week between 7:30 and 9 P.M. there is a *Ramayana* performance at **Sasono Suko People's Park** (THR—Taman Hiburan Rakyat) on Jalan Katamso. Another venue for *Ramayana* and other arts is **Galeri Senisono** on the corner of Jalan Ahmed Dahlan and Jalan A. Yani (opposite the General Post Office and old bank). Check their program for details.

12. The Central Java Address List

Banks—BNI 1946, Jalan Ahmed Dahlan/Jalan Trikora, Jogya. Bank Central Asia, Jalan Urip Sumoharjo 65, Jogya (Tel. (274) 86455). Bank Dagang Indonesia, Jalan Sudirman 67, Jogya. Bank Bumi Daya, Jalan Sudirman 7, Jogya (Tel. (274) 5094, 86918). Bank Rakyat Indonesia, Jalan Katamso 23, Jogya. BNI 1946, Jalan Sudirman 19, Solo.

Bank Bumi Daya, Jalan Slamet Rihyadi 18, Solo (Tel. (271) 3928, 4911).

Embassies and Consulates—The American Embassy is in Jakarta on Jalan Medan Merdeka Selatan, Jakarta (Tel. (21) 360 360). The Canadian Embassy is in Jakarta on the 5th floor of the Wisma Metropolitan Building, Jalan Jendral Sudirman, (Tel. (21) 510709).

Emergency Phone Numbers—Ambulance (118). Fire (113). Police (110).

Ford Foundation—Bulak Sumur, Block A/16, Jogya (Tel. (274) 3325).

Foster Parents Plan, Inc.—Jalan Jogokaryan 113, Jogya (Tel. (274) 87013, 5340).

Garuda Airlines—Jalan Mangkumbumi 56, Jogya (Tel. (274) 4400, 5184). Jalan Suryopranto 22, Solo (inside Kusuma Sahid Prince Hotel) (Tel. (271) 21402). Jalan Adisucipto Km 9.4, Jogya (Tel. (274) 4948).

Hospitals—RS Bethesda, Jalan Sudirman 70/Jalan Wahidin, Jogya (24-hour casualty/emergency) (Tel. (274) 2281). RS Panti Rapih, Jalan Cik Ditro 30, Jogya (Tel. (274) 3333). Rumah Sakit, Jalan Veteran, Solo. (Don't bother trying to call—they probably won't speak English on the phone.)

Merapi Volcano Observation Service—Jalan Cendana, Jogya (Tel. (274) 2685).

Money changers—Alif Int'l, Jalan Pasar Kembang 19, Jogya. Dewata Giri, Jalan Marlioboro 72, Jogya (inside Hotel Garuda). Intan Biru, Jalan Marlioboro 18, Jogya (outside Mutiara Hotel). Win and Son, Jalan Parangtritis 47, Jogya (near Jalan Prawirotaman).

Pharmacy/Apotik—Kimia Farma, Jalan Marlioboro 179, Jogya. Kimia Farma, Jalan Marlioboro 123, Jogya. Apotik Marlioboro, Jalan Marlioboro 141, Jogya. Apotik Merapi, Jalan Mangkubumi 109, Jogya. Apotik Babasari, Jalan Adisucipto 273, Jogya. Apotik Ratna, Jalan Parangtritis 56, Jogya.

Phone (Int'l)—Jalan Yos Sudarso 9, Kota Baru, Jogya. Jalan Sudirman, Solo.

Post Office—Jalan Senopati/Jalan Trikora, Jogya. Jalan Sudirman, Solo.

Postal Agent—Batik Palace Hotel, Jalan Pasar Kembang 29, Jogya.

Telex and Telegram (Int'l)—Jalan Trikora 2, Jogya (next to Post Office).

Tourist Information—Jalan Marlioboro 16, Jogya. Jalan Slamet Rihyadi 235, Solo.

10

West Java and Jakarta

1. The General Picture

The western side of Java is dominated by the metropolis of Jakarta, a fast-moving, hot, and sometimes dirty city of around nine million friendly inhabitants. Jakarta's first impression on you is usually a lasting one, and generates either love or hate. One of the reasons for this is that this is a city of extremes—the tree-lined avenues of Menteng and high-rise office blocks or the pitiful squalor of squatter families along the canals. Unfortunately, the first thing that many visitors want to do when they arrive in Jakarta is leave. Don't worry about the noise and maniacal drivers. There is a great deal of interest and beauty to be found in this capital city of Indonesia. All you have to do is look.

Most visitors choose to stay in the vicinity of Central Jakarta—along Jalan Thamrin, near Gambir central railway station, Menteng, or along Jalan Sudirman, which leads towards Kebayoran—at one of the dozens of hotels that range from the luxurious Hilton or Borobudur to the backpacker dormitories on Jalan Jaksa. In the medium price range are smaller hotels in the suburbs of Kebayoran and Menteng, the Hotel Indonesia (Indonesia's first high-rise), and the colonial-era Transeara Hotel.

Jakarta's two main shopping areas are Kebayoran Baru/Block M and Glodok/Chinatown. Set in the affluent satellite suburb of Kebayoran

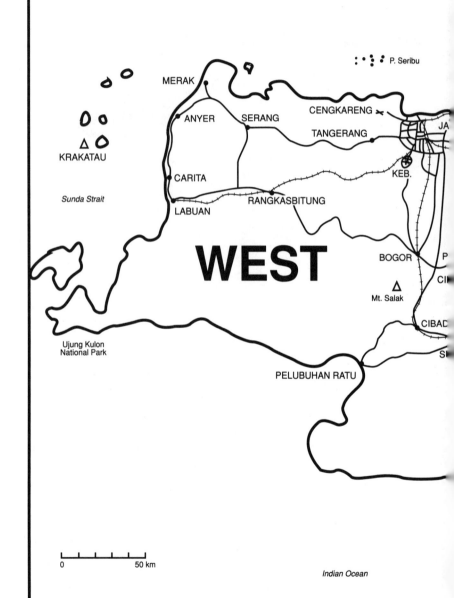

P. Seribu

MERAK

CENGKARENG

ANYER   SERANG

TANGERANG

JA

KRAKATAU

CARITA

KEB.

Sunda Strait

RANGKASBITUNG

LABUAN

WEST

BOGOR

P

Mt. Salak

CI

CIBAD

Ujung Kulon
National Park

S

PELUBUHAN RATU

0   50 km

Indian Ocean

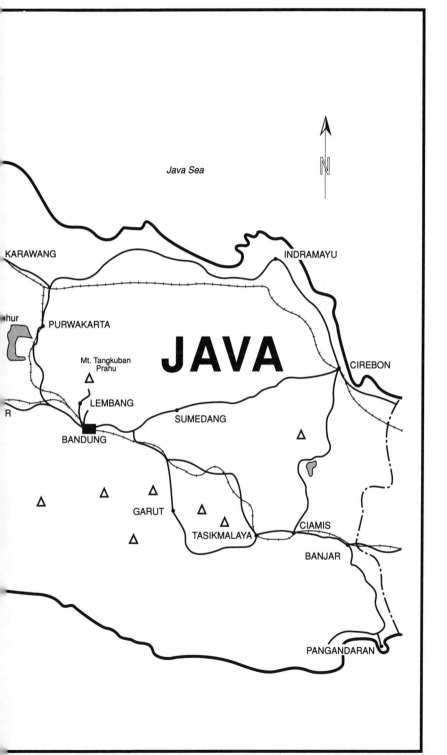

Baru, Block M has restaurants, boutiques, and department stores, all with easy access and off-street parking. Many of Jakarta's expatriate population live in the suburbs near here.

On the northern side of town, extending along and past a long, wide thoroughfare named Jalan Gajah Mada/Jalan Hayam Wuruk is Jakarta's Chinatown, called Glodok. This area is also the location of the original Dutch garrison and port, Batavia.

Glodok is the hub of the Chinese business district. Specializing in retailing, wholesaling, and banking, the Chinese of Jakarta have taken over the old Dutch quarter so that they can be close to their businesses. Outdoor stalls abound in the area after dark, especially on Jalan Mangga Besar, Jalan Pecenongan, and around Pasar Baru.

Not far from Glodok is the old port of Sunda Kelapa, where sailboats off-load their cargoes from the outer islands. Adjacent to Sunda Kelapa is Pasar Ikan, where an old Dutch fort is well maintained.

The Dutch in the form of the V.O.C., or East India Company, first set up operations in the 1620s at the mouth of the Ciliwung River that runs through Jakarta. Earlier, the Portuguese had tried to establish a fort here, but were defeated by the navy of the ruler of Demak in 1527. The local kingdom at the mouth of the river was Pajajaran, and they were going to pay tribute to the Portuguese. The village at that time was called Sunda Kelapa. It is from this Javanese victory that Jakarta was given its name—*Jaya karta* (literally "town of victory").

In the second half of the seventeenth century and the first half of the eighteenth century, Batavia's wealthy citizens and government officials moved outside the city's walls to what is now Jalan Gajah Mada and Jalan P. Jayakarta. Some had mansions near the Ciliwung River where they had built bathing places and landing platforms for boats. Menteng and Senen were also being settled in the area of Jalan Pos, Jalan Senen Raya, Jalan Gunung Sahari, and Gambir, at the center of the new capital of Weltevreden, away from the cramped conditions of the old walled city at Sunda Kelapa and Pasar Ikan.

In 1814, during the British period, Jalan Veteran (formerly Rijswijk Straat) was considered fashionable and respectable, so all Chinese and Indonesian shops were compelled to move away. After the Suez Canal opened in 1869, trade increased, the city flourished, and a new port was built at Tanjung Priok. This wealth financed government buildings that still stand today, from the Presidential Palace through to Senen. In 1873 the railway between Batavia and Bogor (Buitenzorg) began operating. Trains and trams operated in the city, such as from Kota to Harmoni along Jalan Gajah Mada.

After gaining its independence, Jakarta grew steadily until the oil boom years, when development really took off. More recently the impetus of growth has been helped by tourism and manufacturing. As in the past, government decisions and business opportunities are concentrated in Jakarta, so other cities and islands often complain about the unequal distribution of wealth, development, and employment. It is of course a common problem in developing countries.

Make the most of your stay in Jakarta. Visit the islands, the mountains, and find you way around the old Dutch quarter, Chinatown, and the Dutch buildings of Weltevreden. Love it or hate it; Jakarta is certainly a place you cannot easily forget.

Using the phone in Jakarta

Before I forget, you should know that the state-run telephone system in Jakarta is hopelessly overloaded and nearing a state of total collapse. The problem is due to rapid commercial and industrial development without a sufficient growth in infrastructure, such as adding extra phone lines and exchanges. The government is trying to catch up, but is at best standing still. As a result, the success rate of calls is less than 50 percent and you may be cut off when you do get through.

New exchanges and switching systems are being introduced, which has meant that six-digit numbers are being replaced with seven digits. Some of the documented changes are as follows (note that x corresponds to the original number):

1. 671 xxx has become   690 7xxx
2. 412 xxx   "   "   420 9xxx
3. 670 xxx   "   "   690 4xxx
4. 517 xxx   "   "   520 7xxx
5. 76x xxx   "   "   769 xxxx
6. 80x xxx   "   "   809 xxxx

Other changes may have occurred that we don't yet know about. If you're having problems getting through, ask your hotel receptionist to call for you. The same problems apply to a certain extent to the rest of Java and Bali, so you can't always rely on the phone. It may be quicker and easier to jump in a taxi and go straight to the place you're after.

Bandung

If you want to see more of West Java, you could do worse than using *Bandung* as your base, staying at one of the comfortable hotels and doing daytrips across the highlands and the south coast.

Set on a plateau 112 miles (180 kilometers) south of Jakarta, Bandung has cool nights that are a welcome change after the lowlands. Being some 2000 feet (800 meters) above sea level, as soon as the sun sets the

BANDUNG

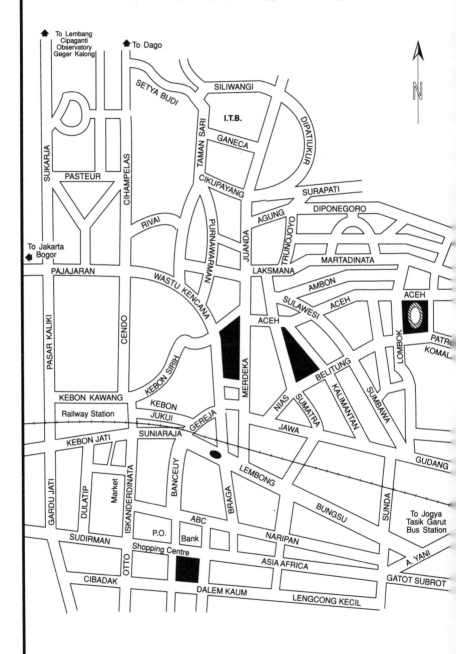

temperature drops pleasantly. At Lembang, which is situated in the hills 11 miles (18 kilometers) to the north, the temperature change is even more pronounced.

The crater of Mt. Tangkuban Prahu can be reached on foot from Lembang. Go early in the morning for a good view over the city. Nearby is Marabaya, with its hot sulphur pool, tea estates, and mountain scenery. Ten miles (17 kilometers) from Lembang is Ciater hot springs.

Bandung as a city is growing fast, and the urban spread is having a marked effect on the environment. Many of the trees that lined the boulevards were removed to make way for increased traffic flow. This and industrial pollution have marred the beauty of a city that was once called the "Paris of Java."

As well as being the administrative capital of the Sundanese people, Bandung is also the traditional cultural and artistic center of the highland race which is often considered peripheral to Central Java. However, this viewpoint overlooks the existence of the kingdom of Pajajaran, which has its court near present-day Bogor, and dates from the fifteenth century.

2. Long-Distance Transportation

Jakarta is Indonesia's most important long-distance travel terminus. Sukarno-Hatta **airport**, which was named after the Republic of Indonesia's first president and vice-president, is over an hour's freeway drive to the west of the city at Cengkarang. Hence it is more commonly known as Cengkarang Airport (pronounced "cheng-car-eng"). It was built in the early 1980s, and all international and domestic flights leave from here, though this may change soon if Halim Airport is used again by a new operator.

Garuda Indonesia Airlines (Tel. (21) 5780014 7:30 A.M. to 5 P.M.; 5701292 5 P.M. to 7:30 A.M.) is at present the only airline that flies direct between Jakarta and the U.S. A DC10 flight, number GA 800, leaves Jakarta at 1:40 P.M. on Tuesday, Wednesday, Friday, and Sunday bound for Los Angeles. There are stops at Denpasar (Bali), Biak (for fuel), and Honolulu. Arrival is at 6:40 P.M. the *same day* after crossing the international dateline. The same plane refuels and returns to Bali at 9 P.M. and arrives in Indonesia at 8:15 A.M. the next day (i.e., a two-hour turnaround).

Qantas has daily flights from Jakarta via Bali to Sydney, where you can connect onto several airlines to North America. **UTA French Airlines** leaves Jakarta each week for L.A. via Sydney and Tahiti. Singapore's Changi Airport is the closest major hub for many other American and Asian airlines that fly from Singapore via Hong Kong or Tokyo. For more information on international flights from Bali and Jakarta, turn back to the first section of Chapter 2.

Domestic flights leave Cengkarang Airport for all major towns in Indonesia, including Bali and several towns and cities in Java. Garuda is once again the preferred airline. **Merpati** (Tel. (21) 413608, 417404) and **Bouraq** (Tel. (21) 655326, 655170) flights are available that are cheaper (though slower) to many of the same destinations as Garuda, as well as more out-of-the-way towns and resource projects. Garuda flies from Jakarta to *Denpasar* (Bali's only airport) seven times a day, starting at 6 A.M. and going until 7:55 P.M.. The 1 hour, 45 minute non-stop flight costs $107 each way. To *Jogya* there are four flights a day, from 6:10 A.M. through 2 P.M., that cost $62 each way for a 1 hour, 10 minute flight. To *Surabaya* costs $88 for a 1 hour, 20 minute flight, the first at 7:30 A.M. and the last at 5:30 P.M., though at certain times there is one as late as 8:45 P.M. Be sure to check which terminal your plane leaves from. Terminal A is for international and regional flights (including Bali), Terminal B is domestic flights other than shuttle services; and Terminal C is for shuttle service flights.

An **airport bus service** operates between Cilandak Bus Terminal, Pulo Gadung Bus Terminal, Block M, Hotel Indonesia, and the airport at regular intervals for around $10.

From the city of *Bandung*, **Garuda Airlines** (Tel. (22) 56936, 52497, 51497) flies once daily to *Surabaya* non-stop at 11:55 A.M. taking 1 hour and 10 minutes, and at 9 A.M. and 2 P.M. via Jakarta. The 11:55 flight continues on to *Bali* each day. At 2 P.M. daily Garuda flys to *Bali* via *Jakarta*, the whole flight with connections taking nearly five hours. To *Jogya* there is one daily flight at 11 A.M. via Jakarta, arriving at 3 P.M.. Garuda's Bandung office is at Jalan Asia Africa 73. **Merpati** and **Bouraq** flights are also available to other cities in Java, to Bali, and other Indonesian islands.

Taking an overnight **express train** to *Jogyakarta* or *Surabaya* should not be overlooked. The trains are comfortable, air-conditioned, and clean, the stations are handy to the center of all cities involved, and while you may not see a lot of the countryside out of your windows except when the moon is up, you do get a better look at Indonesia's life than you would by flying. Why not take the train out of Jakarta and fly the next leg to Bali?

The *Bima Express* (with sleepers) operates between *Jakarta* and *Surabaya*, stopping at *Jogya* after crossing the highlands of West Java. The *Mutiara Utama* (reclining seats only) runs along Java's northern coastline to *Surabaya* via *Semarang*. Both trains start their journey each afternoon at the Kota Railway Station (Tel. (21) 678515), which is in the heart of the Chinese business district on Jalan Stasiun Kota 1, Kota (Glodok). To save you the trouble of going to Kota to buy your ticket, I suggest you buy it from **Carnation Travel** (Tel. (21) 344027, 356278). The extra $1 to $2 (Rp 2,000 to Rp 3,500) that Carnation charges is well worth it. No need to line up—just book in advance and pick up your ticket from Carnation one day before departure at Jalan Menteng Raya 24, Jakarta Pusat. The *Bima* and *Mutiara* have reserved seating, so your seat should be empty when you get on. If someone is in your seat just call the conductor to move them. The *Bima* leaves Kota station first, at 4 P.M. The *Mutiara* departs at 4:30 P.M..

For nearly an hour Jakarta's suburbs line the tracks, then begin the satellite towns, market gardens, and rice paddies. Meals are available on the train, though you would be advised to take with you enough food and drink to last the night, just in case you don't like what's for sale. Cookies, bread rolls, and tetra-pack juice or tea are for sale at supermarkets or at a shop at the stations. The one-way fare to Jogya is $13 (Rp 25,000) and to Surabaya $16 (Rp 31,000).

You should also note that round-trip return bookings are not available. Tickets can only be bought at the town you are leaving from.

There are also day trains out of Jakarta to Central and East Java, but I don't recommend them because they are mostly slow, economy class (meaning very hot) trains that stop at many towns on the way. The same goes for the other economy trains that run at night. They are also overcrowded and without reserved seating. Pilfering of your possessions while you sleep is something else that is much more likely to happen on the economy trains than on the *Bima* or *Mutiara*.

From *Bandung*, the *Mutiara Selatan* goes to *Surabaya* via *Tasikmalaya*, *Banjar*, and *Jogya*. Tickets are available at the railway station on Jalan Kebon Jati and Jalan Kebon Kawung. Carnation Travel has a local office called *PT Pusaka Nusantara* (Tel. (22) 51466) on Jalan Trunjoyo 4, which is in the suburbs on the northern side of Bandung. This ticketing office is handy for advanced bookings.

Overnight express is also the preferred type of **bus transportation** if you are heading east to *Jogya*, *Surabaya*, or *Bali*. If you are going to *Sumatra* you can take a day bus to the **Merak Ferry Terminal**, catch the **ferry**, and look for a bus or train in Sumatra; or you can book a bus that goes through to *Padang*.

Overnight busses to *Jogya*, *Semarang*, *Surabaya*, *Solo*, or *Malang* leave from **Pulo Gadung Bus Terminal** on the eastern side of the city. One-way tickets to these cities average $10 (Rp 20,000). Small booking agents around the Jalan Jaksa backpacker area sell tickets on these buses, known as *bis malam cepat*. One reliable bus company is **Jawa Indah Express** (Tel. (21) 36 4389), which has its office at Jalan Krekot Jaya Block C 11/8. Other recommended bus companies to travel with are **Cakrawala, Lorena, Bali Indah**, and **Bhayangkara**. Tickets are also available at each company's ticket office at **Pulo Gadung Bus Terminal** a few days in advance.

From *Bandung*, there are overnight express buses to *Jogya* and *Surabaya*, though these buses aren't as comfortable as on other routes. Air-conditioning is available. To *Jogya* the one-way bus fare (AC) is around $6 (Rp 12,000), or $7 (Rp 14,000) to *Surabaya*. **Rajawali** and **Jawa Indah** are two of the better companies. Bus ticketing offices are on Jalan Kebon Jati 46-68, near the Melati Hotel. All buses leave from the main bus terminal on Jalan Ahmed Yani.

Those worldwide **car rental** companies, **Avis** (Tel. (21) 331974, 332900) and **Hertz** (Tel. (21) 570 3683) are well represented in Jakarta for self-drive cars to go across Java and to Bali. Roads are generally of poor condition, so you will need plenty of time if you plan to drive around. **Avis** has offices at the Borobudur Hotel (Tel. (21) 323707 ext. 1281) and at Cenkarang Airport (Tel. (21) 311974, 332900). **Hertz** has offices at the Mandarin Oriental Hotel (Tel. (21) 32 1307 ext. 1267-8), the Hyatt Aryaduta (Tel. (21) 376 008 ext. 197), and at Cengkarang Airport Terminal A (Tel. (21) 550 7125) Terminal B (Tel. (21) 550 7086). Two other reliable car rental companies are **Toyota Rent-a-Car** (Tel. (21) 570 3327) at Jalan Surdiman 5, and **National Car Rental** (Tel. (21) 32 2849, 33 3423-5), which has an office at the Kartika Plaza Hotel on Jalan Thamrin.

3. Local Transportation

Included in this section are the different ways of getting around the cities of *Jakarta* and *Bandung*, and how to travel the 112 miles between them. Population experts predict that by early next century, West Java between Jakarta and Bandung will be one continuous urban/industrial belt with some 20 to 30 million people.

Street-level Jakarta is not a particularly pleasant place, so I recommend that you travel by **taxi** at all times on your first visit. Jakarta has many reliable taxi companies with radio dispatched, clean taxis that use meters. In order of reliability I would go for **Jakarta International Taxis** (Tel. (21) 333777), **Steady Safe** (Tel. (21) 333 333), and **Blue Bird** (Tel. (21) 333000, 325607). There are many new radio taxi operators now that are just as good. **Blue Bird** has the best **airport taxis**, but if you call them to come to a private house, they often tell you yes and then don't turn up. If the hotel calls them they're fine. **Jakarta International** is very good for pickups from a private house. If you've been waiting for a while and they still haven't got a vacant taxi, the control room will call you back and let you know that you will need to wait a little while longer.

Taxis can also be hired by the hour or the day. The fee payable varies somewhat depending on the make and condition of the car and whether it is air-conditioned or not. Gas will be extra.

Several companies offer services to *Bandung* from Jakarta. The most reliable of these is **Media** (Tel. (21) 343643, 320343), whose office is at Jalan Johar 15, Menteng. Media's Bandung office (Tel. (22) 82182, 83183) is at Jalan Cihampelas 87 in Bandung's northern suburbs. Other Jakarta operators are **Angkutan 4848** (Tel. (21) 348048, 364488—24 hours) at Jalan Prapatan 34, Menteng; and **Metro Taxi** (Tel. (21) 672827), which is in the Chinatown area at Jalan Kopi 2C, Jakarta Kota.

If you go to the depot you may be able to save some money by going with some other people who are also waiting.

4. Hotels and Lodging

Jakarta and the rest of West Java have a good supply of accommodations to pamper those who want a bit of luxury or to be practical and comfortable for those on more of a budget. In the five-star field, the **Hilton, Mandarin**, and **Borobudur Inter-Continental** are firmly entrenched as Jakarta's best. Close behind in this class are the **Hyatt Aryaduta** and the **Sari Pacific**. There are another 10 or so high-rise hotels that offer similar service though at a slightly less efficient level, and with rooms and restaurants that aren't refurbished as often. Apart from that, they are usually conveniently located and their lower nightly tariff puts them in the moderately priced category. The better hotels of Bandung also fall into this group. Five-star hotels in Jakarta charge around U.S. $150 to $200 per night for a single room. The next group costs $90 to 125 a night in Jakarta or $40 to $100 in Bandung. Not counting backpacker hotels on Jalan Jaksa or cheap Indonesian hotels, budget hotels in Jakarta cost around $50 a night or $20 in Bandung and cater to many Western as well as domestic tourists. Pay as much as you can afford in Jakarta. It will give you a more favorable opinion of the city, to have somewhere to escape to after the hustle and bustle.

EXPENSIVE HOTELS

The **Hotel Borobudur Inter-Continental** (Tel. (21) 370333, 380 5555) thinks of itself as a country club in central Jakarta—23 acres of tropical gardens, 8 tennis and 7 squash courts and one racquetball court, an Olympic-size pool, a Clark Hatch fitness center, and their scenic jogging track (the best in central Jakarta). And there's not only sport but also food. Several restaurants are in the hotel, including seafood, Japanese teppanyaki, and a coffee shop-*cum*-brasserie. Many foreign businesses make the Borobudur their base. At least there they know all facilities will always be working, both in their rooms and at the business center. The Borobudur faces onto a large, tree-covered square which was the center of the second Dutch colonial capital named Weltevreden. On other sides of the square are the Dutch-era cathedral, colonial buildings, and residences. Room rates start at U.S. $200 a night, but you're getting the best that Jakarta has to offer. Book in North America through your local Inter-Continental Hotel, Garuda Indonesia airlines, or write direct to Hotel Borobudur, Jalan Lapangan Banteng Selatan, P.O. Box 1329, Jakarta Pusat 10710, Indonesia (Fax: 62 21 380 9595).

The **Jakarta Hilton** (Tel. (21) 570 3600) is not situated in central Jakarta, but is adjacent to the Semanggi Highway cloverleaf halfway between Menteng and Kebayoran Baru. From here you can easily catch a taxi to the old and new business districts, Chinatown, or the airport. The hotel itself is set in over 30 acres of grounds with 13 tennis courts, a one-mile jogging track, an outdoor eating area, a Balinese theater, and the Executive Club, which has complete sport facilities, function rooms, and restaurants.

The main hotel has the most impressive lobby in Jakarta, the ceiling being a replica of the Sultan's Palace in Jogya, with an ancient *gamelan* xylophone that is played in the afternoons. As well as the usual 24-hour room service, business center, and coffee shop, there is the highly rated Taman Sari Restaurant and the Oriental disco. For outdoor dining in a cool, tranquil setting, walk across to the Pizzeria cafe overlooking a small lake. Room rates at the Hilton start at $150 a night for a single room in the main hotel or $200 for a single room in the garden tower, which offers more spacious and better-appointed rooms and suites. Book through your nearest Hilton hotel, Garuda Indonesia Airlines, or direct to Jakarta Hilton International, Jalan Gatot Subroto, P.O. Box 3315 Jakarta 10002, Indonesia (Fax: (62) 21 58 3089, 58 3091).

Jakarta's **Mandarin** (Tel. (21) 321307) is run by the Oriental Group, the owners of the much-lauded Oriental Hotel in Bangkok, so they know how to take good care of you. It's in a really handy position facing the city's central roundabout. The hotel is a little over ten years old and reputation-wise is standing up well.

Get a room on as high a story as possible and watch Jalan Sudirman snake its way towards Kebayoran Baru. Like Jakarta's other best hotels the rooms are excellent, as is the Club Room French and Spice Garden Sichuan restaurants. Fitness freaks can use the gym, sauna, or squash courts. Afterwards join in on a barbecue at the Pelangi Terrace poolside on the 5th story. The Mandarin's location on the roundabout means you can drive off in any direction, whether towards old or new Jakarta. Single and double rooms cost U.S. $175 a night, though Garuda Airlines can probably get you a better rate than that if you book your room with your ticket. Another option is to phone their North American number 1-800-526-6566, or write direct to the Mandarin Oriental, Jalan Thamrin or P.O. Box 3392, Jakarta Pusat 190, Indonesia. (Fax: (62) 21 324669).

Another recommended hotel in this group which offers excellent service together with a handy location is the **Hyatt Aryaduta** (Tel. (21) 376008, 380 4777), which is on Jalan Prapatan 44-48, not far from Gambir railway station and the U.S. Embassy. In North America you can book by phoning (800) 233-1234, (800) 228-9000, your nearest Hyatt Hotel, or Garuda. The **Sari Pacific Hotel** (Tel. (21) 323707) on Jakarta's main street Jalan Thamrin comes in close behind the others. For food there's a well-stocked delicatessen, a grill, and one of Jakarta's best Japanese restaurants. The popular Pit Stop disco is open till 2 or 3 each night. Book through Garuda Airlines or write direct to Sari Pacific Hotel, Jalan M. Thamirin, P.O. Box 3138, Jakarta, 10340 Indonesia (Fax: (62) 21 323650). In the U.S. you can book by phoning (800) 663-1515.

Jakarta saw a burst of hotel construction start in the late 1980s. Three that have just opened or are about to open are **Le Meridien** on Jalan Sudirman, **The Regent** on Jalan Rasuna Said (Kuningan), and the **Jakarta Grand Hyatt** on Jalan M. Thamrin. I'll give you more about these in the next edition of the *Maverick Guide to Bali and Java*, after I have gotten some local feedback and had a chance to visit.

MEDIUM-PRICED HOTELS

Jakarta

Hotel Indonesia (Tel. (21) 320008, 322008), for many years Jakarta's premier hotel, faces the city's main roundabout, which is named after it (Bundaran Hotel Indonesia). This treasured landmark, when it opened in 1962, was the country's first high-rise building in the new Jakarta that was created in the rice fields that adjoined Menteng. Jalan Thamrin was this new, wide throughfare with a massive water-filled roundabout at one end. In later years this business expansion continued past the H.I. roundabout along Jalan Sudirman towards the distant satellite suburb of Kebayoran Baru. Nowadays it is one continuous high-rise strip. In keeping with this modern era, Hotel Indonesia is undergoing an extensive refurbishment—a new lobby, restaurants, room decor, and a redesigned

Nirwana supper club. Services are similar to a five-star hotel, though at a lower price. Single room rates start at $110 a night. In North America book through Incentive Hotels (Tel. (201) 992 3411), your travel agent, Garuda Airlines, or write direct to Hotel Indonesia, Jalan Thamrin, P.O. Box 1054, Jakarta 10010, Indonesia (Fax: (62) 21 321508).

The **Sahid Jaya** (Tel. (21) 570 4444) is another of Jakarta's better hotels, with rooms and suites in their original high-rise hotel and newer tower. A good selection of places to eat, bars, and a good nightclub attract people from all over Jakarta to the Sahid. Sahid Hotels is an Indonesian group of hotels that succeed in creating an Indonesian feel in their always tastefully appointed hotels. Single rooms start at $120 a night, rising to $300 for the better suites. In North America you can book through Utell International (Tel. (800) 223 9868), in Los Angeles (Tel. (213) 662 4772), (Fax: (62) (213) 666 9929), or through Garuda Airlines. You can also write direct to Sahid Jaya Hotel, Jalan Sudirman, P.O. Box 1041, Jakarta 10010, Indonesia (Fax: (62) 21 583168).

On the seafront next to the yacht club and Ancol recreation park is **Horison Hotel** (Tel. (21) 680008). The water is good for boating and The Thousand Islands are offshore, but I wouldn't swim in Jakarta Bay itself due to heavy metals pollution. The hotel also has one of Jakarta's best golf courses and a floating seafood restaurant. At the end of a day of sight-seeing, the grounds of the Horison Hotel are a delightful place to cool off and relax. Location-wise, while it's a bit far from Menteng and central Jakarta, it is handy to Chinatown and old Dutch Batavia.

Book through your travel agent, Garuda Airlines, or direct to Hotel Horison, Jaya Ancol, P.O. Box 3340, Jakarta, Indonesia.

Set in beautiful gardens on the western side of Jakarta, on the main beltway road and handy to the airport toll road, is the **Orchid Place Hotel** (Tel. (21) 59 6911, 59 3115). This low-rise hotel has some 85 rooms with most modern room and sports facilities at a reasonable price. Single rooms start at $50 a night. Book through Garuda Airlines or send direct to the Orchid Palace Hotel, Jalan S. Parman, Slipi, Jakarta, Indonesia (Fax: (62) 21 599584).

Other moderately priced hotels in Jakarta are the **Kartika Plaza** (Tel. (21) 32 1008), centrally located but a bit seedy at Jalan Thamrin, Jakarta Pusat, Indonesia; **Jayakarta Tower** (Tel. (21) 629 4408, 649 6760), which is on the major thoroughfare (Jalan Hayam Wuruk, Kota) leading into Chinatown and colonial-era Batavia; the **Kemang Hotel** (Tel. (21) 799 3208) on Jalan Kemang Raya, Kebayoran Baru (Fax: (62) 21 799 3492), which aims for the expatriate businessman market, and the **Kartika Chandra Hotel** (Tel. (21) 511008, Fax: (62) 21 520 4238), on Jalan Gatot

Subroto, close to the new business district of Kuningan and the Hilton Hotel.

Bandung

The Art Deco **Savoy Homann Hotel** (Tel. (22) 432244, 43 0083, 43 6187) is the place to stay in West Java's capital. It features comfortable rooms with modern facilities, a bar, a restaurant, a coffee shop, and all have recently been renovated to highlight the Art Deco architecture. The Savoy Homann is centrally located in the Central Business District close to shops, restaurants, and cinemas. Single rooms start at around $50 a night and go up to $100 for deluxe twins. Book through Garuda Airlines or write direct to the Savoy Homann Hotel, Jalan Asia Africa 112, Bandung 40261, Indonesia.

Close by at Jalan Asia Africa 140 is **Hotel Kumala Panghegar** (Tel. (22) 43 2286, 432295), with 200 air-conditioned rooms, coffee shop, gym, and sauna. On the rooftop is a revolving restaurant with views across the city, its suburbs, and up to the Mt. Tangkuban-prahu volcano. Book through Garuda or direct at Hotel Pangehegar, Jalan Merdeka 2, P.O. Box 506, Bandung 40111, Indonesia.

The **Grand Hotel Preanger** (Tel. (22) 430682-3), with a new luxury wing added to the Art Deco original, has a 24-hour coffee shop, pool, and health club, and a central location at Jalan Asia Africa 81, Bandung, West Java, Indonesia (Fax: (62) 22 52197). Also in Bandung is the **Naripan Hotel** (Tel. (22) 59383), at Jalan Naripan 31-33 in central Bandung and the cheapest of this group.

Hotel Papandayan (Tel. (22) 43 0799) is another new hotel that offers four-star comfort and service and is fully equipped for the business traveller. This 243-room hotel is located at Jalan Gatot Subroto 83, Bandung 40263, Indonesia (Fax: (62) 22 430988). Book direct, through your travel agent, or through Garuda Indonesia Airlines.

BUDGET-PRICED ACCOMMODATIONS

This group of hotels in Jakarta will cost you around $30 to $50 a night for your room, which will be air-conditioned, with phone, T.V., and hot shower.

The **Menteng Hotel I** (Tel. (21) 325208, 3104151) on Jalan Gondangdia Lama 28, Jakarta Pusat, has one of Jakarta's most famous pick-up bars—the Hotmen Bar. Apart from that, the hotel is well located in central Jakarta close to many restaurants. The same group has another hotel, the **Menteng Hotel II**, around the corner at Jalan Cikini Raya 105, Jakarta Pusat 10330, Indonesia. Both of these hotels have reasonable rooms, a coffee shop and restaurant, and shopping arcade.

The **Sabang Metropolitan** (Tel. (21) 25 4031-9), at Jalan Agus Salim 11 (Sabang), is close to Jalan M. Thamrin, Jakarta's central square, and Gambir railway station. Do not confuse this with the Sabang Palace Hotel, which is not recommended. The Sabang Metropolitan has a 24-hour coffee shop and room service, a bar, and a swimming pool.

On the eastern side of Medan Merdeka square is the colonial-era **Transaera Hotel** (Tel. (21) 35 1373, 35 9336) at Jalan Medan Merdeka Timur 16, Jakarta Pusat, Indonesia.

From central Jakarta we move south along Jalan Sudirman to the suburb of Senayan. On a side street leading towards the national stadium is the **Asri Hotel** (Tel. (21) 584071) on Jalan Pintu Satu Senayan, Senayan, Jakarta Selatan. Carry on farther, past the Ratu Plaza shopping center into Kebayoran Baru, and there are a few other small but comfortable hotels handy to the Block M shopping area.

Try the **Garden Hotel** (Tel. (21) 79 5808) at Jalan Kemang Raya, Kebayoran Baru, Jakarta, Indonesia; **Interhouse** (Tel. (21) 71 6408, 716 6669) at Jalan Melawai, Raya 18-20, Kebayoran Baru, Jakarta, Indonesia; or **Kebayoran Inn** (Tel. (21) 716028, 7391001) at Jalan Senayan 87, Kebayoran Baru, Jakarta, Indonesia.

Bandung

The budget-priced hotels that I am recommending for Bandung are small establishments with clean rooms and a hot-shower bathroom. A fan keeps the room cool (you don't really need air-conditioning in Bandung), and your room may have a phone. Except for limited meals such as breakfast, you will need to leave the hotel to eat. Single rooms will cost you $20 to $30 for their better rooms. More spartan rooms will cost less, but I suggest you at least have a hot-water shower, as the water will get very cold at night.

The **Hotel Soetie**, on the corner of Jalan Sumatra and Jalan Martadinata, is in a pretty suburban area in the administrative area, as is the **Corner Hotel** (Tel. (22) 59921) at Jalan Wastu-kencana 8. Close to the railway station on Jalan Kebon Jati is the **Hotel Melati**.

5. Restaurants and Dining

Eating out is a treat in *Jakarta*. The wide range of races that have come here to do business ensure that there is a wide range of cuisines with a range of prices to match. There are very upscale restaurants in some of the 5-star hotels and the newer office blocks of Jalan Sudirman and Jalan Rasuna Said. Block M has a good selection of fast food, American and Chinese style; Pasar Baru has Chinese seafood; Japanese restaurants and fast food are all over town; and then there is Indonesian

Jakarta street vendor

food—mouth-watering *sate* sticks, hot and spicy *Padang*, and *rijstaffel* smorgasbord. Be careful with the wandering street vendors and daytime sidewalk stalls (*warung*). These stalls don't have running water or refrigeration, so you may end up with a severly upset stomach. Night stalls are a safer bet, such as along Jalan Pecenongan for seafood and Chinese.

The smaller city of *Bandung* has a limited selection of eating places suitable for Western visitors. For better-quality meals stick to the hotels recommended in section 4 or restaurants along Jalan Braga and Jalan Asia Africa. Budget travellers like **Restaurant Sakardana** on Jalan Kebon Jati near the railway station. For upmarket West Javanese (Sundanese) food in an outdoor setting try **Babakan Siliwangi** on Jalan Siliwangi in the northern suburbs. Here you can choose a fish from a pond and watch as it is grilled.

So-called "American food" is available at the 24-hour **Pakuan Coffee Shop** at Hotel Panghegar (Tel. (22) 432287), Jalan Merdeka 2. Also at this hotel is the **Pasundan Dining Room**, specializing in West Javanese food with a buffet dinner. A Sundanese cultural performance accompanies dinner each Wednesday and Saturday, 7:30 P.M. to 10 P.M.. On top of Hotel Panghegar is a revolving restaurant specializing in French cuisine that opens daily from 4 P.M. to 11 P.M..

At the **Hotel Kumala Panghegar** (Tel. (22) 52141) is the **Sakura Japanese Restaurant** (open 11 A.M. to 10:30 P.M.) and the **24-hour Mawar Coffee Shop** that has Chinese dishes, located at Jalan Asia Africa 140. The **Savoy Restaurant** (Tel. (22) 430082) at the Savoy Homann Hotel at Jalan Asia Africa 112 specializes in Indonesian dishes.

The remainder of this section deals with restaurants and dining in Jakarta.

Credit cards are accepted at the better establishments recommended here, more so than in other cities. American Express is the best known, then Diners and Visa and Mastercard. Even so, you will need to carry around more cash in Jakarta than at other times of your trip, at least Rp100,000 to Rp200,000. Cash advances from restaurants are generally not possible. You will need to go to a bank.

Tipping is one habit that is slowly catching on in Jakarta. In hotels and better restaurants a government service charge is added to your bill. Some of it is supposed to get back to the staff. As a result, tipping is not obligatory, but a thank you for good service. Leave the loose change, an Rp500 or Rp1,000 note.

Drinking water from any tap is definitely a no-no. Don't even brush your teeth with it. Only bottled mineral water should come in contact with your mouth. There are many brands that come in 1-liter and 2-liter plastic bottles. This is also the case for other places in Bali and Java.

Don't even make the mistake of thinking water from a modern hotel tap is drinkable. You will quickly get a severely upset stomach and bowels. However, any water that is served to you in a restaurant is drinkable, and the ice should be okay, too.

Some people get so worried about drinking the water that they only drink **alcohol** or Coca-Cola. This is not surprising after you've tried the local beer, such as *Bintang, Anchor, San Miguel,* or locally brewed *Carlsberg.* Spirits are freely imported, though not always served at restaurants. Wine is quite expensive, especially European labels. American wine is rare. Australian wine is the most widely represented and most reasonably priced. It's a nice drop, too, if this Aussie does say so himself.

Each of the five-star **hotels** recommended in the last section has at least one exceptional restaurant. The cuisine may be French, Japanese, or Indonesian, but you could do worse than only eating at hotels if you're only staying in Jakarta for a few days. Then there are the hotel coffee shops and poolside terraces for quick snacks such as a hamburger and fries in a more informal setting. Hotel coffee shops are a favorite with expatriates for a quick lunch. The "expats" also frequent the hotel restaurants if they are acknowledged as the best in town, such as the French food at the Hyatt Aryaduta or the international menu at the Taman Sari Restaurant at the Hilton.

The **Ponderosa** group is the ruler of the Jakarta **steak** scene. To date there are four Ponderosa Steakhouses, each in a high-rise office block, that also offer Mexican and Italian specials. The steaks come out as you asked for and for light eaters, there's also a salad bar with the buffet lunch. Two of the steakhouses are only open for lunch from Monday to Saturday: the Ponderosa (Tel. (21) 348045) at Jalan Merdeka Selatan 17, Wisma Antara Building, which is close to Jalan Thamrin; and the Ponderosa (Tel.(21)583280) in the Arthaloka Building at Jalan Sudirman 2, less than half a mile from the Hotel Indonesia roundabout.

Two other outlets near the Hilton Hotel are open from 11 A.M. to 10:30 P.M. daily. The Ponderosa (Tel. (21) 587731 ext. 251) in the Widjojo Centre, Jalan Sudirman 57, Senayan; and the Ponderosa (Tel. (21) 5780480) in the Centrepoint Building on Jalan Gatot Subroto 35-36, Senayan.

Memories (Tel. (21) 5781008), open for lunch and dinner Monday to Saturday, has old-style atmosphere and expensive steaks and seafood. Memories is located in the Wisma Indocement Building, Jalan Sudirman 70-71, Senayan. **Gandy Steakhouse** (Tel. (21) 333292) at Jalan Cokroaminota 90, Menteng does it more of an Indonesian way, but comes up with quite edible steaks, as well as coffee and ice-cream. Very reasonable prices too, as it caters more to the local market. Other outlets are at Jalan Melawai VIII/2 Block M, (Tel. (21) 715520); and at Jalan Gajah Mada 82A, Kota (Tel. (21) 6200539).

Jakarta has some excellent **seafood** restaurants (Chinese style). **Yun Nyan** (Tel. (21) 364063, 346434) is considered by many to be one of the best seafood restaurants in Southeast Asia, certainly Indonesia. Excellent shrimp, crabs and whole fish, and reasonably priced. Yun Nyan (also spelled Jun Njan) is situated near Pasar Baru at Jalan Batu Ceper 69 (which runs off Jalan Hayam Wuruk). It opens for lunch and dinner 6 days a week and for dinner only on Sundays. It is recommended you make a reservation. Close by is the **Bahari** seafood restaurant on Jalan Batu Tulis. Here the food is good also and even cheaper. **Lembur Kuring** at Jalan Asia Africa, Senayan serves West Javanese-style seafood in an outdoor setting by a lake. Each group has their own pavilion, though don't go too far away from the entrance in case you have any language problems with the waiter. Specializes in grilled whole fish and green Sundanese salad. Prices are very reasonable.

The Tavern (Tel. (21) 376008) at the Hyatt Aryaduta Hotel is a relaxed place to meet friends or have a quiet drink. **The George and Dragon** (Tel. (21) 325625) has more of an English feel and serves good English pub food. Reasonably priced. The George and Dragon is very close to the Hotel Indonesia at Jalan Teluk Betung 32, and is open from 10 A.M. to midnight daily. For a German feel visit the **Old Heidelberg Bar** in the Prince Building at Jalan Sudirman 3-4. German food, music, and hearty fun. **The Jaya Pub** (Tel. (21) 327508) is an institution in Jakarta, though it's not really a pub at all. There's good live jazz, and regulars sometimes sing along with the band. It's in a handy location behind the Jaya Building at Jalan Thamrin 12 (opposite the Sari Pacific Hotel).

French cuisine is well represented in Jakarta. One of the best is **Le Parisien** (Tel. (21) 376008) at the Hyatt Aryaduta Hotel. **Le Bisto** (Tel. (21) 364277) offers intimate French dining with a piano bar. Located near Jalan Thamrin at Jalan Wahid Hasyim 75, Le Bisto specializes in lobster thermidor and Bouillabaisse. The food is good and prices are reasonable. In the same area is **Cog Hardi** (Tel. (21) 336376), a new trendy place that also serves French cuisine. It's located at Jalan Jaksa 18 among the backpacker hostels. **La Rose**, in the Landmark Centre at Jalan Sudirman 1, is a gold-plate French restaurant.

For **Italian** food, try **Ristorante Rugantino** (Tel. (21) 714727) at Jalan Melawai Raya 28, Block M. It's open from 11:30 A.M. to 10:00 P.M. daily. **Pizza Hut** has several outlets in Jakarta, all of them maintaining the standard you're used to. One is in the central Jakarta Theatre Building at Jalan Thamrin 9 (Tel. (21) 352064) and is open from 9 A.M. to 11 P.M. daily. Another is at Ratu Plaza, Jalan Sudirman (Tel. (21) 711011).

Jakarta's better hotels often have visiting chefs from Europe and America who put on special menus for the duration of their visits. These are called "seasons," and vary from hotel to hotel, week to week.

At the **Green Pub** (Tel. (21) 359322) in the Jakarta Theatre Building on Jalan Thamrin you can listen to live jazz every night except Sunday while you dig into enchiladas and other **Mexican** specialities. Contrary to its name, this eating place is not really a pub, and not especially for the Irish. It is, however, a good place for a cheap meal and a cold beer.

For those who want to try some **local** food, in Jakarta you can find many restaurants that specialize in one of the regional cuisines and are safe to eat at. Then there are thousands of small eating houses (*rumah makan*) and street stalls (*warung*) that may not be so safe and cater mainly to the locals and migrants from other provinces in Indonesia.

One of the finest European restaurants in Jakarta, the **Oasis** (Tel. (21) 347819), also serves a sumptuous smorgasbord of Indonesian dishes called *rijsttafel*. A procession of traditionally dressed maidens bring the banquet to your table. It's all very well done and very expensive. Reservations for dinner need to be made well in advance, which may make it difficult for short-term visitors. Open for lunch and dinner Monday-Saturday, the Oasis is located at Jalan Raden Saleh 47, Menteng in a lovely old house that once belonged to an American admiral.

Club Noordwijk (Tel. (21) 353909) is an old Dutch-style restaurant that serves *rijsttafel* as a buffet lunch on Saturdays. They also have steak on the menu. At night you can dance to the sounds of a Dutch street organ. The reasonably priced Club Noordwijk is at Jalan Juanda 5A, Jakarta Pusat, between Pasar Baru and the Presidential Palace.

In the same vein as the Dutch smorgasboard is the North Sumatran one. Named after a town on Sumatra's coastline, *Padang food* is thought of as hot and spicy. That's not always so, though some dishes certainly are, such as *rendang* beef curry and anything that has a red tinge to it. There is no menu for Padang food. You only pay for what you eat. **Sari Bondo** (Tel. (21) 35843) at Jalan Juanda 27 is one of Jakarta's best Padang restaurants, and is quite reasonably priced, too. It's open from 8 A.M. to 10 P.M. daily. Another Padang restaurant in central Jakarta is **Salero Bagindo** (Tel. (21) 336671) at Jalan Cokroaminoto 76, Menteng. It opens daily here and at several other locations around Jakarta. **Natrabu Restaurant** (Tel. (21) 335668) at Jalan Agus Salim (Sabang) 29A, Mentang has traditional Sumatran decor to add to the atmosphere.

Sate is the favorite dish of many people, locals and foreigners alike. Small chunks of chicken, lamb, goat, beef, or pork on skewers are grilled over charcoal. It comes with soy or peanut sauce and is delicious. **Satay House Senayan** is the city's satay specialist, with several western-style and reasonably priced restaurants around town. Try them at Jalan Cokroaminoto 78, Menteng (Tel. (21) 344248); Jalan Kebon Sirih 30, Menteng (Tel. (21) 326238) and Jalan Pakubuwono IV/6, Kebaryoran Baru (Tel. (21) 712752). The Satay Houses open daily for lunch and dinner.

Javanese **fried chicken** is another mouth-watering dish, without the herbs and spices of KFC. Just look for the sign with *ayam goreng*, the exact translation of fried chicken. Adjoining the central square with the Independence Monument is **Ayam Goreng Monas** (Tel. (21) 362187, 363756) on Jalan Silang Monas/Jalan Veteran I. Jakarta's branch of **Ayam Goreng Pemuda** is at Jalan Tomang Raya 32, Jakarta Barat, on the western side of town.

For **East Javanese** cuisine try the **Handayani Restaurant** (Tel. (21) 373614) at Jalan Abdul Muis 36E, Tanah Abang, which is to the west of the Independence Monument. West Javanese (Sundanese) cuisine was mentioned earlier under seafood.

If you feel like outdoor, informal dining, head for the **Jalan Pecenongan night market**. During the day the shops sell cars and spare parts. In the late afternoon the shops start to close and benches, gas cookers, and stools arrive to create one of Jakarta's favorite outdoor eating places. Prices are low but even the rich come for fresh Jakarta-style **Chinese** cooking, such as noodles, froglegs, and seafood. Give the wandering minstrels Rp100 and they will go away and let you eat in peace. Jalan Pecenongan is near the Pasar Baru shopping area, running off Jalan Juanda/Jalan Veteran. For reasonably priced noodle dishes try **Bakmi Gajah Mada** (Tel. (21) 6294689) at Jalan Gajah Mada 92, Taman Sari. They're also at Jalan Thamrin 21, Menteng (Tel. (21) 310 2092); and Jalan Melawai Raya 3, Kebayoran Baru (Tel. (21) 739 8038). Open for lunch and dinner daily.

Going a little up-market, there's the **Summer Palace** (Tel. (21) 33 3899), serving Sichuan and Cantonese cuisine in the Tedja Building, at Jalan Menteng Raya 29, Menteng. Reservations are recommended for lunch in the large, Hong Kong-style restaurant. Open for lunch and dinner daily.

The **Dragon Gate** (Tel. (21) 36 5293) at Jalan Juanda 19, Gambir, is a reasonably priced Cantonese and seafood restaurant that opens from 6 P.M. to 3 A.M. daily.

Other Chinese restaurants, **Bahari** and **Yun Nyan**, were mentioned under seafood.

The **Omar Khayam** (Tel. (21) 35 6719) specializes in **northern Indian** dishes such as *tandoori*. There is also a buffet lunch. It's good food at moderate prices. Located close to Pasar Baru at Jalan Antara 5-7. Adjoining the George and Dragon English-style pub is **George's Curry House** (Tel. (21) 32 5625) that serves relatively inexpensive Indian, Sri Lankan, and Sumatran curries. George's is at Jalan Teluk Betung, which runs off Jalan Thamrin near Hotel Indonesia's tennis courts. The **Orient Express** (Tel. (21) 380 6676) has an inexpensive buffet of northern Indian dishes as well as ordering off the menu. Open daily for lunch and dinner, The Orient Express is at Jalan Majapahit 28 C-D, Harmoni, not far from the Presidential Palace.

Jakarta's biggest expatriate group is Japanese, so this has led to a profusion of **Japanese** restaurants. Service is always good but prices tend to be expensive and dishes sometimes are on the small side. **Chiku Yo Tei** (Tel. (21) 58 8220-1) is a favorite with Western locals. The menu gives you plenty to choose from, and the location opposite Ratu Plaza shopping center makes it easy to find. Open daily for lunch and dinner, Chiku Yo Tei is at Jalan Sudirman 61, Senayan. Even more expensive is **Tokyo Garden** (Tel. (21) 520 7069), though the decor and the food make it worthwhile. Tokyo Garden opens daily for dinner and Monday through Saturday for lunch. It's located south of Menteng at Jalan Rasuna Said 10-11, Lippo Life Building, Kuningan. A very popular, reasonably priced Japanese restaurant is **Kikugawa** (Tel. (21) 32 7198), at Jalan Cikini IV/13 (formerly Jalan Kebon Binatang), Menteng. Kikugawa is a long-standing favorite with Western residents of Jakarta. **Hana Sushi** (21) 711721) serves *sushi*, *sashimi*, and *tempura* at moderate prices. Reservations should be made for lunch or dinner. Hana Sushi is inside the Ratu Plaza Shopping Centre on Jalan Sudirman, Senayan, and is open daily.

The only **Korean** restaurant recommended to me by my friends in Jakarta is the inexpensive **Koreana** (Tel. (21) 71 3776) which specializes in Korean barbecue. Situated at Block M, Kebayoran, Koreana is open for dinner each day at Jalan Melawi VI/3.

American-style fast food in Jakarta encompasses burgers, Southern fried chicken, and doughnuts. Several of the outlets are at Block M, catering to the expatriate and upper-class local population. **Kentucky Fried Chicken** has outlets at Jalan Melawai Raya 84, Block M, (Tel. (21) 73 1463); Ratu Plaza, Senayan, (Tel. (21) 71 2182); Jalan Cikini Raya 119, Menteng, (Tel. (21) 32 1045); and Jalan Agus Salim 31-33, Menteng, (Tel. (21) 32 2035). KFC is open from 10 A.M. to 10 P.M. daily.

Bob's Big Boy (Tel. (21) 514900) at Kuningan Plaza Tower on Jalan Rasuna Said is open from 10 A.M. to 10 P.M. Monday to Friday and 11 P.M. on Saturdays and Sundays.

Dairy Queen (Tel. (21) 730 7628) opens from 10 A.M. to 11 P.M. daily at Jalan Melawai Raya 72, Block M.

Dunkin Donuts (Tel. (21) 77 4771) are open from 9 A.M. to 6 P.M. daily at Jalan Melawai Raya 8A, Block M.

Pizza Hut, who I have listed under Italian food, has a delivery service or a sit-down menu.

Church's Texas Fried Chicken has outlets at Ratu Plaza shopping center, Senayan, (Tel. (21) 711292); Jalan Samanhudi 14-16 (Pasar Besi Plaza), Pasar Baru, (Tel. (21) 376960); and at Jalan Cikini Raya 60, Menteng (Tel. (21) 32 0370).

Swensen's Ice Cream continues the traditions of old San Francisco at Jalan Cikini Raya 119, Menteng (Tel. (21) 32 1045) and Jalan Melawai Raya 84-85, Block M (Tel. (21) 77 1181). These and other Swensen's outlets open daily from 10 A.M. to 10 P.M..

If you're looking for light and healthy fare, the **Ponderosa Steakhouses** already mentioned have fresh salad bars and other light dishes. **The Thistle** serves Danish open sandwiches at Jalan Sudirman 36 (Wisma Benhil Building), Senayan from 8 A.M. to 7 P.M. Monday to Friday and 8 A.M. to 5 P.M. on Saturday. They're closed Sundays. **Eye of the Wind** (Tel. (21) 712209) has Danish open sandwiches as well as heavier meals such as pizza. It opens from 9 A.M. to 9 P.M. Mondays to Saturdays and 9 A.M. to 5 P.M. on Sundays in the Ratu Plaza shopping center on Jalan Sudirman, Senayan. Danish open sandwiches are also served at **The Shakespeare** (Tel. (21) 321808 ext. 242), a Tudor-style English pub in the Wisma Kosgoro Building on Jalan Thamrin, Menteng that's open from 11 A.M. to10 P.M. Mondays to Saturday. Light snacks are also served in the coffee shops of most of the four- and five-star hotels, such as Hotel Indonesia, the Hilton, and Borobudur.

6. Sightseeing

Jakarta's most interesting sights are the reminders of the colonial era, when it was called Batavia. In the area between the Kota railway station and the old Dutch fort at Pasar Ikan there are many original buildings, some of which house museums. This part of Jakarta was the center of the city until the mid-1800s when it started spreading south toward Menteng. Nowadays Jakarta Kota is a vibrant **Chinatown**, so it is worth visiting for this reason also, especially Jalan Pancoran. As the city outgrew old Batavia, new government buildings were constructed at Weldevreden, in the area between the Borobudur Hotel, Pasar Baru, and the Presidential Palace.

For a part of Jakarta that reflects the non-Western element of Indonesian life, you can visit **Tanah Abang**, **Senen**, or **Jatinegara**. These are three lower middle class shopping areas where foreigners are not normally seen.

Heading away from Jakarta, you can go west toward **Carita Beach**, **Merak**, and **Sumatra**, north into the **Java Sea** and the **Thousand Islands**, or south to **Bogor**, into the **highlands**, **Bandung**, and the southern coastline on the Indian Ocean.

If you plan to spend a few days exploring the areas to the south you would be better off setting up base at *Bandung*. Otherwise you will waste too much time traveling along the congested roads that lead out of Jakarta. In Bandung, many colonial administrative buildings remain, as well as a line of **Art Deco buildings** along Jalan Asia Africa that were built in the 1920s by Dutch architects. The Savoy Homann Hotel, the Grand Hotel Preanger original building, Gedung Merdeka Building, and also the Gedung Sate Building are the best examples.

Old Jakarta

Taman Fatahillah, just off Jalan Pintu Besar Utara (opposite the station), is the heart of the original Batavia. On the southern side of the square stands the restored *stadhuis*, or town hall, built in 1710. This building is now the **Jakarta Historical Museum**, with a collection of maps, coins, furniture, stoneware, weapons, and household items. The **Jakarta Art Gallery**, on the eastern side of the square, is housed in another colonial building. On the western side of the square is the **Wayang Museum** with a huge collection of *wayang* leather puppets. These and other museums are open 9 A.M. to 2 P.M. Tuesday to Thursday; 9 A.M. to 11 A.M. on Friday; to 1 P.M. Saturday; 3 P.M. Sunday, and are closed Monday.

Pasar Ikan has an old **Dutch fort**, the **Maritime Museum**, and shops selling souvenirs and handicrafts. At dawn this area is the main fish market. Across a small inlet of water near the fort is the old port of **Sunda Kelapa**, where sailing boats unload their shipments from the other islands. The shoreline used to be much closer to the entrance to the port and Pasar Ikan, but continuous land reclamation has been used to make space for warehouses.

Kota railway station is another colonial era building, as is the **Bank Indonesia** building. **Jalan Kopi** is a busy street of wholesalers with some original buildings still standing.

The second major area of colonial buildings was the suburb known as **Weltevreden**. This is a very open, spacious area so if you plan to walk

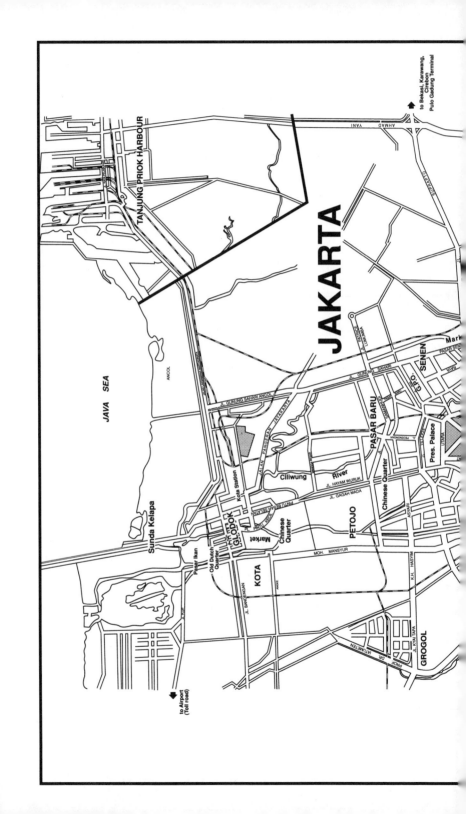

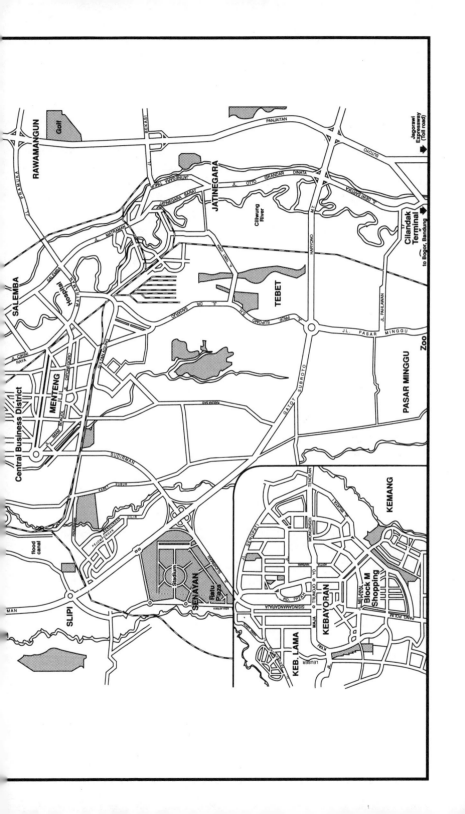

around you would be advised to start at 9 A.M. or 3 P.M. to avoid the heat. A good place to start is the **National Museum** on Jalan M. Merdeka Barat (west) which is an extension of Jalan Thamrin. The museum building, housing a vast collection of Hindu-Buddhist pieces, has been designated as a museum itself. Walk away from Jalan Thamrin to the corner of the square. Straight ahead is the **Presidential Palace**, formerly the governor-general's residence. This is about as close as you can get to the palace because it is not open to the public. Follow the road to the left as it changes its name to Jalan Majapahit. On the right is the Majapahit Hotel. Continue along the right-hand side of the street (with the traffic) for 200 yards to a large intersection called Harmoni. The building you are standing next to is the **Gedung Harmoni** building, which was once the terminus for a tram service that ran from here along Jalan Gajah Mada to Kota railway station and the old town hall. From Harmoni turn right without crossing the street. Continue along Jalan Veteran (Jalan Juanda on the other side) past the rear of the Presidential Palace compound. Look towards the **Monas obelisk** and you will notice that from here the gold flame on top takes on a different shape—that of a woman. President Sukarno was instrumental in having it built that way. The Monas obelisk has a museum at its base and a lookout on top. At the end of Jalan Veteran, in front of you stands **Istiqual Mosque**, completed in the 1970s.

A little farther on, on your right is the **General Post Office** and **Stadsschouwberg**, a former theater. Meanwhile, the street has changed names to Jalan Pos. Here you can cross the street and canal and enter the **Pasar Baru** shopping area, where there are some old shops, but mostly newer and uninteresting. Better to turn right into Jalan Gedung Kesenian to the **town square** of Weltevreden, now Lapangen Banteng. On the far side is the modern Borobudur Hotel. Turn right as you come to the square, and on your right is the Catholic Cathedral. Continue around the park to your left, past the Borobudur Hotel, and follow the traffic to your right into Jalan Pejambon. One hundred yards on you cross the Ciliwung River, which flows into Sunda Kelapa port. On your left is the round-topped **Protestant Church Emmanuel**. Straight ahead of you is the **Gambir railway station**.

Turn left into Jalan M. Merdeka Timur and on your left is the Transaera Hotel. You are now coming to the end of Weltevreden, though interesting colonial buildings are sprinkled throughout the suburb of Menteng. One of the more beautiful streets is Jalan Tengku Umar. Just past the Transaera Hotel is the Petroleum Club. Here you need to cross the street, not an easy matter whether on street level or by pedestrian overpass. Once you do cross, you pass the American Embassy on your left. Continue along Jalan M. Merdeka Selatan (south) and you will come back to Jalan Thamrin.

For me, these two areas are by far the most interesting in Jakarta. And they are alive—integral to today's Indonesia. Less so is **Taman Mini Indonia**, with houses and exhibits from the other islands of Indonesia. Taman Mini is quite far from central Jakarta, just off the Bogor toll road (Jagowari). Also on this side of town at Pasar Minggu is the **Ragunan Zoo**. Here you can see the Komodo dragon, orangutan, birds, and other Indonesian animals. Both the zoo and Taman Mini should be visited Monday through Thursday to avoid the weekend crowds. Jakarta's Disneyland-style playground is called **Ancol**, and is on the Java Sea beachfront. Here is fantasy world and other attractions such as an art market, water sports, cottages, and the Horison Hotel.

OUTSIDE JAKARTA

Bogor is about an hour's drive south of central Jakarta, somewhat less from Kebayoran Baru. Known as Buitesborg by the Dutch, this town at the base of the highlands has always been a retreat from humidity or sicknesses for Jakarta's inhabitants. The old summer palace and botanical gardens (Kebun Raya) are open to the public. Sukarno spent a lot of time at Bogor in this palace.

It rains almost every day in Bogor, so visit the gardens early in the morning. A *Patas* express bus runs from the Cililitan bus terminal in Jakarta to the Bogor bus terminal along the Jagowari toll road. To get to Cililitan take a taxi or a Patas bus from outside Hotel Indonesia or Block M.

Puncak (literally "peak") is at the top of the range between Bogor and Bandung. There are hundreds of cottages for rent, small hotels, swimming pools, lots of trees, fresh air, and cool nights. Puncak is a favorite place to relax away from the city and work. Many Jakarta residents have holiday houses at Cibodas and Cianjur.

A longer and less windy (meaning less dangerous) road from Bogor to Bandung goes through the medium-sized town of **Sukabumi**. To the east of town are Mt. Gede and Mt. Pangrango. Not far from town there are picturesque **sulphur baths** at Sakah.

Pelabuhan Ratu (Queen's Harbor) is a natural harbor named after the goddess of the South Seas, Nyai Loro Kidul. The sea here is especially dangerous, and tourists regularly drown in front of the *Samudra Beach Hotel* (Tel. (21) 340601), so be careful. The rips and crosscurrents will give even the best surfers a real swim for their money. There are strange tales of scrub fires on the headland at night, but in the mornings there is no sign of there having been a fire! For budget rooms, try any of the *losmen* on the waterfront as you enter town.

To get to Pelabuhan Ratu, take the turn-off at Cibadak if coming from Bogor, or turn off at Sukabumi if coming from Bandung.

OUTSIDE BANDUNG

The highlight of most people's visit to Bandung is looking down into the **volcano** Mt. Tangkuban-prahu, just outside the city. At the base of the mountain is the small village of **Lembang**. Try some of the hot corn from the street vendors. From Lembang you can drive or walk two and a half miles (4 kilometers) to the crater and geysers. It is best to leave Bandung at 7:00 A.M. so that you can get to the top and look back over Bandung before the mist sets in. For trekkers, get off at Jayagiri village before Lembang and walk 5 miles (8 kilometers) through the forest to the volcano. Just outside Lembang towards Bandung is the colonial-era Grand Hotel, and at Gegar Kalong is an astronomy observatory. To get to Lembang and the mountain you can catch a taxi, or travel with the locals in an *opelet* from outside the southern entrance to Bandung's railway station on Jalan Kebon Jati.

Dago Tea House is a pleasant place for refreshments in the northern suburbs. The outside terrace overlooking Bandung is beautiful, but it gets quite chilly as soon as the sun sets, so have something warm with you if you go there for afternoon tea.

The best-known **hot sulphur springs** near Bandung are at Ciater and Maribaya. Ciater has a number of pools ranging in temperature from 95 degrees F.(35 degrees C.) to 108 degrees F.(42 degrees C.). At Maribaya there are bath houses and a hot river. To get there you can go by taxi from Bandung, or by public transportation. To Ciater, an *opelet* leaves from the terminal (near the southern entrance to the railway station) on Jalan Kebon Jati. To Maribaya, catch a minibus from the same terminal.

Garut is a small town set in a highland valley, a few hours' drive from Bandung. The scenery is beautiful and the hot baths at Tarogong are a pleasant walk from town.

BEACH RESORTS IN WEST JAVA

On the southern coast of Java, halfway to Jogyakarta from Bandung, is the mainly domestic-tourist resort area of **Pangandaran**. There are guesthouses and a small hotel on the beach facing the sunset (*pantai barat*). Watch the local fishermen and women pull in their nets on the eastern beach in the mornings and the western beach in the afternoons.

Carita Beach, West Java

Pangandaran Beach, south coast of Java

Westerners that go to Pangandaran are mostly backpackers, catching the train from Banjar, then a minibus to Pangandaran market, and then a *becak* to the beach. From Cilacap harbor there is a ferry to Pangandaran.

Carita is the closest beach resort to Jakarta, some two to three hours to the west. Cottages can be rented from Jakarta or you can stay at the basic **Krakatau Beach Hotel** (Tel. (254) 81206, 21043); (21) 320252). Closer to Jakarta at the village of **Anyer** is the moderately-priced Patra Jasa-run *Anyer Beach Hotel* (Tel. (254) 367838); (21) 510322, 410608). At **Merak** is the *Merak Beach Hotel* (Tel. (21) 771240). Merak is the port for ferries going to Sumatra. In the ocean off Carita is the new **Krakatau Volcano**, having risen again from the sea floor after it was totally destroyed in the 1883 eruption. Boat trips can be organized from Krakatau Beach Hotel if the volcano is not too active at the time. When it is active, flames and smoke are visible from the beach.

The **Ujung Kulon National Park** (literally "west cape") can only be reached by boat from Labuan harbor. Prior permission from the Jakarta office of the Department of Parks and Wildlife is needed to visit the last sanctuary of the Javanese rhinoceros. You would need to be lucky to see one, as there are few left.

Taxi is the easiest way to the Carita coast, or by bus from the Grogol or Kalideres terminals. Buses go to Carita in the morning and return in the afternoons. By bus the trip takes some four hours to Carita or three hours to Merak.

The One Thousand Islands Group off Jakarta's coastline is the city's most popular getaway. The name is a literal translation of their Indonesian name *Pulau Seribu*, though actually there are only 128 islands. Some of the islands, such as **Pulau Putri**, are open to daytrippers. Others are private islands that offer package tours which include transfer to the island by fast boat or even helicopter. All of the islands and resorts listed below have bungalow-style accommodations for overnight or several-night stays. Coral reefs and abundant fish life, two things that are missing from public islands such as Putri, are the main attractions of these more secluded islands. Tour operators can organize a trip for you to *Pulau Seribu Marine Resort, Southern Cross Marine Club, Burung Indah, New Saktu, Sepa Island,* or *Kotok Island.* Package prices range from US$35 to $100 per person per day, depending on the quality of your accommodations, amount of diving included, and mode of transfer to your island. Prices should be lower during the week for rooms, but the transfer may cost more. Whenever you go you'll be sure to enjoy yourself.

The distance of the islands from Jakarta ranges from 25 miles to 50 miles. Slower boats take about two hours from Ancol Marina, faster ones less than an hour.

7. Guided Tours and Going It Alone

Several of the national tour operators that you may have (or will) come across in other towns and cities of Bali and Java have their head offices in Jakarta. Different tour companies have different schedules for tours, so you can pick and choose to make the most of your day. **Natrabu** (Tel. (21) 332876) at Jalan Agus Salim 29A, Menteng, (Fax: (62) 21 322386); **Pacto** (Tel. (21) 346634) at Jalan Surabaya 8, Menteng and at Hotel Borobudur (Tel. (21) 356952); and **Panorama Tour** (Tel. (21) 350438, 376718) at Jalan Balikpapan 22B, Petojo (Fax: (62) 21 36 3977) are some of the better tour operators that run city tours and further afield to Bogor, Bandung, The Thousand Islands, and the Krakatoa (Krakatau in Indonesian) volcano. As well as these tour operators, each of the major hotels has a tour operator on hand that will be able to show you around.

In Bandung, try **Interlink** (Tel. (22) 50614, 51251) at Jalan Wastuken-cana 5; or **Surya Budaya** (Tel. (22) 52029) at Jalan A. Yani 25.

CITY TOURS

Panorama has a comprehensive cultural tour of old Jakarta, including museums, Pasar Ikan, and Sunda Kelapa, as well as a quick visit to a *batik* factory. This five-hour tour starts at 9 A.M. daily (except Mondays, when the museums are closed) and costs US$15 per person. Tour code is PT 02.

HIGHLAND TOURS

The same company does a sweep through Bogor and Bandung that is recommended if you don't want to make your own arrangements. See Bogor's Botanical Gardens, tea plantations at Puncak Pass, Ciater hot springs, and drive to the top of Mt. Tangkuban-prahu volcano. This two-day tour costs $125 per person for a single room. One-day tours cover the same territory. An 8-hour return trip to Bogor, Puncak, and a safari game park costs $30 per person. This one leaves at 9:30 A.M.. An early start at 7 A.M. is needed for the 12-hour trip to Bandung via Puncak. After a brief city tour you drive to the top of the Tangkuban-prahu volcano and then to some Ciater hot sulphur pools for a swim.

KRAKATOA VOLCANO

Krakatau Ujung Kulon Tours & Travel (Tel. (21) 320252) is in the Wisata International Hotel on Jalan Thamrin, behind Hotel Indonesia. They specialize in tours out to the volcano and wildlife-viewing safaris into Ujung Kulon National Park on the southwestern tip of Java, facing Sumatra and the Indian Ocean. This tour operator has another office at Jalan Gondangdia Lama 28, Menteng (Tel. (21) 330846).

Panorama Tours also visits Krakatau Island, which broke the surface in 1929 after the original volcano was blasted into oblivion in the 1883 eruption. You stay overnight in a cottage at Anyer, have a picnic on the island, and explore Kratatau for $275 per person.

Sometimes it is not possible to go out to Krakatau Island because of the intense and dangerous volcanic activity. So active is the volcano that this island continues to grow at an extraordinary rate.

Batemuri Tours (Tel. (21) 320807, 320982) runs three- and four-day adventure trips to Krakatau and Ujung Kulon. The longer you spend in the park the better your chance of catching a glimpse of the rare Javanese rhinocerous. The price for the trips depends on the number of participants. The four-day trip costs $400 per person if you have two people in your group, or $350 per person if there are three or four. A three-day trip costs from $220 to $300 per person. Batemuri Tours also has their office at the Wisata International Hotel on Jalan Thamrin (behind the Hotel Indonesia).

WATER CRUISES

The Thousand Islands is the favored destination of most water cruises. By water cruises I mean one-day tours; for overnight stays check the last entry under Sightseeing. Day cruises usually leave from the Ancol Marina, which is adjacent to the Horizon Hotel. The islands (actually only 128) range from 25 to 50 miles offshore, and travelling time is 2 to 3 hours each way depending on the type of boat.

Panorama Tours (Tel. (21) 350438) runs a cruise to Pulau Anyer Island, which is 25 miles offshore. This ten-hour cruise leaves at 7 A.M. from the marina and costs $40 per person. An overnight stay costs an extra $60 per person. Panorama also has a day cruise to Sepa Island for $50 per person that leaves from the marina at 7 A.M. and returns at 4 P.M..

Hovermarine (Tel. (21) 325608) operates hovercraft cruises and shuttle services to The Thousand Islands, Ujung Kulon, and Lampung in South Sumatra. Contact them for departure time and to check where they leave from. Their office is at Jalan Gondangdia Lama 26, Menteng.

8. Water Sports

The waters off Jakarta are the best way to escape the city heat. Pulau Seribu, or **The Thousand Islands**, are a couple of hours offshore from Ancol Marina or Tanjung Priok Harbor. Many of the islands have cottages or lodges available for rental on a nightly or weekly basis. The coral and fish in this part of the Java Sea are both colorful and abundant. Some of the lodges are constructed of natural materials and are set amidst rainforests. Others are modern cottages facing white sand beaches with a pool and jetty for your boat on hand. Use the boat to search for other coral reefs or just snorkel 25 yards offshore.

Jakarta's other marine playground is along Java's **west coast**, starting at Merak and extending past Anyer to Carita Beach, some 100 miles (160 kilometers) from Jakarta. A good highway now goes most the way to Merak, so the trip takes 1 to 2 hours, depending on the number of city people with the same idea. As would be expected, the roads are packed on Saturdays leaving Jakarta and Sunday afternoons coming back.

SWIMMING

For water sports in the city, several hotels have **swimming pools** open to the public for an entry fee of $3 to $4 (Rp6,000 to Rp8,000) per person. Jakarta's largest aquatic complexes are at the Senayon Sports Centre and at Ancol (Tel. (21) 68 2521). Pools that are open to the public are at the following hotels: *Hotel Indonesia* (Tel. (21) 32 0008) on Jalan Thamrin; *Kartika Plaza* (Tel. (21) 32 1008) also on Jalan Thamrin; *Sahid Jaya* (Tel. (21) 58 7031) at Jalan Sudirman 86 Senayan; and also at the *Pondok Indah County Club* (Tel. (21) 764906) at Pondok Indah.

DIVING

Close by to Jakarta, Pulau Seribu (The Thousand Islands) offers the best coral and the clearest water. Along the Carita coast visibility is often poor due to water turbulence, wave action, and riptides. Diving conditions for Bali are covered in detail in Chapter 5. Bali has far better coral, and dive companies there can arrange dive trips to distant reefs. For the Thousand Islands though, these PADI-certified companies will be able to help you out with equipment rental and repair, and trips to the islands. *Divemasters* (Tel. (21) 58 3051, ext. 9037) and *Jakarta Dive School & Pro Shop* (Tel. 58 3051, ext. 9008) are both in the Bazaar shopping arcade at the Hilton Hotel on Jalan Sudirman. Divemasters also has an office at Ancol Marina (Tel. (21) 68 0385). *Dive Indonesia* (Tel. (21) 36 0209; 37 0108, ext. 76024-5), at the Borobudur Hotel, sells, rents, and repairs equipment and fills air tanks.

SAILBOARDING/WINDSURFING

The Thousand Islands are a beautiful area to windsurf, looking down into the water as you go along. The water is clear, though winds are not always strong. There's also the problem of coral, so wear some old tennis shoes. The private resorts recommended under Sightseeing have boards for guests. On **Pulau Putri** you can rent boards, but they are generally old and poorly maintained. There is a windsurfing club at the *Horizon Hotel* at Ancol, but winds near the coast tend to be light and the water not too clean. If you want to rent a board and are able to travel with it, try *P.T. Far East Trading Indonesia* (Tel. (21) 489 4272, 489 9774) at Jalan Tawes 6, Rawamungun (East Jakarta). They sell and rent Mistral boards.

9. Other Sports

PARTICIPATION SPORTS

"Members-only" clubs and the major hotels have the best **sports facilities** in Jakarta and Bandung. For short-term visitors this means that you will need to stay at the *Hilton, Borobundur Inter-Continental, Hotel Indonesia,* or the new *Grand Hyatt,* as these have tennis and squash courts, a jogging track, and a gym.

The *Ancol Golf Course* (Tel. (21) 68 2122) at Ancol by the sea is one of the better-maintained **golf courses** in Jakarta that is not restricted to members only. Others are the *Kebayoran Golf Club* (Tel. (21) 58 2508) at Jalan Asia Africa, Pintu 9, Senayan, and the *Halim Golf Course* (Tel. (21) 80 0793) on Jalan Halim Raya, Jakarta Timur. You will need to check whether these courses rent clubs.

These **bowling** centers are open from 10 A.M. to 12 midnight daily. They are best visited during the day as evenings they are quite busy with competitions. Lane fees are very reasonable. Try *Jaya Ancol Bowl* at Ancol recreation park; *Kebayoran Bowling Centre* (Tel. (21) 71 3208) at Jalan Melawai IX, Block M, Kebayoran Baru; *Kartika Chandra Bowling Center* (Tel. (21) 51 1008) on Jalan Gatot Subroto; and *Jakarta Bowling Center* (Tel. (21) 34 4876) on Jalan M. Merdeka Selatan in central Jakarta.

SPECTATOR SPORTS

Soccer and **badminton** are Indonesia's favorite sports for the average person. The country rates very high in the badminton stakes and invariably holds the world title for singles and doubles. The National Sports Stadium at Senayan is the best venue for viewing soccer and other sports.

10. Shopping

Jakarta people love to shop. The markets and shopping centers are busy from early morning into the evening every day and the shelves are always well stocked. Quality may at times be questionable for locally made goods, but prices are low to compensate. Imported goods, on the other hand are usually expensive, especially for luxury consumer items, though that doesn't seem to deter wealthy Indonesians who are able to make fortunes producing foreign goods under license and supplying them to the largely closed local market.

Arts and crafts from all over Indonesia are sold in Jakarta. The best buys are **batik** from Jogya and Pekalongan; **wood carvings** and **jewelry** from Bali; **woven rugs** from Sumba, Timor, and Roti; and **tribal art** from Borneo and New Guinea. However, the same items could also be bought at Jogya or in Bali, and prices there are lower.

In Jakarta, *batik* cloth and clothing are best bought in the traditional markets at Tanah Abang and Cikini. Both are in central Jakarta and service a largely middle class Indonesian population. The *batik* there is what the locals and domestic tourists prefer, though there are usually one or two Westerners shopping there, too. *Pasar Tanah Abang* market is at the western end of Jalan Wahid Hasyim at the corner of Jalan Fakhruddin in the suburb of Tanah Abang. Not far from here is Museum Textil on Jalan Tubun 4, which has old *batik* on display.

Pasar Cikini is on the left side of Jalan Cikini Raya, Menteng. Refer to Chapter 2 for techniques on bargaining and price haggling, which are the normal way of doing business in traditional markets and shops. Another market that you shouldn't miss in central Jakarta is the *Jalan Surabaya* street market, with dozens of kiosks selling colonial antiques, Chinese ceramics, leather goods, and plenty of fakes. *Caveat emptor.*

The major *batik* companies have their own showrooms in Jakarta, and it is there that you will find high-quality modern designs in both *sarong* lengths and ready-to-wear clothing. *Batik Keris* (Tel. (21) 33 0834) is at Jalan Cokroaminoto 87-89, Menteng; the President Hotel, 1st floor, Jalan Thamrin (Tel. (21) 32 0508, ext. 2221); the Ratu Plaza, ground floor, Jalan Sudirman, Senayan (Tel. (21) 71 1579); and at Golden Truly, 2nd floor, Jalan Fatatehan 68, Block M, Kebayoran Baru (Tel. (21) 71 7371). *Batik Danar Hadi* (Tel. (21) 32 3663) has showrooms at Jalan Radeh Saleh 1A, Menteng; Jalan Melawai Raya 69-70, Kebayoran Baru (Tel. (21) 77 3319); Jalan Tanah Abang II/1A, Tanah Abang (Tel. (21) 35 3839); and at Sarinah Pasar Baru, Jalan Pasar Baru 41-43 (Tel. (21) 35 4658). *Batik Semar* (Tel. (21) 59 3514) has its main showroom at Jalan Tomang Raya 54, Tomang; and a branch at Jalan Hanglekir II/23, Kebayoran Baru (Tel. (21) 77 1849). Other independent *batik* shops are at Block M and Pasar Baru.

Art shops are the best places to find **Balinese carvings** and **tribal art** such as **woven rugs** and **baskets**. There are several of these at Block M, Menteng and at Gajah Mada Plaza on Jalan Gajah Mada, Petojo. You will also find these goods at Jalan Surabaya market. At Block M, on Jalan Melawai V, the *Aldiron Plaza* building devotes its third floor to handicraft stores. *Shinta Art Shop* (Tel. (21) 71 5788) is at Jalan Melawai VI/17; and *Pasar Raya Sarinah Jaya* (Tel. (21) 71 1269) at Jalan Iskandarsyah II/2 has one floor that sells handicrafts. In central Jakarta, *Jakarta Handicraft*

Centre (Tel. (21) 338157), at Jalan Pekalongan 12a, sells **statues, carvings, precious stones, Bangka tin**, and other metal objects. *Ardjuna*, (Tel. (21) 34 4251) at Jalan Majapahit 16A, sells **artifacts** from Bali, Jogya, and China. *Sarinah Department Store* on Jalan Thamrin has one floor for handicrafts and *batik*. *Pasar Seni*, in the Ancol recreation center, has shops selling a wide range of arts and crafts.

Jakarta has several comprehensive **bookshop** chains which stock a good range of English-language titles. *Ayumas Agung* (Tel. (21) 35 4563) is at Jalan Kwitang 6, Menteng, and has branches at Rata Plaza, 1st floor (Tel. (21) 739 5382); and T.J. Plaza at Jalan Melawai Raya I (Tel. (21) 71 3958). *Gramedia* (Tel. (21) 629 7809) at Jalan Gajah Mada 106-9 is one of Indonesia's best chains. They have another branch on Jalan Pintu Air at Pasar Baru. Jalan Kwitang, at the Senen end, is the original bookshop street. As well as *Ayamas Agung* at number 6, there is *Gunung Agung* (Tel. (21) 310 2004) at number 37/38.

Newsagents in the major hotels have a good range of English-language **newspapers, magazines**, and some **paperbacks**. Try *Hotel Indonesia, Borobudur*, and the *Hilton*.

Traditional markets are the best place to buy **fresh fruit**. *Pasar Cikini* on Jalan Cikini Raya, Menteng, and *Pasar Melawai* at Block M both have a good range. Imported fruit such as apples are sold on Jalan Pinangsia in Glodok. Packaged foodstuffs, local and imported, are sold at most shopping plazas and in the smaller shops at Pasar Baru and Block M. *Supermarkets* in Jakarta have a good range of food items. There is a group of supermarkets on Jalan Cokroaminoto in Menteng, namely *Hero, Galeal*, and *Safeways*. Hero has branches on Jalan Gondangdia Lama, Menteng, and on Jalan Tomang Raya, Tomang. Galeal is also at Block M. *Golden Truly* is an excellent supermarket in the Jakarta Theatre Building on Jalan Thamrin. *Kem Chicks* on Jalan Kemang Raya, Kebayoran Baru is one of Jakarta's best.

Alcohol is cheapest at Hero, Galeal, or Safeways.

IN BANDUNG

Art shops in Bandung are congregated along Jalan Braga and near the square on Jalan Asia Africa. *Sarinah* is at Jalan Braga 10; *Tatarah* at Jalan Braga 75; and *Sukama* at Jalan Braga 88. *Bapika* is in the Miramar Shopping Centre on Jalan Alun-Alun Timur, and *Karya Nusantara* is at Jalan Asia Africa 94.

Two of the bookstore chains previously mentioned have branches in Bandung. *Gramedia* (Tel. (22) 50 835) is on Jalan Merdeka 43, and *Ayumas Agung* (Tel. (22) 43 0797) is in the Gedung Pelaguna Nusantara building.

Where the Shops Are

The two favorite shopping areas with Westerners in Jakarta are Pasar Baru near the General Post Office and Block M in Kebayoran Baru. *Pasar Baru* (literally "new market") extends all the way along Jalan Pasar Baru to Jalan Samanhudi and the Metro Department Store. Side streets off Jalan Pasar Baru, such as Jalan Pintu Air, specialize in sporting goods. Pasar Baru is good for daily necessities, clothing, and toiletries. Try the Matahari Department Store. *Senen* is an important wholesale and commercial area bordering central Jakarta, but it is not recommended due to a problem with pickpockets. *Tanah Abang* market has wholesale *batik* and textiles. In central Jakarta, the better shopping centers are *Menteng Plaza* on Jalan Cokroaminoto 79, Menteng, and *Plaza Indonesia* on Jalan Thamrin near the Hotel Indonesia, which has over 400 upmarket shops. The *Ratu Plaza* is a large, modern supermarket shopping center at the Kebayoran end of Jalan Sudirman. It has a bookstore, department store, and restaurants.

Block M is favored by foreigners and expatriates because goods sold are of a higher quality and are the type of things they consider daily necessities. Indonesian and Western tastes do not always coincide. Another attraction of Block M is the ordered street layout and plentiful parking. Block M is bounded by four main roads: Jalan S. Hassanndin as you enter Kebayoran from the city, Jalan P. Polim on the western side, Jalan Melawai Raya on the southern side, and Jalan Melawai I to the east. *Melawai Plaza* and *Sarinah Jaya* are on Jalan Melawai I, and *Aldiron Plaza* fronts Jalan Hassanudin. In the center of Block M on Jalan Melawai IV is *Pasar Melawai*, a traditional market, though cleaner than most. Department stores at Block M include *Grand Duta* at Jalan Melawai Raya 93 (second floor); and *Matahari* on Jalan Melawai III/24, which specializes in clothing.

Jakarta's **Chinatown**, called *Glodok* or *Kota*, is the city's busiest commercial district, but Westerners don't usually go there to shop. This is probably due to the fact that they usually live on the other side of town and traffic jams in the area are horrendous and getting worse due to the sheer volume of traffic and the attraction of cheap prices. The vibrancy and energy of Glodok makes it one of my favorite places in Jakarta. Also its location adjoining the old Dutch city means that there are constant reminders of the past.

The wide thoroughfare that leads from the Harmoni intersection (near the Presidential Palace) into Glodok has a different name on each side of the central canal. Jalan Gajah Mada runs northwards into Glodok and Jalan Hayam Wuruk runs southwards. At Harmoni is the *Duta*

Merlin Department Store, the longest-established, high-rise prestige department store in the area. Halfway along Jalan Gajah Mada is the *Gajah Mada Plaza*, another upscale department store. At the end of Jalan Gajah Mada, where it changes names to Jalan Pintu Besar (literally "main gate"), is the center of Glodok. *Pancoran Market* leads off to the left through the tollgates. This street changes into Jalan Pintu Kecil (small gate), and on the left is *Pasar Pagi*, an important wholesale area for textiles. From Jalan Pintu Kecil, turn right back towards Taman Fatahillah, the old Batavia town square.

Jalan Hayam Wuruk has the worst traffic jams around noon when school is out and all the kids are being picked up. This is the time to find a restaurant and wait until 1:30 to 2 P.M. for the traffic to clear. Or do some more exploring to pass the time, such as to Pasar Ikan and Sunda Kelapa.

IN BANDUNG

Bandung's premier shopping area is Jalan Asia Africa and around the main square (Alun-Alun). The central market is on Jalan Iskandardinata, between Jalan Asia Africa and the railway station. Jalan Braga is another commercial street with mainly art shops and nightclubs. Bandung's wholesale district is behind the General Post Office on Jalan ABC and Jalan Banceuy. Another old commercial street is Jalan Dulatip, near the railway station.

11. Night Life and Entertainment

Jakarta shows a reasonable level of sophistication in its night life. Each of the major hotels has a cocktail bar where live Indo-Jazz is played, and most also have a late-night disco, night club, or supper club. As well as these, there are other bars and clubs in central Jakarta. Nightlife in Bandung will be covered at the end of this section.

Ancol Recreation Park on the beach facing Jakarta Bay, is the city's biggest entertainment area, with bowling, watersports, restaurants, an art market, a Disneyland-style Fantasy Land, a golf course, and an Oceanarium. Ancol gets quite busy with locals on weekends and holidays, so visit during the week. Take a taxi to get there, otherwise you'll have to do a lot of walking from Jalan Martadinata to the beachfront. You will need to pay for admission to the park itself and then also to the individual attractions.

TIM, an abbreviation of Taman Ismail Marzuki, is Jakarta's **Arts Center** (Tel. (21) 34 2605, 34 1665). Performances are held just about every night. It has modern and traditional local acts, as well as overseas visitors. There is an exhibition hall of paintings by contempory Indonesian artists, as well as a Graphics Gallery. In one of the buildings there is a classical dance school. TIM is located at Jalan Cikini Raya 73, Menteng.

PUBS, TAVERNS, AND BARS

These are covered in Section 5. Notable are the **George and Dragon**, the **Tavern**, and the **Jaya Pub**. Bars are in the bigger hotels.

NIGHT CLUBS, SUPPERCLUBS, DISCOS

It's sometimes a bit difficult to categorize Jakarta night life, so I've put everything together. In the hotels, Hotel Indonesia (Tel. (21) 32 0008) has the formal **Nirwana Supper Club** and the Hilton has the **Oriental Disco** (Tel. (21) 570 3600), part of the Juliana's of London group. **Pit Stop** (Tel. (21) 32 3707) at the Sari Pacific Hotel is also managed by Juliana's of London. These are open nightly until late, and hotel guests are admitted free. On weekends members and guests get first preference, so you may not get in.

Tropicana International Night Club is more of a supperclub-style place at Jalan Manila, Senayan. Very establishment. A restaurant and nightclub that caters to a Chinese clientele is **Blue Ocean** (Tel. (21) 36 6650, 36 1194) on Jalan Hayam Wurnuk 5, near Harmoni. The Chinese food is good, as are the singers from Taiwan. Showtime is nightly from 8:30 to 11:30.

Aiming at a younger market are **Hollywood East Discotheque** (Tel. (21) 34 4434, 34 6214) in the Harmoni Plaza Building at Jalan Gajah Mada 1; and **Ozone Discotech** (Tel. (21) 36 5443, 36 3332) next door in the Duta Merlin shopping center. At the other end of Jalan Hayam Wuruk in Glodok is **Stardust Disco** (Tel. (21) 649 6760) on the top floor of the Jayakarta Tower Hotel.

Not far from Menteng on Jalan Rasuna Said is the Kuningan Plaza Building. Here is another supperclub, **Casablanca** (Tel. (21) 51 4800), serving dinner from 7 to 10:30 nightly, and **Ebony Videotheque** (Tel. (21) 51 3700, 51 7979) which has a large screen for video clips and old movies. Both are open nightly.

A sleazy but popular club is **Tanamour** (Tel. (21) 35 3947) at Jalan Tanah Abang Timur 14, Tanah Abang.

MOTION PICTURES

Indonesia is way behind in terms of local release of foreign movies (including American), so don't expect too much. Movies are sometimes dubbed, and can have showings in Indonesian or in English with Indonesian subtitles. The best cinemas are **Jakarta Theatre** on Jalan Thamrin/corner Jalan Wahid Hasyim; **Odean** at Taman Ria, Jalan M.

Merdeka Selatan, and **Studio 21** on Jalan Thamrin. You would be just as likely to see a good movie on your hotel's in-house movie program.

TV AND RADIO

Until recently, Indonesia had only one TV station—a government operation with very basic programming. Now Jakarta has a private TV station with paid advertising, so things may get a bit better. Radio is mostly Indonesian-language D.J.'s playing easy-listening music. Not so good.

CLASSICAL ARTS

Classical arts, such as *wayang kulit, wayang-orang* dance-drama, and traditional dance, are performed at a number of venues in Jakarta on a regular basis. For more information on the *wayang* stories turn back to Chapter 4. At the Hilton Hotel, a Javanese *gamelan* orchestra plays in the lobby to welcome guests. On the hotel grounds is the Balinese garden, where traditional Balinese dances are performed at 7 P.M. each night except Monday. Bookings are done through the hotel reception at (570 3600).

Museum Wayang (Tel. (21) 67 9560) at Jalan Pintu Besar Utara (on Taman Fatahillah, Jakarta Kota-Glodok) stages a *wayang kulit* puppet play each morning at 10 A.M.. The **National Museum** (Tel. (21) 36 0976) on Jalan M. Merdeka Barat stages *wayang kulit* or *wayang golek* twice a month. In Jakarta these *wayang* performances are condensed versions of the all-night epics staged in Bali and Jogya. The **Museum of Fine Arts** (Tel. (21) 681 685) on Jalan Pos Kota, Glodok has a nightly dinner show with traditional dance at 7 P.M..

Wayang orang dance-drama is staged most nights at the **Bharata Theatre** on the corner of Jalan Gunung Sahari and Jalan Kalilio, Senen. Showtime is from 8:30 to 12 P.M..

TIM Arts Centre (Tel. (21) 34 2605) on Jalan Cikini Raya, Menteng also has traditional dance and *wayang* performances. You will need to check their monthly program for details.

R.R.I. (Radio Republik Indonesia) on Jalan M. Merdeka Barat next to the National Museum has a large auditorium which is sometimes used by visiting groups from other parts of Indonesia. Check their schedule to see whether you can buy tickets.

The classical arts of Central Java and Bali are much better when seen away from Jakarta, such as at Jogya, Solo, or Ubud. So, if you have already been or plan to go to these towns I really wouldn't bother seeing them in Jakarta. This doesn't mean that the Jakarta performances are bad—just that the others are better.

NIGHT LIFE AND ENTERTAINMENT IN BANDUNG

Bandung is a pretty quiet city as far as nightlife goes. Nightclubs are mostly in the better hotels on Jalan Asia Africa or on Jalan Braga. The **Latin Quarter** (Tel. (22) 59 378) is at Jalan Braga 35; and **Capri Disco** (Tel. (22) 58 689) is at number 37. Near the Grand Hotel Preanger at Jalan Tamblong 14 is the **Aneka Plaza** nightclub (Tel. (22) 51552).

West Java has its own form of traditional arts, though these are in many aspects similar to Central Javanese arts. For a look at the Sundanese (i.e. West Java) classical arts, visit the **Purwa Setia Building** on Gang Tegellega for nightly performances of Sundanese dance from 9 P.M. to 2 A.M.. *Wayang kulit* is performed at the **Yayasan Building** on Jalan Naripan (near the corner of Jalan Braga). **Hotel Panghegar's Pasundan Dining Room** (Tel. (22) 43 2287) has a cultural show with dinner on Wednesdays and Saturdays at 7:30 P.M., or you may hear of a special troupe playing during your visit.

12. The West Java Address List

Airlines—Bouraq Indonesia, Jalan Angkasa 1-3, Kemayoran (Tel. (21) 659 5326). Cathay Pacific, 3rd floor, Hotel Borobudur, Jalan Lapangan Benteng Selatan, Menteng (Tel. (21) 380 6660). Delta Airlines, Hotel Indonesia, Jalan Thamrin, Menteng (Tel. (21) 310 1351). Garuda Indonesia, B.D.N. Building, Jalan Thamrin 5, Menteng (Tel. (21) 334425, 334429-30). Merpati/Garuda Airlines, Jalan Asia Africa 73, Bandung, (Tel. (22) 54563). Merpati Nusantara, Jalan Angkasa 2, Kemayoran (Tel. (21) 413608). Northwest Airlines, Wisma Bumiputera Bldg, Jalan Sudirman, Kav 75 (Tel. (21) 520 3152). Qantas Airways, B.D.N. Building, Jalan Thamrin 5, Menteng (Tel. (21) 326707, 327707). Singapore Airlines, Chase Plaza, Jalan Sudirman, Kav 21 (Tel. (21) 584041, 584021). Thai Airways Int'l, B.D.N. Building, Jalan Thamrin 5, Menteng (Tel. (21) 320607, 330943). U.T.A French Airlines, Summitmas Tower, Jalan Sudirman Kav 61-62 (Tel. (21) 520 22623). United Airlines, Borobudur Hotel, Jalan Lapangen Banteng Selatan, Menteng (Tel. (21) 361707).

Banks—Amex Bank, Arthaloka Bldg, Jalan Sudirman 2 (Tel. (21) 5702389). Bank Bumi Daya, Jalan Iman Bonjol 61, Menteng (Tel. (21) 333721). Bank Central Asia, Wisma BCA, Jalan Sudirman Kav 22-23 (Tel. (21) 570 3711). Bank Dagang Negara, Jalan Thamrin 5, Menteng (Tel. (21) 321707). Bank Duta (Visa Card), Jalan Kebon Sirih 12, Menteng (Tel. (21) 38009001). B.N.I. 1946, Hotel Indonesia branch, Jalan Thamrin, Menteng (Tel. (21) 326996). Bank of America, Wisma Antara Building, Jalan M. Merdeka Selatan 17, Menteng (Tel. (21)

347031). Chase Manhattan, Chase Plaza, Jalan Sudirman Kav 21. (Tel. (21) 5782213), and Jalan M. Merdeka Barat 6, Menteng (Tel. (21) 374008). Citibank, Landmark Center, Jalan Sudirman I (Tel. (21) 5782007). Hong Kong Bank, Wisma Metropolitan II Building, Jalan, Sudirman Kav 31, Senayan (Tel. (21) 5780075). B.N.I. 1946, Jalan Asia Africa, Bandung.

Consular Offices—Australia, Jalan Thamrin 15, Menteng (Tel. (21) 323109, 330824). Britain, Jalan Thamrin 75, Inteng (Tel. (21) 330914). Canada, 5th floor, Wisma Metropolitan, Jalan Jendral Sudirman, Jakarta (Tel. (21) 510709). Malaysia, Jalan Iman Bonjol 17, Menteng (Tel. (21) 336438). Singapore, Jalan Rasuna Said Block X/4, Kav 2, Kuningan (Tel. (21) 5201489-92). United States, Jalan M. Merdeka Selatan 5, Menteng (Tel. (21) 360360).

International Telegraph—Jalan M. Merdeka Selatan, Menteng.

International Telephone—Jakarta Theatre Building, Jalan Thamrin, Menteng.

Int'l Telephone & Telegraph-Jalan Lembong, Bandung.

Medical Services—General Hospital, Jalan Diponegoro 71, Menteng (Indonesian language) 24-hour. The Medical Scheme, Setia Budi Building, Jalan Rasuna Said, Kuningan (Tel. (21) 51 5481) 24-hour. Medika Loka, Kuningan Plaza, South Tower, Jalan Rasuna Said, Kuningan (Tel. (21) 578 1267). S.O.S. Medika Jalan Prapanca Raya, Kebayoran Baru (Tel. (21) 73 3094) 24-hour. General Hospital, Jalan Kebon Jati, Bandung.

Money Changers—Ayumas Gunung Agung, Jalan Kwitang 24-25, Menteng (Tel. (21) 349490). Sinar Iriawan, Jalan Irian 3, Menteng (Tel. (21) 321115, 322644). Sinar Iriawan, Jalan Palatehan I/1C, Kebayoran Baru, (Tel. (21) 712376).

Police—Kodak Metro Jaya H.Q., Jalan Sudirman, Senayan (Tel. (21) 510 110).

Post Offices—General Post Office, Jalan Pos, Pasar Baru. Menteng P.O., Jalan Cikini Raya, Menteng. Kota P.O., Jalan Pos Kota, Kota (Glodok). Postal Agent, Hotel Indonesia, Jalan Thamrin, Menteng. G.P.O., Jalan Asia Africa, Bandung.

Tourist Information—Jakarta Theatre Building, Jalan Thamrin, Menteng. Central Square (Alun-Alun), Jalan Asia Africa, Bandung.

Index

THE MAVERICK GUIDE TO AUSTRALIA: 1992-1993 EDITION

By Robert W. Bone
Edited by Kevin Voltz

"One of the best guides on Australia to hit the bookstores in a long time." **Los Angeles Times**

"For travelers heading down under . . . almost required reading." **Booklist**

A fully updated version, the 8th edition of *The Maverick Guide to Australia* portrays the country as an alluring, yet accessible, vacation destination. A lengthy chapter on the Australian people provides wonderful background, including a glossary of the "Strine" dialect. The growing cities of Sydney, Melbourne, Perth, and Canberra are fully described, with candid evaluations of hotels and restaurants. With 28 useful maps, this enjoyable guide offers recommendations on every travel aspect, from sightseeing and recreation to dining and transportation. Suggestions for hiking and camping in the great Outback are also included.

408 pp. 5 ½ x 8 ½ Maps Index
ISBN: 0-88289-847-7 $12.95 pb

THE MAVERICK GUIDE TO HAWAII: 1992 EDITION

By Robert W. Bone
Edited by Carol Greenhouse

"One of the best travel guides I've ever read."
Chicago Sun-Times

"More helpful than any of the others I packed."
The Travel Book: Guide to the Travel Guides

"It may well be one of the most complete guides to these paradisiacal islands in the Pacific. . . .An invaluable handbook."
Washington Times

Hundreds of valuable tips are offered in this handy guide to the fiftieth state. Written from the *kamaaina* (native) perspective, it abounds with suggestions on what to see and do in Hawaii: hiking, camping, fishing, swimming, diving, and much more! Beach lovers will delight in the book's listings of beaches, including many secluded spots unknown to most visitors. Tips for swimming and diving tell when the waters are safe to enter. Current prices and honest evaluations of hotels and restaurants make this a must for travellers who want to know before they go.

480 pp. 5 ½ x 8 ½
Maps Appendix Index
ISBN: 0-88289-864-7 $12.95 pb

THE MAVERICK GUIDE TO NEW ZEALAND: 8TH EDITION

By Robert W. Bone
Edited by Susan Buckland

*"A lively and informative guide to travel in New Zealand. . . .
This is the best guide to New Zealand ever seen by this New
Zealander."* **Library Journal**

*"Bone's paperback is a solid where-to-go-and-what-to-see
guide. . . ."* **Booklist**

"Robert Bone's The Maverick Guide to New Zealand *offers
almost all of the practical information you'll need to plan a
trip. Besides lots of nitty-gritty observations, it touches upon
bits of history, language, personalities."* **Los Angeles Times**

New Zealand is a paradise of endless beaches,
breathtaking mountains, ancient glaciers, lush forests, and
friendly people. This guide contains fascinating and
complete information on the island nation, from the
charming cities of Auckland and Wellington to the remote
splendor of Mt. Cook. Newly updated price information
for all hotels, restaurants, and attractions is included, as
well as ideas for exciting activities like safari tours with
native Maori guides or whitewater rafting expeditions on
the country's many swift rivers. The only way to travel in
New Zealand is with the Maverick Guide.

368 pp. 5 ½ x 8 ½ Maps Index
ISBN: 0-88289-752-7 $12.95 pb

THE MAVERICK GUIDE TO THAILAND

By Len Rutledge

About five million people travel to Thailand each year, making this unique country one of the most popular destinations in the East. From Chiang Mai and the North to Phuket and the South to Pattaya and the East, Thailand offers romance and adventure to quench the thirst of even the most adventurous traveler. The newest addition to the Maverick Guide Series, *The Maverick Guide to Thailand* offers everything the traveler to Thailand could ever want to know. This comprehensive guide includes information on where to go and what to do in each large city and throughout the countryside, clearly describing tours, restaurants, sports, and other entertainment available. Also included are maps and helpful address lists to aid the reader and tips on what to wear, as well as currency exchange, Thailand weather, and more.

Organized like the other Maverick Guides, *The Maverick Guide to Thailand* is more complete, up-to-date, and has more usable information than any other guide to Thailand. It allows the traveler to make the most of Thailand, and to enjoy all that this beautiful, exotic destination has to offer. This book is sure to become the definitive guide to the area.

336 pp. 5 ½ x 8 ½ Photos Color maps Index
ISBN: 0-88289-792-6 $14.95 pb

THE MAVERICK GUIDE TO MALAYSIA AND SINGAPORE 1992-1993 EDITION

By Len Rutledge

Len Rutledge has been traveling to Singapore and Malaysia for 20 years. In the last twelve months he has walked the streets of both countries' major cities, driven thousands of miles to the hill resorts, historic centers, and beaches of peninsular Malaysia, traveled to exotic island paradises, and tramped the jungles of Borneo in search of orangutans and forgotten tribal people. From his travels comes this exciting insider's account of Singaporean and Malaysian traditions, cultures, and modern lifestyles which is essential reading for anyone with an interest in the region.

Sections on the geography, history, and culture of Malaysia and Singapore as well as general travel tips and recommendations offer the traveler the most up-to-date information available on these two exotic countries. Within each region, there is a comprehensive discussion of transportation options, accommodations, restaurants, guided tours, sports, shopping, and entertainment.

Packed with detailed maps, telephone numbers, and excellent address lists, this complete guide will smooth your travels and ensure a unique experience as you explore these two intriguing countries.

Len Rutledge is an Australian travel writer and photographer. Rutledge is also the author of the acclaimed *Maverick Guide to Thailand*.

480 pp. 5 1/2 x 8 1/2 Photos Maps Index
ISBN: 0-88289-851-5 $14.95 pb

TRAVEL NOTES

TRAVEL NOTES

Please tell us about your trip to Bali and Java
(This page can be folded to make an envelope.

THE MAVERICK GUIDES
Pelican Publishing Company
1101 Monroe Street
P.O. Box 189
Gretna, Louisiana 70054